ARGUMENT OF LAUGHTER

So it may prove an argument of laughter
To the rest, and I 'mongst lords be thought a fool.

Timon of Athens, III. iii. 20-1

ARGUMENT OF
LAUGHTER

D. H. MONRO

Lecturer in Philosophy
University of Otago, N.Z.

UNIVERSITY OF NOTRE DAME PRESS • 1963

First published 1951
Reprinted by permission of the Melbourne
University Press, Victoria, Australia

To my companions at Paiaka, 1942-5,
where most of this book was written.

FOREWORD

THERE is no lack of books on humour. But as a rule each writer contents himself with developing a theory of his own. The result is that there is no single book which can be recommended to the reader who wants a general survey of all the theories. The only exception I know is Sully's *Essay on Laughter*, which is now out of date.

This book attempts to give such a survey. But it is meant to be a critical survey: I have not been content merely to summarize the views of other men. Obviously, some standpoint is needed from which to criticize. In Part 1, I have tried to find such a standpoint, by setting out, as objectively as possible, the facts about humour for which any theory must account. In Part 2 I have tried to estimate how far the various theories do in fact account for them. Inevitably this has led me to develop certain views of my own. These are set out, tentatively, in Part 3, which thus becomes (I must confess) the outline of yet another theory.

In spite of this, I hope that my standpoint has remained objective.

It is obviously not possible to give a complete account of every theory that has been advanced to explain humour. I have had, therefore, to make a selection. At first sight, it may seem an arbitrary selection. Some of the writers included are of patriarchal standing; others are recent and comparatively obscure.

The selection has not, however, been arbitrary. All theories seem to me to fall into four main classes. I have tried to give representative theories in each class. While it was obviously not possible to exclude some of the classic writers, like Hobbes and Kant, it seemed better to choose my representatives from comparatively recent works, since these generally take account of at least the more important points urged by their predecessors.

I have not, however, paid much attention to the large number of recent writers who have adopted an experimental, laboratory approach to the subject. 'Sense of humour tests' and the like may eventually throw light on the essential nature of humour, and some of the facts already discovered are no doubt valuable. But, so far as I know, the use of such tests has not yet resulted either in the development of a new theory or the confirmation of an old one.

I wish to thank the University of New Zealand for a grant towards the cost of typing the manuscript.

ACKNOWLEDGEMENTS

The following authors and publishers are thanked for granting permission to quote from copyright material:

George Allen & Unwin Ltd. and the authors for quotations from V. K. Krishna Menon, *A Theory of Laughter* and J. Y. T. Greig, *The Psychology of Laughter*. Edward Arnold & Co. and the authors for quotations from E. M. Forster, *Aspects of the Novel* and Harry Graham, *Ruthless Rhymes*. J. M. Dent & Sons for quotations from G. K. Chesterton, *The Defendant*. Gerald Duckworth & Co. Ltd. and the authors for quotations from Hilaire Belloc, *Sonnets and Verses* and Edith Sitwell, *Selected Poems*. Hamish Hamilton Ltd. and the author for quotations from Max Eastman, *The Enjoyment of Laughter*. John Lane Ltd. for quotations from Stephen Leacock, *Humour: its Theory and Technique*. Mr. A. M. Ludovici for quotations from his *Secret of Laughter*. Macmillan & Co. Ltd. for quotations from Bergson, *Laughter* and W. S. Gilbert, *Savoy Operas*. Methuen & Co. Ltd. and the author's executrix for quotations from G. K. Chesterton, *Tremendous Trifles*, and Methuen & Co. Ltd. for quotations from Robert Lynd, *The Pleasures of Ignorance,* from C. W. Kimmins, *The Springs of Laughter,* and F. Anstey, *Burglar Bill*. Routledge and Kegan Paul Ltd. for quotations from Schopenhauer, *The World as Will and Idea,* and Routledge and Kegan Paul Ltd. and the author for quotations from J. C. Gregory, *The Nature of Laughter*. Martin Secker & Warburg Ltd. and the author for quotations from George Orwell, *Critical Essays*. C. A. Watts & Co. Ltd. for quotations from Herbert Spencer, *Essays*. I also thank Mr. Bernard Shaw for pointing out that it was not legally necessary to obtain his permission for the quotation from the preface to *Plays Pleasant*.

8

CONTENTS

PART 1

WHAT WE LAUGH AT

1

THE PROBLEM OF LAUGHTER

L AUGHTER is one of the unsolved problems of philosophy. It is not, indeed, one of the larger and weightier stumbling-blocks, like Being or Knowing; yet some very great men have stubbed their toes upon it. Aristotle, Kant, Hobbes, Bergson, Freud are among them; and there are many lesser names. They have, of course, contributed a great deal; and yet it can be said that the problem is still largely unsolved.

One reason for this is, perhaps, that the great men have been somewhat preoccupied with weightier matters. Bergson's theory of laughter fits in magnificently with his general doctrine of creative evolution; Freud's provides remarkable confirmation of his own theories of dream analysis. Both are ingenious and illuminating; but perhaps it is not surprising that neither explains all the facts about laughter.

What are those facts? We should start with them, not with a theory or a formula. Let us suppose the phenomenon of laughter were to be encountered for the first time by a visitor from some planet where they do not laugh. His report (to the Martian Society for Terrestrial Research) might read like this:

Laughter is a phenomenon almost universal among men. According to some investigators, it exists also among the other animals, at least in a rudimentary form. It is marked by easily recognizable physical manifestations, and almost certainly by accompanying bodily changes, such as the oxygenation of the blood. It is also marked by a peculiar mental, or psychical, condition. In this it does not differ from the other emotions manifested by this unstable animal. Anger, or fear, may also be described by their physical symptoms (the paling or flushing of the cheeks, the chattering or grinding of the teeth, and so on) and each is recognizable also as a mental state, though this is not so easy to describe. But these emotions can also be defined in terms of their causes. Many things may cause fear; and different men will fear different things. But the causes of fear all have a common characteristic: they are all regarded by the man who fears them as a source of impending pain or discomfort. Teleologically, fear may be described as the psycho-physical concomitant of the impulse to flee. The other emotions can all be disposed of in the same way. But the peculiarity of laughter is that its causes have not yet been summed up in any simple formula.

There, in the rather pompous language of learned societies in every planet, is the crux of the problem. We all know laughter, as a change in the physical appearance of others, as a peculiar sensation, and emotion, in ourselves. We all say, as a matter of experience, that such and such is funny, or laughable. But what does that mean? What is the common characteristic of the things that make us laugh? Why, in fact, do we laugh at them?

It is sometimes said that this statement of the problem already prejudges it. To begin with the laughable, with the objects at which we laugh, is to presuppose that the cause of laughter is in them, not in ourselves. But is it not possible that laughter is subjective? The search for a common characteristic may have failed simply because none exists.

Says Mr. V. K. Krishna Menon:

It is well known, and indeed observable by all, that what makes one man laugh may even make another angry. Sugar is sweet, but it is sweet to everybody. You may not like it overmuch, but you cannot deny that it is sweet . . . . In this sense, a situation, if it is laughable, must be so to everyone, whether he is pleased to recognise it to be so or not. That this, however, is not so has been recognised by all. It is then fairly obvious that in assuming that persons laugh *at* a situation we are assuming more than the facts. We may assume only that *in* certain circumstances or situations people feel impelled to laugh. This fundamental and very obvious point of fact has been missed or ignored in all discussions about the nature of laughter, probably because it is too obvious. Hence all the various divergences of opinion among even the acutest minds.

I do not think this argument is really conclusive. We have already seen that it applies equally well to fear. All men do not fear the same things. Yet we understand pretty well what we mean by 'fearsome'. We do not have to define this *merely* as causing fear. We can give it an objective characteristic as well: a sign of impending pain or discomfort. Furthermore, we know the effects of fear on a man's behaviour. We know that it will result, generally speaking, in flight or avoidance.

There is plenty of room for variation here, of course. All men do not feel pain or discomfort at the same things. We may often be mistaken when we judge that something forebodes pain; our fear will be none the less real. Or you may, if you like, make more difficulties by citing instances of irrational fear, where we tremble even though we know that no disaster impends. The woman who shrieks at a mouse (if, indeed, she exists off the stage) doubtless knows quite well that mice are harmless. It would be easy, by arguing on these lines, to cast doubt on our definition of 'fearsome'. But nevertheless, there is no real doubt that it does correspond, however roughly, to the facts. The varied things we fear do have a well understood common characteristic. We have to allow for a subjective element when we define it. We may have to allow also for odd, inexplicable eccentricities, like mouse-fearing women. But the point is that the causes of fear, speaking generally, are well understood. We know where fear fits in with our general behaviour.

It is just this that we do not know about laughter. We cannot find any common characteristic for the laughable, even though we take care to allow for subjective terms, like 'sign' or 'pain'. We cannot say that laughter leads to any behaviour, like flight, or is connected with any 'impulse', such as 'avoidance'. The laughable is what we laugh at. We laugh because we have seen something laughable. That seems all we can say.

Mr. Menon recognizes this problem, of course. He, too, is seeking a formula which will serve as a common characteristic of the laughable. Indeed, he offers us one. His point may be merely that we must be careful to allow for subjective terms. But I think he means to go further than this. I think he means to condemn our whole approach to the subject; that he feels it futile to compile a list of things at which men laugh, and then try to find what they have in common. Yet this seems to be the only safe procedure. It is the only way to make sure that we are really attacking the problem of laughter, and not something of our own manufacture which we choose to call by its name. Many writers on laughter do wander very far from the subject, simply because they do not keep such a list before them as a kind of touchstone. If we wish to test a theory of laughter it seems reasonable to apply it to some joke and see whether it explains it adequately. It is hardly enough to condemn it out of hand because it does not conform to a particular metaphysic. Yet some writers have done just that.

Mr. Menon, however, is right in seeing dangers in this

approach. Let us suppose a similar list were compiled of the
fearsome. We solemnly note everything that men fear or have
feared: mice, earthquakes, Socialism, wars, dragons, marriage,
triplets, prison, and so on. We might indeed seek far for the
magic formula which would bind them all together. No doubt
M. Bergson would demonstrate some inelasticity, some fatal lack
of flexibility, in each in turn. No doubt Freud would find infantile repression in them all. But ingenious as both explanations
would certainly be, we would still feel that, however convincingly they demonstrated that the chosen formula fitted each and
every example, it was still not *that* element in it that made us
afraid.

Professor Greig, for example, wishing to discover why we
laugh at a man chasing his hat, remembers that the hat is a
sexual symbol, and decides that that is the reason. If this is the
sort of thing Menon has in mind, he is quite right. Obviously
this is to concentrate too much on the object. One feels that
Greig has been poring too minutely over his list of laughable
objects, trying at all costs to find some thread, however slender,
which will link hats with Punch and Judy (Punch's humped
back is another phallic symbol) and both with drunkenness and
mothers-in-law, so that he has forgotten altogether what it feels
like to laugh.

Many theories of laughter are full of just this kind of wrong-
headed ingenuity. It is impossible not to admire the skill with
which the author makes his formula fit so many diverse examples
of laughter; but we continue to feel, unshakeably, that he has
somehow missed the real point of the joke.

Nevertheless, the objective approach still seems the best. We
will proceed, then, by compiling a list of the laughable, as complete as we can make it. We will then use it as a touchstone
with which to test the theories of laughter that have been
advanced.

Perhaps, however, our question is not correctly stated as: what
is the common characteristic of the objects we laugh at? Let
us take the parallel with fear a little further. Feared objects,
we said, are all regarded as signs of impending pain or discomfort. But this is not strictly a characteristic of the objects
themselves, or, at any rate, it is not a quality *in* the objects. We
fear toothache because of qualities it has, and we fear bores

because of qualities they have, but the qualities are not the same. It is not, then, so much a question of finding common characteristics of the objects we laugh at, as of finding common elements in the situation when we laugh at them. It follows that we have not merely to examine the objects of laughter, but also to analyse our own feelings when we laugh at them. And this involves analysing such concepts as 'humour' or 'the laughable'. But we can hardly do this without paying very careful attention to the actual objects of laughter.

There is, however, another objection to our suggested procedure, one that we have already touched on in referring to mouse-fearing women. To say: 'Aunt Matilda is afraid of cats' is not the same thing as saying 'Cats are fearsome'. Even if we could say 'Most people are afraid of cats', we might still add, without contradicting ourselves: 'but cats are not fearsome', though perhaps we would more naturally say: 'not *really* fearsome'.

To call something 'fearsome', then, does not merely mean that we (or most people) feel a particular emotion in its presence. It means further that we regard the emotion as peculiarly appropriate to objects of a certain kind. 'Fearsome', in short, means not so much what people do in fact fear, as what they ought to fear. If A says that what B is afraid of is not really fearsome, he means that B has made a mistaken judgment, not that he is not afraid. In exactly the same way, it may turn out that some of the things people laugh at are nevertheless not laughable.

If we are going to explain away some objects of laughter in this fashion, it will probably be desirable, though it may not be strictly necessary, to explain how such mistaken judgments can arise. I say it may not be strictly necessary, because the existence of irrational fear does not seriously cast doubt on our definition of the fearsome. We may know a woman who is afraid of mice, and we may not in the least understand why. We may not even be able to say that her *judgment* is mistaken, because she may know quite well that mice are not dangerous. I think we can say that in some sense this is a mistaken *emotion,* though there are difficulties in regarding emotions as being subject to error, apart from errors of judgment which give rise to them.

What such aberrations suggest is that our account of fear has not been completed when we have defined 'fearsome'. 'I am afraid of X' does not mean the same as 'I regard X as dangerous'. But the two are related, and the relation is such that when the first proposition applies the second usually applies also. In the odd case when this is not so, we can say 'X is feared, but it is not fearsome'. This corresponds with ordinary usage, and it means that we can be satisfied with our definition, even though we cannot explain irrational fears. But I think we would be more completely satisfied if we could explain them.

Similarly, an analysis of 'funny' or 'laughable' should normally be applicable to all the things at which we laugh. If we find some to which it does not apply, we can still save our analysis by supposing these to be cases of mistaken judgment or the more mysterious phenomenon we have called mistaken emotion. To investigate these is not to analyse the laughable, but may, then, be relevant to the analysis.

The way to investigate irrational fears is presumably to enquire into the life histories of those who have them. No doubt A's fear of spiders or B's fear of red-headed sailors could be understood if we knew enough about their lives and surroundings. Parallels in the field of humour are laboratory investigations into the difference between the reactions of A and B to a set of printed jokes, or a discussion of 'national' humour.

This type of inquiry is part of what we mean by asking how laughter fits into the rest of our behaviour. I say part of what we mean, because we may ask this question about men in general as well as about particular individuals or selected groups, such as nations. We know how fear fits into human behaviour in general, because we know what pain and danger mean in the human situation. If we did not know this we would not feel satisfied with our definition of the fearsome. If we are presented with some similar definition of the laughable, we will probably not feel satisfied unless we can see how laughter, so explained, fits in with the rest of our behaviour. But, as with the fearsome, we shall probably be fairly satisfied if we know this in quite general terms.

How laughter (or fear) fits in with the rest of our behaviour might mean something else as well. Fear is an emotion: it has its physical concomitants. If we can explain these as the result (for example) of adrenalin being pumped into the blood-stream in order to prepare the body for the physical action necessary to cope with danger, we will feel that we understand more precisely just what fear is. Laughter, too, is of course a physical phenomenon as well as a mental one. One of the things we mean when we say that something is funny is certainly that we feel a peculiar emotion towards it. That emotion has its physical concomitants, which are what we mean, primarily, by laughter, and which the physiologist no doubt investigates by his special methods. A full account of laughter should, I think, demonstrate the connection between laughter as a physical phenomenon and as a mental experience.

The foregoing discussion is an attempt to distinguish various questions which may be asked about laughter. To recapitulate, they are:—

(a) What is the common characteristic of the things at which we laugh?

This, we have suggested, should be re-stated as:—

(b) What is the common element in laughable situations? That is, granted that laughable objects may not have a common characteristic, what is the common relation between us and the varied characteristics at which we laugh?

(c) How does laughter fit in with the rest of our behaviour? This, we saw, may mean:—

(c.i) How does the common element in laughable situations fit in with human behaviour in general?

(c.ii) What is the relation between the objects at which an individual laughs and his life history, temperament, etc.?

(c.iii) What is the relation between the common element in laughable situations and the physical concomitants of laughter?

The question with which we shall be concerned is (b). But, as we have seen, we can hardly avoid considering (c.i). The other two are largely outside our scope, but here and there it may be necessary to refer to them. We shall be largely concerned with analysing our meaning when we call something 'funny', but in doing so we shall find it necessary to keep our eyes constantly on what people actually laugh at.

2

NON-HUMOROUS LAUGHTER

F EW WRITERS on laughter have made any systematic attempt to list the things we laugh at. The reason is obvious: we laugh at almost everything. A man may laugh exultantly at winning a contest of some sort; his opponent may laugh (bitterly, or to show he is a good sport) at losing it. We laugh when at ease among our friends; we laugh with embarrassment in the company of strangers. We laugh when somebody does something odd and unexpected. We also laugh when he does something entirely characteristic and 'just like him'.

Obviously, any catalogue of the laughable which began thus— (a) success in contests, (b) failure in contests, (c) ease and security, (d) embarrassment and insecurity, (e) the unexpected, (f) the familiar'—would drive the earnest investigator to distraction before he had finished his first chapter. Yet every instance I have given, and many more equally contradictory, have been advanced by some writer or other in support of some theory of laughter. And almost invariably the contradictory instance has been seized upon by his critics to refute him.

The difficulty seems to be that laughter is, or may be in special circumstances, expressive of a number of emotions. Embarrassment, despair, exultation, and so on may all cause laughter. But when we call a situation 'laughable' we are not thinking of these kinds of laughter. Over and above them, there is an ill-defined but recognizable emotion which we may call 'seeing the funny side of things'. It is this funny side that we are really trying to focus here.

We could, of course, get out of this difficulty easily enough by saying that our subject is not laughter, but humour. This also relieves us from trying to explain tickling and nitrous oxide, which generally give difficulty to even the most ingenious formula-framers. Unfortunately, humour is too narrow a term. It is nearly always distinguished from wit (though nearly everybody disagrees about the exact difference), and frequently from buffoonery, the comic, the farcical, the grotesque. What is needed is some satisfactory term which will include all these. This is purely a verbal difficulty, and may be overcome. 'The ludicrous' might do; or we might simply use 'humour' in this broad sense.

But the difficulty goes deeper. We know so little of our subject that we cannot say in advance what we want to exclude. The laugh of embarrassment, the phenomenon called 'laughing it off', may after all turn out to be closely linked with the laugh of humour. The laugh of triumphant exultation is regarded by many as the archetype of all laughter and the key to all comedy.

We must not, then, ignore the non-humorous laugh altogether. But we should clearly recognize the difference between the two. Or as clearly as we can, because there is often no hard and fast line between them. W. S. Lilly speaks of 'that ringing laugh of pure human happiness which one sometimes hears from the lips of young girls; is there any music like it? They laugh as the birds sing.' This laugh of mere gladness is often peculiarly difficult to distinguish from the laugh of humour. But the important point is that it is the ludicrous, humour in the broad sense, that is the core of our subject. Primarily it is the varieties of this that we are trying to list. Other types of laughter may be noted, for they may help us; but we will not be very upset if we cannot frame a definition of the laughable which allows for nitrous oxide, tickling and embarrassment as well as ludicrousness.

All this may seem to labour the obvious: but the difficulty of determining the field of investigation is perhaps the main stumbling-block in our path. There is so much that is obviously and legitimately included in the laughable, and so much more that can be included if we juggle with terms a little, that one can find examples to support almost any theory. Writers not unnaturally choose the ones that support their views, and ignore the rest.

Let us begin by listing the main types of non-humorous laughter. We will then have them safely pigeon-holed, ready for reference if they turn out to be relevant, but powerless to divert us from our main problem.

(a) Tickling

With the probable exception of laughing-gas, tickling is the most obviously non-humorous stimulant of laughter. It may be, of course, a pure coincidence that tickling causes the same physical response as a joke. It may be no more relevant to theories of humour than the onion is to theories of tragedy. But there are at least two reasons why we cannot ignore it. It was possible, in

1896, for Lilly to dismiss the physical side of the subject entirely
with the grandiose dictum: 'The laugh of the soul and the laugh
of the body are distinct. Only a gross superficial analysis will
confound them.'

We are no longer quite so scornful of the physiological
approach to psychology. On the face of it, it seems promising
that laughter can be induced by a simple technique of tactile
stimulation easily mastered by any schoolboy. It should be possible, one feels, to isolate the physical causes of laughter at least.

But, unfortunately, the physiologists do not help us very much.
Tickling has produced almost as many theories as laughter itself.
It has been suggested by Dr. Louis Robinson that ticklishness is
a special sensitiveness bestowed by nature on those parts of the
body which are specially vulnerable in warfare, or, alternatively,
peculiarly liable to attack by parasites. Havelock Ellis regards
ticklishness as a defence against premature sexual advances. The
young girl instinctively wishes to hide the armpits, the breasts,
and other ticklish regions, so that tickling ensures modesty.

Professor J. Y. T. Greig urges against all three theories that
they do not explain why tickling makes us laugh, and, against
Robinson, that he forgets the sole of the foot, a peculiarly ticklish spot which is neither sensitive to parasites nor vital in warfare. This objection obviously applies with equal force against
Ellis, but Greig cannot say so, because he wishes to accept the
view that the ticklish spots are the 'erogenous zones' and to deny
only the connection between ticklishness and modesty.

The second reason why we cannot ignore tickling is that it has
been advanced to support various theories of laughter. Thus
Sully gives a tentative explanation which suggests a general connection between laughter and play. There is always, he suggests,
an element of the unknown in tickling. That is why it is impossible to tickle oneself. Moreover, the ticklish parts of the body
are all rarely touched, and usually difficult to see. But touches
of unknown origin at places not closely observable have a dis-
turbing effect. This must be neutralized by a sense of the harmlessness of the attack. Tickling, then, is a special case of teasing,
which may be defined as a playful attack well understood to be a
pretence. Its emotional essence, for the person being teased, is
'the swift inter-action of moments of nascent fear with a joyous
recognition of harmlessness'.

If tickling is a special case of teasing, teasing is in turn a special case of play. And when play takes the form of mock combat, laughter ensures that the aggression will not be taken too seriously. Even dogs realize the need for some signal of this sort. A puppy at play springs on his adversary with tail wagging and with short, joyful barks. When the fight is serious, he growls and bares his teeth.

As a theory of laughter, this cannot be dismissed out of hand. All practical jokes and most witticisms can be described accurately enough as a playful attack. But it does not explain tickling, because it is not the tickler, but the person tickled, who laughs. Sully, who never commits himself definitely to the play theory of laughter, though he gives it his general approval, probably recognizes this. He is satisfied to establish a general connection between tickling and play. The laughter of tickling he attributes rather to the joyous dissolution of momentary fear.

But is the fear dissolved? Although Sully says that 'the feeling-tone of tickling may be pleasant or unpleasant' and that 'it depends on circumstances whether pleasure or unpleasure predominates', his conclusions require that the sensation should be on balance pleasurable. The nascent fear must be overwhelmed by a joyous recognition of the harmlessness of the attack. My own experience is that tickling is almost entirely unpleasant. As a child, I have often been intimidated by the threat: 'If you don't do so-and-so, I will tickle you.' This was just as effective as if my companion had said: 'I will hit you.' In other words, tickling may be felt as intensely disagreeable, may be feared as such, and yet still evoke laughter.

Greig's theory obviously owes much to Sully's. He defines tickling as 'the intermittent tactual stimulation of an erotogenic zone'. Since the ticklish spots are erogenous, touching them inevitably sets off 'love responses'. In an infant this is the only response. Babies do not become ticklish until they are at least two months old. But as soon as the child is old enough to recognize in the person who touches something that may hurt as well as soothe, the love responses will be obstructed by fear and, if the stimulus recurs more rapidly than the normal rhythm of nervous conduction, by pain. But Greig's general theory of laughter is that it always occurs whenever love responses are obstructed by some other emotion, which is eventually swamped by the love response. When tickled, therefore, the child will laugh, provided the obstructions are overcome from moment to moment.

Unlike Sully, Greig does not think that the fear is caused by the element of the unknown in tickling. Indeed, he claims that it does not make any difference whether the child knows beforehand or is left guessing where he is going to be tickled. It is the intermittency of the tickling that is important. Every time the threatening finger is raised once more, the child feels a fresh upsurge of fear, which is swept away when he finds that the touch is after all only a light caress. But it is not, as Sully thinks, mere relief at the baselessness of his fears that causes laughter. There is also the positive erotic pleasure caused by the stimulation of the erogenous zone.

We have seen reason to doubt whether the ticklish parts of the body really coincide with the 'erogenous zones'. One may doubt also whether the intermittent touch is really enough to cause a continual upsurge of fear, which is as continually overcome. This might happen at first; but one would expect the child to become conditioned to the process, so that his fears would vanish entirely. Conditioning, however, does not seem to enter into Greig's calculations. He believes firmly that first experiences establish a pattern of behaviour which will persist even after it has become inappropriate. Thus he suggests that laughter at being tickled is a habit, established in infancy, which will persist even though, on some later occasion, pain predominates over erotic stimulation.

This addendum suggests that the objection we have already brought against Sully, that tickling is often an unpleasant sensation and feared as such, had also occurred to Greig. As a defence his argument is not very convincing. It means that we laugh not because the situation confronting us is laughable (in Greig's rather odd sense of the term) but because it brings the unconscious memory of an earlier situation that was laughable. Greig uses this theory more than once when he gets into difficulties. It always seems a little far-fetched but possibly it is at its most plausible when applied to tickling. For the laughter of tickling does seem to be involuntary and instinctive.

Finally, we may note that Greig does not help his case by introducing pain as an alternative obstruction which the love responses may have to overcome. For, while one may readily grant that baseless fears would soon be swept away by the pleasurable erotic sensation, one would hardly expect real pain to succumb so readily.

Enough has been said of tickling to show that it provides no easy way out of our difficulties. Evidently we know as little about it as about the laughter of humour. It has evoked quite as much controversy, and although it seems a simple physical phenomenon, it is apparently just as difficult to investigate.

(b) Laughing-gas

Nitrous oxide sometimes figures in theories of laughter because it has been called laughing-gas. But this seems to mean little more than that taking it results in a feeling of general light-heartedness, which may or may not be accompanied by laughter.

It is interesting, though of course quite well known, that lightness of heart may be the result of chemical changes in the body. It is equally well known that mere lightness of heart may be a cause of laughter, even if it is not usually a sufficient cause. When we feel good we may be ready, as we say, to laugh at anything. We may even say that on such occasions we laugh at nothing. Usually, however, we find that some external stimulus is needed to set us off, even though it may be a very slight one (a very weak joke, for example).

But though there may be a general connection between physiological changes and euphoria, and between euphoria and laughter, it does not seem that this gets us very far. We can hardly suppose that hearing a joke, or seeing someone slip on a banana-skin, causes any direct chemical change in the organism.

(c) Nervousness

Tickling and nitrous oxide are not merely non-humorous stimulants of laughter; they are, at least at first sight, purely physical and mechanical, even though most theories of tickling rapidly desert physics for psychology. But nervousness is psychological from the beginning.

Nervousness is no joke; and yet nervous people do frequently laugh. The shy child confronted by a stranger can often utter no sound but a giggle. A shy man on a public platform will often laugh a good deal. Hysteria may be only an extreme case of this. These phenomena are, however, so closely connected with our next class, that it may be as well to consider them together. We pass on, then, to

(d) Relief After a Strain

Most writers add to the examples above the laughter that occurs in churches, schoolrooms and law-courts. Sully groups these with nervous laughter, and remarks that the common factor is a preceding period of intense and concentrated strain. This attitude is hard to maintain and tends to collapse more or less automatically. Hence laughter; for laughter is a relief, which allows an escape of the nervous energy concentrated to meet the strain. The relief may indeed be largely physical. Physically, laughter is essentially a deep prolonged inspiration followed by a series of short, explosive expirations. This has a 'flushing' effect, both on the air in the lungs and the circulation of the blood. But it is well known that intense strain affects the breathing. 'I held my breath' we say, to denote fearful expectation; and we use 'breath-taking' in the sense of startling or thrilling. The self-conscious decorum, then, which we maintain in church, may actually affect our breathing; and when we giggle our harassed lungs are snatching at the simplest means of relief.

It is a little odd that the simple, physical explanation which eluded us when dealing with tickling and laughing-gas should turn up now we have moved into realms which seem purely psychological. As an explanation, it is at least plausible; but I am not sure that we can apply it without question to all cases of nervous laughter.

There is no doubt that relief from strain does explain some laughter. The clearest case I know occurred in a New Zealand school. A workman doing some repairs to the roof dropped a hammer, which crashed through the ceiling of a classroom, narrowly missing the teacher's head. The workman waited in terrified suspense; no doubt he 'held his breath'. For a moment there was complete silence; then a great shout of laughter came up from the children, and the workman concluded (correctly) that his carelessness had had no serious results.

The laughter which more commonly occurs in the schoolroom, or in church, is fairly obviously of this type. True, there must usually be some joke, however weak, to set it off. The child, or the church-goer, does not laugh involuntarily, out of mere nervousness, but he seizes at the slightest excuse for legitimate laughter. It may be fairly assumed that he is under a strain, and is seeking relief. The laughter of soldiers after battle, cited by Kline, is another example.

But can we say that the child giggling at a visitor, or the shy speaker on the platform, is feeling relief *after* a strain? The strain is still going on. Sometimes, indeed, he may even try to check the nervous laugh, and its persistence may add to his embarrassment. For this reason it seems better to regard laughter during strain and laughter after a strain as different, though doubtless closely related, types.

Sully's explanation, however, applies equally well to both. For even when the nervous giggle actually adds to the embarrassment of its author, he may still obtain some physical relief. The labouring lungs may insist on fresh supplies of oxygen, even at the expense of the social prestige of their owner. On the one hand, then, if no other relief is forthcoming, laughter may force itself out for purely physical reasons. And on the other hand, if mental relief has already come, and there is no longer any need to check the breath, we would expect the physical organism to resume its normal course as quickly as possible. And laughter may well be the shortest route to the restoration of the *status quo*.

(e) 'Laughing it Off'

Laughter is often a defence mechanism. We may laugh deprecatingly when referring to our own achievements. 'Don't take me too seriously; I am not really boasting' is what we mean to convey. Naïve people will occasionally say hastily 'I was only joking' in a desperate attempt to retrieve a *faux pas*. But it is more usual to convey the same idea more subtly, by continuing the conversation in a facetious tone, and with occasional bursts of somewhat forced laughter. The modern distrust of all highfalutin' sentiments is responsible for much defensive laughter. If we do find it necessary to utter a high-sounding phrase or a sentiment that sounds priggish, we preface it with a laugh.

Like the laughter of relief, defence mechanism laughter has been put forward as the basic type which explains all laughter. Ludovici, who takes this view, gives some interesting examples of defensive laughter. He points out that when a man chases his hat, he will often join in the laughter which his discomfiture evokes. This, of course, is a desperate attempt to persuade the spectators that he can take a joke against himself, can see the funny side of things, as well as any man.

A rather extreme instance of this was furnished Ludovici by a smartly dressed woman, who slipped on the pavement one wet day in Bond Street. The contents of her handbag were scattered over the footpath, and her gloves, stockings and skirt were covered with mud. Yet she laughed heartily all the time Ludovici and other bystanders were helping her to her feet.

Something of this may be present in the laughter of the shy man on the public platform. He may be trying to persuade his audience that he is entirely at ease. So may the giggling child. But the fact that nervous laughter is often involuntary rather tells against this theory. Defensive laughter, on the contrary, is forced. And it is obvious that this explanation cannot apply to the laughter of relief. On the whole, defence mechanism laughter would seem to be entirely different from these other two types. There is nothing instinctive about it: it is a conscious attempt to take advantage of the fact that laughter is commonly associated with joy.

(f) Joy

And this leads us to another distinct type. We all know that laughter is often no more than an expression of high spirits, of a feeling that life is good. Laughter and joy are indeed linked so closely that it is often difficult to distinguish the laughable from the merely pleasurable. Thus Stephen Leacock, who believes, brave soul, that man is becoming steadily more humane, tells us that the modern clown is merely a more humane version of the Roman spectacle. But, while the Romans found pleasure no doubt in the sight of criminals being mangled by lions, there is no evidence that they found it funny. Fox-hunting or bull-fighting or lynching are closer modern equivalents than the circus clown.

But, if pleasure is not the same as humour, it is certainly one source of non-humorous laughter. The happy laughter of children at play suggests itself as an obvious example, but perhaps it had better be rejected. The laughter may be caused by play in particular, and not by pleasure in general, or it may be an example of freedom from restraint.

Lilly's 'ringing laugh of pure human happiness which one sometimes hears on the lips of young girls: is there any music like it?' is a safer, if vaguer example. Ludovici, writing in a more cynical decade, tells us that the laughter of girls will be particularly ringing if they are conscious of being well-dressed. Sully cites as examples of sheer joyousness the laughter of children at a burst of fireworks, of adults at suddenly meeting an old friend after a prolonged absence, of children or savages at the sight of a new toy or bauble.

Examples do not, actually, present themselves very readily. Mere pleasure, or well-being, or satisfaction, will cause a smile perhaps, but not a laugh. But they often cause a predisposition for laughter; they put us in the frame of mind where any joke, however feeble, will be greeted with gales of laughter. We may be tempted to say here that the mood of well-being is the 'real' cause of laughter; but this type of reasoning has its pitfalls. Ludovici makes a great point of the fact that we laugh more readily at a joke in a foreign language than at one of equal merit in our own tongue. The real cause of laughter here, he tells us, is our feeling of superiority over those who are not linguists. But if laughter is only an expression of superiority we should laugh at any passage we translate successfully, whether it is a joke or not. No doubt our pride in our linguistic ability does reinforce our laughter, but only because, by giving the correct response, we are anxious to show that we have really understood. If the passage happened to be tragic, the correct response might be tears, and not laughter, and no doubt each of us would then be anxious to outweep the other. But it would be absurd to base a superiority theory of tears on such evidence.

Well-being, then, is a frequent predisposing cause of laughter; but it is important to remember that an immediate cause, a joke of some kind, must also usually be present. Nevertheless, joyous laughter pure and simple does occur, as in the examples already given. Sully suggests that it is a sudden onset of joy that makes us laugh, where its more gradual approach will only make us smile. The fireworks, the toys, the old friend, must burst suddenly upon us, causing 'a sudden accession of pleasurable consciousness, which raises the feeling-tone of the subject to one of joyous excitement'.

(g) Play

Children at play laugh a good deal. So for that matter do adults, on the occasions when they play like children. A group of men at a seaside bach romping, wrestling and skylarking generally, will certainly laugh as they romp. The same men playing cards will not laugh, at least not at the mere act of card-playing. But then neither will children laugh when playing ludo or snakes and ladders.

We might infer that it is the more active play that causes

laughter. But activity alone is not enough. Football players seldom roar with laughter as they take the field; even wrestlers, whose sport perhaps comes closest to the lighthearted hooliganism of the seashore, are not noticeably merry in the ring. What is necessary is release from restraint, even the restraint imposed by the rules of an organized game, which sets its players a goal that is, at least for the moment, taken seriously.

Here apparently, is a link with the laughter that occurs after a strain. But there are some important differences. It is plausible to suppose that the snicker in church is a physical relief; but the man who laughs while playfully pummelling a comrade can hardly be easing the strain on his lungs. It may be, of course, that civilized life, in which we have few opportunities to run or leap or wrestle, does impose a strain, conscious or otherwise; but it can hardly be the type of strain that requires a simple physical device for the oxygenation of the blood. Freedom from restraint is a particularly promising formula for laughter; but Sully's simple physical explanation applies only to its very simplest manifestations.

It has been suggested that any manifestation of playfulness is likely to cause laughter, such as the gambols of a lamb or a lively kitten. These certainly do strike us as laughable; but 'any manifestation of playfulness' is perhaps going too far. Chess tournaments and cricket matches are also manifestations of playfulness. It is not easy to see exactly why a kitten is laughable. But its antics do suggest exuberance raised to the nth degree. They resemble the boisterous skylarking of holiday-makers; in comparison, the disciplined jollity of the chess-player is not only too restrained, but too earnest. Playfulness must be divested of any hint of seriousness before it is laughable; it must be, not only ultimately, but immediately and palpably, indulged in 'for fun'.

Linked with this is the theory, already mentioned, that laughter is the outward sign that our doings are not to be taken seriously. Max Eastman makes a big point of this. He quotes the hero of Owen Wister's novel *The Virginian*, with his ominous injunction: 'When you call me that, smile!' The Southern code allowed only one response to an insult, meant seriously; it could be ignored only if 'in fun'; only, in fact, if accompanied by a smile.

This does not of course explain why a man or an animal obviously 'in fun' should call forth instant laughter. But, on the other hand, if laughter is an immediate and spontaneous reaction to very obvious fun, we can readily understand why it should be adopted as a symbol of innocent intentions.

It does not seem, then, that we can support the theory that laughter originated in this way, as a convenient means of distinguishing mock combats from the genuine article. It looks rather as if this function is secondary and derivative.

At the same time, the connection between play and laughter is certainly worth noticing. Playfulness, that is, not taking things seriously, is certainly one element of almost all laughter. And it may be noticed that here we have approached the border-line between humorous and non-humorous laughter. It is difficult to distinguish accurately between what is funny and what is merely in fun.

(h) Make-believe

There is one type of play which deserves special treatment. 'Let's pretend' is of course a popular children's amusement; but it is also common enough in adult fooling. An apprentice makes some trivial blunder; his work-mate pretends that the error is very serious, trying to convince him, by a grave commiserating tone, that he is due for a reprimand, or even dismissal. We are all familiar with such miniature pieces of acting. In part, of course, this is a practical joke. But not entirely: the victim may often be led to believe something that is not to his personal disadvantage, and need not cause him concern. He may, indeed, enter into the spirit of the thing, and carry on the dialogue in the same vein, inventing new details. Here, of course, no-one is deceived; but both participants enjoy a piece of sheer make-believe.

This type of fooling is not unlike a mock fight. Relief from restraint may play some part in it: it is at least an attempt to vary the monotony of the daily routine by placing a new interpretation on familiar facts. But it has more kinship with what we will find to be the source of much humorous laughter, the twisting of things out of their familiar context so that they fit as smoothly as possible into a very different one.

It must of course be admitted that, just as simple boisterousness ceases to be laughable when it becomes an organized sport, like wrestling, so stage performances do not, in themselves, cause laughter. But this is because the acting has been deliberately harnessed to the service of other emotions. Eliminate all the devices which make this possible, and consider an actor simply as a man dressed up in someone else's clothes, or assuming somebody else's voice and manner, and laughter usually does follow. Certainly in ordinary life mimicry is one very fruitful source of laughter. And in general we may say that anything masquerading as something else is a good formula for laughter. But this time we probably have crossed the border-line.

(i) Contests

At first sight it would not perhaps occur to us that contests, whether mental or physical, are likely to cause much laughter. Nature, red in tooth and claw, may by her very redness produce those higher evolutionary types which march breast forward towards civilization, to that happy consummation when teeth become machine-guns and claws are replaced by high explosive bombs. Ruthless competition in commerce may be the one infallible road to plenty and security for all. Strife, in short, may produce all good things; but not, one would have thought, much merriment.

Yet laughter, if not merriment, does sometimes come from contests. It is not the exuberant laughter of play; that, we have seen, is inhibited whenever it becomes earnest enough to be regarded as a contest, as in wrestling or chess. It is the laugh of triumph, the 'Ha!' of the stage villain when foreclosing a mortgage or trussing a maiden to the teeth of a circular saw. It has, naturally enough, been made much of by those who think, with Hobbes, that laughter expresses a feeling of superiority. The oldest and most primitive form of laughter, says Professor Leacock, is the shout of triumph with which the savage exulted over his fallen foe; giving him, as we still express it, the merry 'Ha-ha!'

The laugh of triumph does no doubt occur. And it occurs as a rule when we have scored off an opponent, not when we have merely scored. We do not, that is to say, expect a man to laugh when he hears that he has passed an examination, or won the Nobel Prize. It is apparently the fallen foe, not the mere feeling of triumph, that is essential.

I do not, as a matter of fact, find it easy to remember, from my own experience, examples of triumphant laughter. I suspect that it is a somewhat literary concept. Probably not even Professor Leacock has actually seen many savages guffawing over the slain. Children, it is true, will laugh at an adversary reduced to tears. Very often, however, this is an attempt to laugh off their own feeling of guilt; it is very close to the defiant laughter of a naughty child who knows he is being naughty. Yet genuinely exultant laughter does, as we have said, no doubt occur; and it is, as we have seen from Leacock, very important to some theories of laughter.

Mental contests often cause laughter; the attraction of a debate is hearing one protagonist score off the other. This sort of thrust and parry is generally good for a laugh; but it usually comes from the spectators, not the debaters. The usual explanation of this is that the spectator gets a vicarious feeling of superiority, through identifying himself with the victor. It is difficult to prove or disprove this. My own feeling is that the satisfaction is much more intellectual than this; it is the neatness and skill of the riposte that delights us. Eastman, who maintains strongly that the humour of repartee is in the contest and not in the superiority, points as proof to amorous repartee, in which the conversation is twisted into mischievous compliments rather than mischievous insults. I am not sure that this proves the point. Any Freudian will at once retort that such compliments are only a form of 'sexual aggression', and Freud himself uses this concept to explain obscene wit. It is perhaps an over ugly phrase for harmless love-making, but it can after all hardly be denied that the tradition of female coyness and male pursuit is essential to the existence of amorous repartee.

Amorous repartee is indeed only one type of mock combat which adults invent for their amusement. We all get a good deal of sport out of teasing each other about our foibles, our opinions, our professions. 'Old So-and-so loves to get one on to me', we say. Often enough there may be a half serious intent behind our sparring. The real source of it all may be an instinctive attempt to smooth over, or laugh off, the real frictions which must occur in any society. If we accept this explanation, we will have to regard the feeling of superiority, if it exists, as a sort of catharsis.

This survey probably does not include all types of non-humorous laughter. But it does, I think, list the main ones. And while our main object in pigeon-holing these varieties was to get them out of the way, so that we could get some order into our discussion of humour, we have already discovered a good many topics which will meet us again. In particular, we have seen that various emotions seem to accompany our different types of laughter. There is the feeling of relief from strain, of joyousness, of superiority over others. Each of these is an important ingredient in some theory of laughter.

3

TYPES OF HUMOUR

NOW WE COME to the much more difficult task of listing the main types of humorous laughter. And here we are faced with a dilemma right at the beginning. Our object is to set down the causes of laughter, quite objectively, uninfluenced by any prior theory, so that we can then examine the list and try to find a characteristic common to each item on it. But obviously we could only do this fully by including every joke that has ever raised a laugh. We can only avoid this superfluity by grouping many of them together in broad classes, and we cannot do this without a basis of classification. And a basis of classification, if it is to be at all adequate, cannot altogether avoid a prior theory of humour.

One realizes the effects of this difficulty in reading C. W. Kimmins' book, *The Springs of Laughter*. The author has asked some thousands of school children, in Britain and the United States, to write down their favourite funny stories, or the sights that have made them laugh most. Obviously this is valuable material. But it is not easy to get any definite result from Kimmins' account of it, simply because he has not worked out any adequate classification for his mass of data. Again and again he groups together, because of some quite extraneous resemblance, stories whose appeal is obviously quite different. Such groups as 'jokes about children', 'domestic incidents', 'street happenings', and so on, obviously tell us nothing at all about their appeal as jokes.

Unfortunately this classification often vitiates Kimmins' conclusions about humour, when he does venture to draw any. For instance, he tells us that at about the age of ten, children begin to delight in stories of class-room incidents. Their appeal, he suggests, indicates the growth of a critical attitude to authority. But his examples hardly bear this out. He cites the story of a schoolboy caught lounging at his desk, his feet projecting beyond it, while busily champing at a sweet. 'Sit up, Billy,' snaps the teacher. 'Take that sweet out of your mouth, and put your feet in!'

Now some of the appeal of this story may lie in the discom-

fiture of the teacher, who has been trapped into making an
absurd remark. No doubt the familiar classroom background
does make it more popular with children than with adults. But
the main point of the story certainly lies elsewhere. It consists
in the fact that a form of words, meant to convey one meaning,
has become capable of conveying another and wildly inappropriate one. Added to this is no doubt the ludicrous image of a
boy with his foot crammed in his mouth—an action which would
certainly cause roars of laughter if performed by a clown at a
circus or a funny man on the films. Certainly it is inadequate,
from our point of view, to classify it as a classroom incident, and
we are only doubtfully justified in deducing from it a growth in
critical attitude toward authority.

Again, Kimmins says that children at this age often delight in
the stupid answers of younger children to questions asked in
class. Here are three of his examples:

(a) The teacher told the class about an Indian rajah who
brought the king a present of rich and beautiful silks. 'And,
children, what do you suppose the king said when all these
beautiful things were spread out before him?' There was a
pause, and then a child at the back piped up: 'Ow much for the
lot?'

(b) The teacher was giving a lesson about the wind. She began by saying: 'This morning, when I was sitting on top of the
bus on my way to school, something came very lightly behind
me, gently ruffled my hair, and then kissed my cheek. What do
you suppose it was?' 'Please, miss, the conductor!'

(c) The class was told: 'You have ears to hear, eyes to see, a
nose to smell, and feet to run.' 'But, please, sir,' said one child,
'my nose runs and my feet smell.'

It is pretty safe to say that none of these stories depends at all
on a feeling of superiority at the stupidity of the children's
answers. The point of (a) lies in the intrusion into an exotic,
romantic, courtly setting of the blunt, suspicious attitude (and
incidentally the accent) of a street-corner huckster. In (b)
there is a similar incongruity between the romantic, highfalutin' tone of the teacher and the sordid realism of the child.
There is also, as in the 'put your feet in' story, the twisting of a
set of words so that it becomes equally appropriate to each of
these two startlingly different interpretations. Finally, there is
the mention of the forbidden subject of love-making. In (c) we

have the verbal twisting again, together with the mention of another forbidden subject. Probably there is room for argument about all these stories. But it can hardly be doubted that 'mistakes of younger children' is inadequate and misleading as a label for any of them.

This hasty labelling throws doubt on what is probably Kimmins' main conclusion. He tells us that at 'the period of rapid growth' (12 to 14 years) there is 'a considerable lowering of the sense of humour'. He means by this a fondness for 'extravagant' stories, involving gross exaggeration or wild improbability. One example he cites is a boy's story about a bicycle running away down a steep hill. In an effort to save himself, the cyclist steers up a wide plank, stretching from the ground to the roof of a house. He plunges off the top of the roof, but is providentially caught on the other side by people beating carpets in the back yard.

Now whether or not we agree with Kimmins in condemning this story, we can hardly deny that its humour does depend entirely on its extravagance. But Kimmins quotes alongside it, as being exactly in the same category, other stories of which the same cannot be said. One of these is the old classroom favourite: 'Lost, umbrella, belonging to gentleman, with bent rib.' This is surely utterly different in its appeal. It can hardly be called extravagant at all—certainly not in the sense in which the term applies to the first story. And elsewhere in the book Kimmins gives, as examples of extravagance, stories which, while they may have an improbable setting, do not depend on this for their point. One of these, which Kimmins stigmatizes as grossly absurd, is the well-known O. Henry story about the poor lovers who wanted to give each other Christmas presents. The man sells his most prized possession, his watch, in order to buy a handsome comb for his sweetheart's beautiful hair. Meanwhile the girl cuts off and sells her hair in order to buy a chain for her lover's cherished watch. We may grant that this story is improbable. But it does not, like the bicycle story, depend for its appeal on the sheer exuberance of its improbability. On the contrary, it must appear to be plausible while you are reading it. If it is felt as absurd, it will fail. The point, of course, lies not in its absurdity, but in the neat symmetry by which the two acts of self-sacrifice cancel each other out.

We must remember of course that Kimmins was not dealing

with the original O. Henry story, but with a bare précis of its plot presented to him as a comic anecdote by an American schoolboy. It is interesting that this story should be retailed in this way, because most readers of O. Henry probably do not think of it as funny, but as pathetic. But in any case, it hardly helps to substantiate Kimmins' conclusions about extravagance and absurdity.

Here are two more stories, both regarded by Kimmins as extravagant, and both cited by him as typical favourites of twelve-year-old boys:

(a) A girl, asked her fiance's profession, said: 'Well, he's a bit of a musician and a bit of a lawyer. The musicians think he's a lawyer, and the lawyers think he's a musician.'

(b) A man went to a charitable lady and said he wished to interest her in the sufferings of a poor family. He drew a harrowing picture of their plight, saying that they would be turned out of their home unless they could find £10 to pay their back rent. 'How did you come to hear of them?' asked the lady. 'Are you their parson?' Brushing away his tears, the man replied: 'No, their landlord.'

Of these (a), although a fairly slender joke, is the reverse of extravagant. It is, in fact, rather quiet and 'dry', and poles away from the exuberance of the runaway bicycle story. While (b) is no doubt inherently improbable, this does not in the least determine its appeal. The point lies in the neat reversal of the stock situation. It is after all eminently reasonable that the landlord should be deeply affected by the inability of a poor family to pay its rent. The tears of disinterested benevolence turn out to be after all only self-pity, and, as in some of the previous examples, behaviour which seems appropriate to one role turns out to be even more appropriate to a very different one.

There are times when Kimmins shows a positive genius for missing the point of the story he quotes. Thus he mentions in passing that certain conventions are fairly rigidly observed in all these stories. Meanness is invariably attributed to a Scot or a Jew, and the hero of stories turning on absence of mind is bound to be a professor. As an example of the latter, he quotes the story of the professor who was held up by a gunman. 'If you move,' said the gunman, 'you're a dead man!' 'On the contrary,' replied the professor, 'if I move it shows that I'm alive.'

It is hard to think of a story less suited to Kimmins' purpose.

Obviously it is no mere convention that the hero of this story is a professor. The point indeed is precisely that he is a professor —that is to say, a pedant, and that he clings to his pedantry even in the least appropriate situation. Absence of mind, on the other hand, at least in the usual sense of the term, does not figure in the story at all.

In dealing with Kimmins at this length, I am not, I hope, merely indulging in the sport, common among writers on humour, of lacerating everybody else's contributions to the subject. These examples do bring out the difficulty that faces us. A classification of humour by merely extraneous features, like 'domestic incidents', 'classroom incidents', and so on, is worse than useless, because it will tempt us to draw false conclusions. Even groupings that may seem to describe the jokes considered as jokes, like 'extravagance and absurdity', 'children's mistakes', and the like, will mislead us unless we analyse our examples with care. Yet any really thorough analysis will in practice amount to laying down a theory of humour. In other words, we will have prejudged the whole issue, and any subsequent conclusions drawn from our preliminary list will be invalid, or at least suspect.

This is probably the real reason why attempts to classify humour have been fairly rare. If you are, like most writers on laughter, a formula-framer, you will be driven to the conclusion that, in the last analysis, there is only one type of joke. They will all turn on release of inhibitions or on superiority at others' misfortunes, or whatever the formula may be. Any other basis of classification will depend on characteristics which are really extraneous and misleading. So you might as well begin by stating your formula and then cite as many examples as possible to prove it. And this is, roughly, the usual procedure.

It is nevertheless rather surprising that as late as 1896, W. S. Lilly could still claim that 'cataloguing the main varieties of the ludicrous' was 'a thing, so far as I am aware, not previously attempted'. His own catalogue is an excellent example of what we need to avoid. It relies largely on terms like humour, the farcical, the comical, the grotesque, and so on. As headings these are not likely to help us much, without very precise definition, which Lilly, incidentally, does not provide. Scattered oddly among these large, vague concepts, and apparently on an equal footing with them, are minutiæ like charades, conundrums, bulls, alliteration. It is obvious that we need classes which will be more precise than humour, and wider in scope than alliteration.

In what follows, I have attempted to provide such a classification. It is not especially original: in many respects it is not much more than an adaptation of the list put forward by Sully. And it should be remembered always that this is a preliminary list. Further analysis may show that many of these classes overlap, and that the differences between them are quite superficial.

On a broad, superficial view, then, we may say that humour falls into the following ten classes:

(a) Any breach of the usual order of events.
(b) Any forbidden breach of the usual order of events.
(c) Indecency.
(d) Importing into one situation what belongs to another.
(e) Anything masquerading as something it is not.
(f) Word-play.
(g) Nonsense.
(h) Small misfortunes.
(i) Want of knowledge or skill.
(j) Veiled insults.

It may be objected that we do not always laugh at each of these. This is one of the main difficulties of our subject: to evolve terms which will describe what is funny without also covering a good deal that is not. Some writers make the general proviso that humour may always be inhibited by the presence of other emotions. Thus our laughter at the misfortunes of others may be inhibited by pity for the victim. To some extent we imply this by limiting laughter to *small* misfortunes; but even then we may sometimes feel more concern than amusement. It will all depend on the circumstances of the individual case, and, to some extent, on our own temperamental peculiarities. This helps to explain why one man's joke is another man's poison.

This is a general objection which applies to all our classes. Other difficulties may best be resolved by considering each class in turn.

(a) Any Breach of the Usual Order of Events

Anything novel or unusual is almost enough in itself to cause a laugh. If you are used to eating with a knife and fork, you laugh the first time you see someone eat with chopsticks. If you are used to chopsticks you laugh the first time you see the knife and fork in use. Unusual dress is another simple example. The costume of any period looks funny to the people of any other period. Bodily deformities, which Sully treats as a separate class, are probably only a special case of this. If you have grown to expect noses to be of a given shape, or ears to be of a certain maximum size, a crooked nose or an over-large ear may make you laugh.

But the case of bodily deformities at once suggests some qualifications. In the first place, pity may easily inhibit laughter here. Or the particular deformity may rouse associations which will also check laughter. To a child a face disfigured by disease may be merely a face with irregular patches of colour on it, and he will laugh. But an adult cannot regard it in quite that way, because, apart altogether from his pity for the victim, he knows that these patches spring from disease, and disease has a definite place in his scheme of things and rouses a definite attitude in his mind. On the other hand, the same adult might laugh at a Maori's tattoo marks, because these seem to him merely a pointless disfigurement. But the Maori will not laugh at them, because to him each mark has a definite meaning. They are signs of rank, fitting into his scheme of things, and as such they are no funnier to him than the judge's wig is to us. But the judge's wig, in its turn, is funny to the American, who has no place for it in his conception of the trappings proper to the dignity of justice.

The point of all this is not merely that we cease to laugh at a novelty once we get used to it. There is more than that involved. Getting used to it usually means that we somehow incorporate it into our general scheme of the universe. Take period costume, once more. So long as a toga is just an outlandish nightgown, you will probably laugh at it. Once it becomes associated in your mind with the glory that was Greece and the grandeur that was Rome, it will evoke quite a different response. Costume drama is not usually regarded as a means of getting laughs from an audience. On the contrary, it is one way of evoking the attitude of romantic nostalgia which past times usually conjure up. But if the costume is not convincing, or if the settings and stage effects generally are not in keeping, the audience certainly will laugh.

This leads to the conclusion that novelty is only funny in so far as it is somehow out of place in some general mental structure. This would suggest an incongruity theory of humour, which it would be premature to pursue at this stage. Without going so far, however, we may note that novelty is not so simple a concept as may at first appear. But, however we explain it, novelty, freshness, unexpectedness does enter in some form into almost every joke. On this ground alone it deserves attention. And, in addition, it does occur often enough in isolation to be regarded as a distinct class.

(b) Any Forbidden Breach of the Usual Order of Events

Oddity takes on a special flavour when it is not merely strange, but wrong. We do not usually think of vice as comic, and yet stage comedy has long regarded vice as an important part of its stock-in-trade. The drunkard, the glutton, the hypocrite, the miser, are all stock figures of fun. Yet all stage villains are not, of course, funny. Why not? The answer seems to be that we laugh only if our attention is not focused on the possibly tragic consequences of the vice, either to its possessor or to others. Nor must we, as we might in a pathological study, consider too closely the causes of the vice. We must not concern ourselves with the way this irregular behaviour fits in with other features of personality, or with other lives. We must regard it simply as a departure from a given norm of conduct.

Is comic vice, then, merely a special case of novelty? There is a clear distinction between the two. Vice is not of course unusual in the simple sense. It has its special character not because it is rare and strange, but because it breaks a rule. And it rouses our interest because rules, whether we take kindly to them or not, have a special importance for us.

We might, however, reverse the question and ask whether novelty is not really a special case of rule-breaking. There is, of course, a clear logical distinction between oddity, as in an unusual costume, and a comic vice, like drunkenness. But they are not always felt as different. Many people do regard oddity in dress as morally reprehensible, even though not all of them will admit it. The difference between morals and *mores* has never been very clear. Most people would rather be accused of immoral behaviour, like selfishness or boastfulness, than of uncustomary behaviour, like eating peas with a knife. It is at least arguable that most oddities are obscurely felt as immoralities. A colonial accent is not only odd and amusing: it is 'wrong'. And while few people would admit that they mean morally wrong, they often act as if they did.

From the simple, unreflective point of view, the only difference is between the forbidden breach and the permissible one. Eating peas with a knife is no less forbidden than lying; indeed a child may easily find that he is reprimanded more severely for the first. Moreover, a breach of custom may easily be a moral breach, even if our standards are not conventional. Wearing plus fours at a funeral, for instance, is more than an instance of unusual costume. It may be interpreted as showing a lack of proper respect, and consequently may hurt the dead man's relatives.

Novelty, then, is not easy to distinguish from breach of custom, and breach of custom shades off into moral breach. Indeed, it is often argued that laughter is a kind of spontaneous punishment imposed on the nonconformist, and is thus a means by which society protects itself against innovation. If so, it is of course quite unjust that long ears or a crooked nose should be punished equally with deliberate wrong-doing. The answer would be, of course, that laughter is an instinctive activity which is not concerned with justice; and that in humour eccentricity of any sort is felt, however unfairly, as a moral breach.

At the moment we are not concerned to affirm or deny this view. Our point is merely that novelty and breach of rule are both, under certain circumstances, the cause of laughter, and that there is at least some connection between them.

(c) Indecency

Indecency quite obviously is a special case of a forbidden breach of the usual order. It is treated here as a separate class because it does appear to be different, at least to the immediate perceptions of the laugher. Our laughter at a smutty story has quite a different flavour from our laughter at the sight of a fat man over-eating. One reason for this is almost certainly that the smutty story allows us to give rein to thoughts that are normally inhibited. It is possible of course that this is part of our laughter at all comic vice. This will be discussed later. But indecency deserves a special place in any analysis of laughter simply because it raises this question in a clear and unequivocal form.

George Orwell, in a thoughtful essay on the comic postcard, says:

A dirty joke is not, of course, a serious attack upon morality, but it is a sort of mental rebellion, a momentary wish that things were otherwise. So also with all other jokes, which always centre round cowardice, laziness, or some other quality which society cannot afford to encourage. Society always has to demand a little more from human beings than it will get in practice. It has to demand faultless discipline and self-sacrifice, it must expect its subjects to work hard, pay their taxes, and be faithful to their wives, it must assume that men think it glorious to die on the battle-field and women want to wear themselves out with child-bearing. The whole of what one may call official literature is founded on such assumptions. I never read the proclamations of generals before battle, the speeches of fuhrers and prime ministers, the solidarity songs of public schools and Left Wing political parties, national anthems, temperance tracts, papal encyclicals and sermons against gambling and contraception, without seeming to hear in the background a chorus of raspberries from all the millions of common men to whom these high sentiments make no appeal. Nevertheless the high sentiments always win in the end, leaders who offer blood, toil, tears and sweat always get more out of their followers than those who offer safety and a good time. When it comes to the pinch, human beings are heroic. Women face childbed and the scrubbing brush, revolutionaries keep their mouths shut in the torture chamber, battleships go down with their guns still firing when their decks are awash. It is only that the other element in man, the lazy, cowardly, debt-bilking adventurer who is inside all of us, can never be suppressed altogether and needs a hearing occasionally.

We may or may not accept this as a general theory of humour, or even of all comic vice. When we laugh at cowardice, laziness, and so forth, we may possibly be rejoicing, as Hobbes supposed, at our own freedom from these failings. But nobody supposes this of indecency.

The indecent may be defined, briefly but adequately, as the mention of the unmentionable. Whatever else society may or may not demand of us, it certainly insists that some natural functions, notably copulation and excretion, should be kept in the background. When they are dragged out into the light of day, we laugh. The formula for the smutty joke is as simple as that.

There are, of course, many refinements on the formula. One of them is the element of contrast. If the revealing phrase can be put in the mouth of a parson, if it can even be obtruded into a religious service, so much the better. 'The bishop and the barmaid' is itself, without any elaboration, a mildly suggestive phrase; and a highly popular comic novel has been written with the title 'The Bishop's Jaegers'. It is funny to point out that even the supreme upholders of the official attitude are not immune from what Orwell calls 'the other element in man'.

The other main refinement is allusiveness. That is what is usually meant by those people who say that they don't mind a smutty joke provided it is witty. The indelicate reference must be smuggled in as neatly and unobtrusively as possible, so that only the keen eye can detect it. Like hypocrisy, this may be vice's tribute to virtue: an attempt to observe the conventions even while enjoying the thrill of flouting them. It must be remembered, however, that allusiveness also occurs in humour which in no way depends on the indecent. This may mean that there are other classes of humour which also depend on release from restraint; or it may mean that there is some quite independent way in which allusiveness contributes to humour.

(d) Importing into One Situation What Belongs to Another

In discussing the stories of Kimmins' schoolchildren, we have seen that they often depend on the intrusion into one sphere of an incident or attitude of mind which is appropriate only to an utterly different sphere. The Indian rajah spreads his costly silks before the king with all the courtly ceremony which accompanies Oriental gifts. And the king, instead of responding with similar courtliness, is represented as exclaiming: 'Ow much for the lot?'

It is usual to call this incongruity. Sully makes incongruity one of his classes, and gives such examples as a tall and a short man together, or climbing a mountain in high-heeled shoes. But incongruity has often been regarded as the whole explanation of humour, and it is possible to analyse almost any joke so as to make incongruity its main feature. It is probably because of this that in his preliminary list Sully confines the term to 'cases where the mind is focused on the relation'. And by this he seems to mean superficial effects of contrast, like the short man and the tall man.

But the story of the rajah does not depend merely on contrast. There is here the mental shock of being jolted out of a whole frame of mind, a whole universe of discourse, with all sorts of rich associations, all sorts of stock responses leaping to the fore-front of consciousness. We are all creatures of habit: and this applies to thought as well as to action. We put kings in one mental compartment, and costers in another. We surround each of them with different associations, and we respond to each with a particular attitude. Each of these structures is largely artificial: it is built up out of carefully selected materials. We leave out of account those facts about kings which would be more appropriate to our attitude towards costers, and vice versa. There is a type of humour which consists in shattering these mental structures by obtruding the inconvenient, inappropriate fact.

Not all of this applies to the story of the rajah. It would be absurd to find here any profound criticism of the real behaviour of monarchs. The point is merely that a particular atmosphere has been built up, an atmosphere that does depend largely on stock responses. And this atmosphere is suddenly destroyed by a single inappropriate remark. It is this which gives the sensation of being suddenly hurled from one universe into another.

This may explain another feature of the Kimmins stories we attempted to analyse. In the story of the landlord pleading for the poor family, the point lay, we decided, in behaviour appropriate to one role turning out to be even more appropriate to an utterly different one. This crops up, too, in the story of the teacher talking about the wind. The point here is not merely that the teacher's romantic discourse about 'Nature' was understood by the pupil to be a prosaic and slightly improper anecdote about a bus conductor. There is a certain delight in realizing that the description really was appropriate to either; that the two universes have not just got mixed, but really are linked to each other. Where the connection depends on the ambiguity of a form of words, of course, the linking is obviously more apparent than real. That is why such stories are often unsatisfactory. The story about the landlord is a better story, because here the connection between disinterested benevolence and commercial greed is rooted in the whole situation and does not depend on verbal ambiguity.

Universe-changing is a very important element in humour: we may even find that it is the key to all humour. For this reason it should perhaps be left till we come to discuss the whole incongruity theory of humour. But even a preliminary list would be incomplete without some mention of it.

(e) Anything Masquerading as Something it is Not

One of Sully's headings is 'pretences', and he defines this as any situation in which we feel that we are peeping behind the mask. 'The harmless make-believe of a child sets us laughing in one key, the detection of half unconscious humbug in another, of an artful impostor in yet another.' Since he gives 'moral sense' as the counteractive, Sully was probably thinking chiefly of trickery and hypocrisy, whether conscious or in the more complex form of self-deception. But most of this could have been included under comic vice, of which hypocrisy is indeed one of his own examples. We need to extend the term to include mimicry, which is a fruitful source of laughter, and the whole field of impromptu acting, of conscious fooling, that we mentioned when discussing playfulness. It can probably be laid down as a general principle that anything which masquerades as another thing is *ipso facto* laughable.

Even those articles of commerce in which a cake of soap appears as a lemon, or a box of cigars as a book, are mildly funny, or at least 'quaint'. A man disguised as a woman, or vice versa, has been a favourite stage device from 'Twelfth Night' to 'Charley's Aunt'. And other types of masquerade, such as a duke pretending to be his own butler, or a prostitute appearing as a Salvation Army lassie, are scarcely less common. There is room here, of course, for all sorts of overtones. Sometimes the masquerade may be a convenient device for introducing indecency, or small misfortunes, or universe-changing, or some other type of humour. It may be a means of derision, as when mimicry becomes parody. But, apart from all this, there is a certain direct pleasure to be obtained from masquerade, simply in itself: and at least in this stage of our inquiry, it deserves to be regarded as a separate class.

(f) Word-play

Playing with words is of course a familiar type of humour, and one which children delight in at a very early age. Almost any distortion of words can be amusing, at least to children. The simplest forms are misspelling and mispronunciation. Much of the pleasure in word-play is probably the mere delight of exploration: of finding out the possibilities in words. There is a delight in merely noticing that a form of words meant to have one meaning can also have an entirely different one. Much of

Lewis Carroll's fooling consists in this sort of mental exploration.

'Take some more tea,' the March Hare said to Alice, very earnestly.

'I've had nothing yet,' Alice replied in an offended tone, 'so I can't take more.'

'You mean you can't take *less*,' said the Hatter. 'It's very easy to take *more* than nothing.'

This sort of word-play shades off into playing with ideas, and cannot always be distinguished from it. It is even possible to play, in much the same way, with figures: mathematical puzzles and problems are not essentially different in their appeal.

This intellectual pleasure remains part of the appeal of word-play even when, as so often, it is pressed into the service of other kinds of humour. Most puns turn out to be either veiled insults or veiled allusions to sex. Sully's example, the term 'a moving discourse' applied to a speaker 'whose oratory had power to clear the fullest hall in half an hour', gains most of its force from being a veiled insult (or better, perhaps, an insult masquerading as a compliment): but it still has some appeal simply as a pun.

(g) Nonsense

According to Sully, a subdivision of the incongruous is 'the absurd, or logically incongruous'. His example is the Irish bull; and he seems to have in mind the union of two things which are logically incompatible, like a square circle. This is of course the strict sense of absurd: and there is certainly a case for linking it with incongruity. For even if we take Sully's example of incongruity in general (climbing a mountain in high-heeled shoes), it can be argued that this is not merely an odd addition to mountaineering costume, outlawed by custom only, like wearing a tweed cap with a dinner suit. The shoes really are, in more than a conventional sense, incompatible with mountaineering. The two things really cannot, in the nature of things, be united, or at least not for long.

Can we say, then, that there are two ways of importing into one situation what belongs to another? We may be bringing together what man has, quite arbitrarily, put asunder: the world of the king and the world of the coster, with the codes and conventions belonging to each. Or we may be bringing together what is inevitably sundered by the laws of nature. Obviously the line between the two will not be clearly defined. There can be endless argument about whether a particular cleavage is natural or artificial. It will follow, then, that a joke which turns on the one cannot always be clearly distinguished from a joke which turns on the other, and that the two had better be regarded as belonging to the same type of humour.

This is all plausible enough: and yet there is a case for regarding absurdity as a distinct type of humour altogether. The notion of a square circle does not give us quite the mental jolt which accompanies universe changing. It is true that this mental jolt may be followed by the Euclidean reflection—'which is absurd'; and that this may enhance the joke. But it is also true that universe changing may be accompanied by the opposite reflection: that the world of our emotions does not after all square with the world of hard fact; and it may well be that this, too, gives point to the joke. The paradoxes of W. S. Gilbert are usually of the first type: those of Bernard Shaw are of the second.

Further, while one can define absurdity as the bringing together of what is logically incongruous, it is doubtful if its appeal depends on any direct perception of incongruity. It may be argued that nonsense appeals directly and immediately just because it is nonsense; because it frees us from the restraint of reason. Consider a typical verse of Edward Lear:

> On the top of the Crumpetty tree
> The Quangle Wangle sat
> But his face you could not see
> On account of his Beaver Hat.
> For his hat was a hundred and two feet wide
> With ribbons and bibbons on every side
> And bells, and buttons, and loops, and lace,
> So that nobody ever could see the face
> Of the Quangle Wangle Quee.

In the notion of the hat obscuring the face, it might be argued, you have a typical reversal of logical relations. But for the most part it can hardly be said that the reader's mind is focused on relations at all. He is led away by a riot of odd-sounding words, which mean nothing in particular but are somehow satisfying. There is no unity of incompatibles in Quangle Wangle, bibbons, or Lear's favourite word runcible. True, they sound as if they mean something, whereas in fact they don't, which is a kind of incongruity; but this does not explain their appeal. It is largely the appeal of fantasy; of that novelty and oddity which raises the feeling-tone of the observer to joyous excitement.[1]

This type of wild fantasy is possibly only an extension of the shock of surprise that is generally regarded as essential to all humour. Humour always provides us with a release from the too familiar pattern of everyday events. What is distinctive about nonsense, at least in its extreme form, is that it does nothing else. It does not merely twist events into a slightly different pattern: it breaks the pattern altogether.

(h) Small Misfortunes

This is a very familiar source of laughter, which requires no elaboration at this stage. The banana-skin, the custard pie, the thumb beneath the hammer, are among the first things we laugh at in childhood. They are the stand-by of the hoariest vaudeville act, and they continue to be good box-office in the newest and shiniest of picture theatres. There may be argument about whether a particular joke belongs to this class or not. Is the hen-pecked husband, for instance, just a man in a jam, or is he something more subtle, an example of the reversal of what is (in theory, if not in fact) the normal order? But there can be no doubt that, all refinements aside, misfortunes are funny, simply in themselves.

(i) Want of Knowledge or Skill

Simple ignorance is generally good for a laugh. We would certainly be amused if we heard someone declare, in all good faith, that New York was the capital of England. We would probably not even smile if he said that New York was the capital of the State of New York. The ignorance, then, must be gross and obvious. This suggests that something more than pride in our own knowledge is involved. If that were all we would laugh loudest at the more pardonable mistakes, because then our pride at detecting them would be the greater. At the same time, there is certainly some tinge of superiority in our laughter at the mistakes of others, but probably our laughter here also has something in common with our delight in absurdity or nonsense.

---

[1] I am informed that 'runcible' may not be a nonsense word, but, since most of Lear's readers think it is, the point is hardly affected. Of the dictionaries I have consulted, only Webster assigns it a meaning; the *Oxford English Dictionary* omits it altogether.

The same can hardly be said of lack of skill. Sully's example here is the clumsy attempt of the circus clown to imitate the agility of the acrobat. Any similar exhibition of ineptitude—the golfer who foozles his shot, the marksman whose bullet misses the target altogether, the paperhanger who gets covered with paste and tangled up in his own paper—may make us laugh. One factor may be the contrast between the conception and the execution—the fact that the butt is setting out to do something for which he is obviously unfitted—but on the whole our laughter seems to be largely at the misfortunes of others.

Another of Sully's examples is quite differently interpreted by Bergson. This is the story of the tourist who, when told of an extinct volcano in the neighbourhood, said in disappointed tones: 'They had a volcano and they let it go out!' Bergson sees in this, not ignorance, but egotism. To the tourist nature is just a spectacle stage-managed for his especial benefit. To Bergson, therefore, this is an example of comic vice, or would be if he were following Sully's classification. Actually, of course, he sees it as just one more example of mental inelasticity, which explains all humour. There is probably much to be said for either explanation: the moral is that even the simplest joke may be surprisingly difficult to classify.

Rather oddly, Sully puts exaggeration in this class, as showing ignorance of what is credible. Exaggeration may of course result from *naïveté*: but it is more often a weapon of caustic wit, and it is then that it is most likely to seem funny. Consider Margaret Halsey on an English tea-party: 'Forcing a way into one of those tight little clusters seemed about as practicable as approaching the Archbishop of Canterbury and asking him if he were doing anything tonight.' Exaggeration here is the typical caricaturist's device of enlarging a defect so as to call attention to it. And even where it is not pointed or caustic, exaggeration need not suggest lack of knowledge. The typical tall story, like the old chestnut about the farmer whose scarecrow 'scared the crows so badly that they brought back the corn they stole two years before', raises a laugh, but not at the narrator's ignorance.

(j) Veiled Insults

Among children it is considered screamingly funny to shout: 'You're a donkey!' Adults continue to be amused at this type of humour, provided that it is wrapped up a little. Freud quotes a gibe at a retiring politician: 'Like Cincinnatus, he has now returned to his place before the plough', which is really just a roundabout way of saying the same thing.

There are differences, however, and they may be important. There is the fact that the insult here just misses—by half a word—being a particularly fulsome compliment. This may be the real point of the joke, and the spice of malice may be an additional, non-humorous source of satisfaction. The fact remains, however, that most witticisms are simply veiled insults. Certainly the veiling is important, as well as the insult: any theory will need to account for both.

The parallel with indecency—veiled sexual reference—is quite close. In childhood, after all, our spitefulness is repressed just as thoroughly as our curiosity about sex. 'Don't be rude!' carries either implication. It may be, then, that veiled insults, like indecency, give rein to a side of our nature that is normally repressed. But in any case it is certainly a common, and a distinct, type of humour.

So much, then, for our preliminary classification. In the following chapters these classes will be discussed more fully.

4

COMEDY OF CHARACTER

T WO of our classes—breach of order and rule, and forbidden breach, or comic vice—may lead us on to comedy of character in general. Not every comic character in fiction or drama is either an eccentric or a villain; but a fairly large proportion of them are.

Certainly the comic villain is a fact of stage comedy and of literature generally. The outstanding example is Falstaff. Falstaff can best be described as a man who consistently and shamelessly breaks both moral laws and social conventions. He is a liar, a glutton, a drunkard, a fornicator, and a coward. Why, then, is he not simply a villain, like Iago? The comparison brings out one important difference. Falstaff has no malice; Iago has little else. Falstaff's vices are the amiable ones that do little harm to anyone but himself. On the whole, we feel that he does much less actual harm in the world than the heroic Henry V. His boastfulness, his love of pleasure and his frank cowardice are all traits we recognize in ourselves, and have repressed more or less unwillingly. It is easy, therefore, to interpret our delight in him as our relief in throwing aside these repressions. Everything is made easy for us: our moral sense is lulled by the fact that nobody is harmed very much by his vices. Or if they are, their suffering is not obtruded on our sympathies; and he has many other qualities with which we gladly identify ourselves—wit, resourcefulness, and a great zest for living.

But, it will be said, not all comic villains content themselves with gluttony and the other self-regarding vices. The comic swindler is a favourite figure; and swindling is pretty obviously harmful to others. Consider O. Henry's gentle grafter, another sympathetic and amusing villain: he is a confidence trickster who sells gold bricks to farmers. But here again the author minimizes the vicious side of his actions. Various devices keep our minds off the suffering of the victims; we are left to assume that they can afford the loss; and in one story, where Jeff Peters has taken part in a piece of fraudulent company promotion, he disgorges the proceeds when he discovers that the victims are the traditional widows and orphans. There is an implication here, of course, that a professed swindler is more honourable than many highly respected financiers; and no doubt this is important. Much of our pleasure in comic villains lies in the feeling that their code is after all no worse than the accepted one. This may be merely a rationalization to stifle our consciences; but it certainly plays a part in our total emotions. That is why humour often plays round departments of morals where we all feel that the accepted code is somewhat shaky: notably sexual behaviour. Here, of course, the irksomeness of the repression is an obvious reason why we welcome a chance to rebel, if only vicariously; but we do so all the more readily because we feel it is easy to justify the rebellion.

At the same time, Lamb is only partly right when he explains Restoration comedy as a dream world to which moral standards simply do not apply. If we were altogether oblivious of current morality, it is doubtful if we would laugh at all. The Restoration drama itself is usually regarded as a reaction from the strictness of the Puritan code. We need to be able to lull our moral indignation sufficiently to enjoy an escape from the tyranny of our customary repressions; but a holiday owes much of its pleasure to the consciousness of the usual daily round waiting to claim its own.

Here we have an explanation which covers many types of humour. Not only comic villains like Falstaff and Jeff Peters, but our delight in indecency and veiled insults can be plausibly regarded as escape from repression. But is all comic vice of this kind? Is the comic villain necessarily a sympathetic figure? Do we always laugh with him, and never at him?

Once we raise this question, we realize that moral deformity, as Sully uses the term, means a good deal more than this. We may laugh at vice without in the least identifying ourselves with it. To Elizabethan audiences, Malvolio and even Shylock were figures of fun as well as Falstaff. It is perhaps significant that later critics have been able to work up much sympathy, and even some admiration, for both of them; but if we defend them, it is only out of patronizing pity for the underdog. We are always conscious of condescending to them, of being extraordinarily magnanimous in finding excuses for them. Nobody ever feels like patronizing Falstaff.

This is the classic view of the place of vice in comedy. The comic figure in the early morality plays was the Devil; though it is true that this was the comedy of incident, of custard pies and banana-skins, rather than the comedy of character. But when comedy of character did develop, it grew out of the notion of 'humours'. The whole point of Falstaff is that he is well-balanced, 'integrated', with a rich philosophy of life all his own. The whole point of a humour, in the early sense of the word, is that it is a kink, a quirk, a mental oddity that throws a man off his balance and twists his view of life. Molière's comic characters are of this type, as can be seen from the titles of his plays: *L'Avare, Le Misanthrope*. And it was largely from Molière that Bergson got his notion of the *idée fixe* as the clue to all comedy. The comic character, on this view, is simply a man with an obsession. The joke is to see how this obsession crops up again and again in the most varied situations, so that he always behaves in a manner wildly inappropriate to the circumstances as others see them, but entirely appropriate to his own ruling passion.

This view of comic vice does not leave much room for getting rid of repression. We may laugh at Don Juan (Byron's or Mr. Linklater's) with a pleasant sense of gratifying our own lusts; but when we laugh at a stage miser or a comic-paper Scot we do not feel that we are giving rein to our own parsimony. Our attitude here gives more support to the superiority theory; and the notion of the fixed idea persisting inappropriately also impinges on the incongruity theory.

Any Scot or Jew story fits the Bergson formula fairly well. The comic Scot allows his love of what the comic-papers archly call 'bawbees' to over-ride everything else. He likes dining in restaurants because there are twopences under all the plates. He takes his girl out and heads for a theatre with 'The Woman Pays' over the entrance in neon lights. Asked how much whisky he can drink, he replies: 'Any given quantity.'

Formally, there are other elements in all these stories, from incongruity to puns. But it is this notion of an overwhelming obsession that gives them point. And the same simple formula explains the stereotypes that serve as comic characters in most popular fiction. Mr. George Orwell has given us a masterly analysis of the school stories that are turned out week after week in the boys' weeklies. Each of the comic characters in these stories has a single oddity that the author exploits endlessly. Often enough this is tied to some supposed national characteristic, like the Scotsman's meanness. There is a comic American boy who seeks every opportunity to make money. There is a comic Indian who transposes the remarks of his companions into long-winded Babu English. There is a comic lord whose single characteristic is laziness, who spends most of his time asleep on a sofa. This simple mechanical comedy of character is also common on the films. Something of it is present in our minds when we exclaim delightedly of our friend's conduct: 'isn't that just like Old So-and-so?' There is, in short, plenty of evidence to support Bergson (or Molière, or Ben Jonson) when he defines vice in comedy as a single obsession, recurring endlessly in varied situations.

This view of comic vice affords the clearest possible case of comic characters who are laughed at, and not with. But even apart from these stereotypes, immorality can occur in comedy without evoking the half-envious toleration inspired by Falstaff or Don Juan. In the schoolboy stories just discussed, I have left out the favourite, and easily the best, comic character, Billy Bunter. He is better than the others, because in him the technique has been carried a step further. He has three or four comic vices instead of one. He is a glutton, a liar, and a coward. Above all, he is incurably selfish. These characteristics all recur, after the same fashion as the single foibles of the others, so that his behaviour in any situation can be pretty confidently predicted. But the different sides of his character have to fit together. The result is that he is something like a fully-rounded character, more of a person and less of an animated mannerism. The character drawing is still at a very low level. But it is precisely because the technique is childishly transparent that this cardboard comedy is instructive. Mature, adult comedy carries the technique a stage further still, gives the character more and more facets, each of which must be consistent with the others, until we have no walking puppet but a real man or woman. But he still has this in common with the stereotype. We still expect to see this character, this many-sided character, reacting to a situation. We do not expect to see the situation moulding him. We still have the confident feeling that we know and understand him through and through.

It is this, I suggest, that really makes the comic character comic. Our emotion is still perhaps superiority — Hobbes's 'sudden glory' — but it is more than just a sneering contempt for some failing we think we have not got. We are conscious rather of seeing the whole human scene from some godlike level at which all men and women look pretty much alike: all weak, all lovable, all transparently obvious in their petty pretences. In a word, all childlike. We feel at home in a cosy little world that we thoroughly understand; and it is pleasant to sit back and watch the children play.

There is a story by H. G. Wells, 'A Vision of Judgment', which exactly describes the god's-eye view: which attributes it, indeed, to God.

The story deals with the Day of Judgment, and we are given the traditional picture of saints and sinners answering the charges of the Recording Angel. Only the picture is not quite traditional. Saint and sinner alike, in the eyes of God, are merely ridiculous. The posturings of vice, the self-congratulation of virtue are both regarded with the tolerant charity which we give to the rather endearing silliness of children.

This is essentially the attitude of humour. Wells is here of course only describing it: the skill of the humorist consists in showing us life as it appears once that viewpoint is adopted. His own handling of Kipps or Mr. Polly is very much the attitude of God to the saints and sinners described in this passage. It does not make much difference whether the humorist surveys the whole field of human endeavour, like Swift or Voltaire, or whether he takes a small cross-section of it, like Jane Austen. In both you will find the same aloof, impartial appraisal.

What he must not do, however, is to assume too completely some partial viewpoint. Nothing could miss the spirit of Swift more completely than the Russian film called 'The New Gulliver'. In this version, Gulliver takes the side of the Lilliputian proletariat and uses his size and strength to help them throw off their oppressors. But Swift's satire goes much deeper than this: like God in Wells' fable, he sees beyond all the fussing about saints and sinners to the absurdity of all human vanity and human pretensions.

The same difference in attitude marks off the more subtle comedy of character from the comic stereotype. The stereotype has some special quirk that makes his behaviour odd in the judgment of ordinary common sense. Thus we have the long procession of diverting cranks whom Peacock assembles at his country houses. But to a keener eye we are all cranks of one sort or another; and every place where men foregather is a Headlong Hall or a Nightmare Abbey.

For in comedy we have, not a mighty clash of wills as in tragedy, but a constant series of dimly discerned misunderstandings. We are all slightly at cross purposes with our neighbours; our values are never quite their values, and our language never quite the same as theirs. Add to this the constant effort on everybody's part to keep his end up, to justify his own behaviour and outlook according to the current codes, and we have the human comedy.

There is a passage in E. M. Forster's *Aspects of the Novel* which describes one such comedy of cross-purposes. It occurred after H. G. Wells had parodied Henry James in *Boon*:

Wells sent 'Boon' as a present to James, apparently thinking the master would be as much pleased by such heartiness and honesty as was he himself. The master was far from pleased, and a most interesting correspondence ensued. James is polite, reminiscent, bewildered, deeply outraged and exceedingly formidable: he admits that the parody has not 'filled him with a fond elation', and regrets in conclusion that he can sign himself 'only yours faithfully Henry James'. Wells is bewildered too, but in a different way: he cannot understand why the man should be upset. And, beyond the personal comedy, there is the great literary importance of the issue.

The root of our pleasure in this type of humour may of course be vanity. It is no doubt flattering to feel that we are above the dust and struggle of human conflicts. Urbane, impartial, amused detachment can certainly be irritating. *The New Yorker*, with its eighteenth-century exquisite who surveys the world genially, quizzically, and a little cynically through his eye-glass, probably typifies fairly well the attitude we have been describing. And *The New Yorker* at its worst can undoubtedly be smug, smart-alecky and short-sighted. At the same time it is, I think, inadequate to regard the god's-eye view as merely an expression of our own vanity. At its best it is rather a sense of the eternal inappropriateness of all human endeavour when measured by the best we know.

The chief delight of the god's-eye view is the penetration of shams. Perhaps nine-tenths of comic vice is really pretentiousness. Deliberate, brazen, unabashed wrong-doing may occasionally make us laugh, but it is the half-envious laugh evoked by Falstaff, the laugh of liberation from restraint. It is vice masked as virtue that most commonly brings the laugh of superiority. The most obviously comic villains are the Mr. Pecksniffs. Part of this may be due to another type of humour: the intellectual pleasure of finding connections where none seem to exist. But another part of our pleasure is certainly the peculiar luxury of the god's-eye view, enabling us to detect the very simple passions and trivial vanities which human beings hide under an elaborate mumbo-jumbo of rationalization.

As a category of humour, then, comic vice is by no means simple. It is, indeed, as question-begging a label as 'classroom incidents'. For comic vice may contain each or all of these ingredients:

(a) The simple contrast between the expected and the actual: in short, novelty and oddity, which is regarded as funny because it is felt to imply this contrast, to be 'unfitting'.

(b) Liberation from the restraint of morality, which always involves some repression.

(c) The god's-eye view, which enables us to penetrate the petty pretences of human behaviour.

Nor can we say that (a) is peculiar to breaches of custom, and that (b) and (c) belong to comic vice. At first sight, it is true, merely odd behaviour seems unlikely to give us this god's-eye view. But often enough the motives behind the oddity will be laid bare. Adolescent shyness, for example, will probably lead to nothing worse than a few harmless breaches of etiquette. But when we laugh at the behaviour of a shy boy at some social gathering, it is not merely because we enjoy the contrast between bungling awkwardness and the assured grace which convention demands. We also have a pleasant sense of penetrating behind the social façade to the simple emotions of the unsophisticated.

This applies even more strongly to (b). Convention may be a tyrant no less than morality, and its victims may call no less urgently for liberation. A stock figure in popular fiction is the gruff eccentric, badly dressed, brusque in manner, lacking all the social graces, but definitely winning the sympathy, as well as the laughter, of the reader. He is to convention what Falstaff is to morals.

Our two original sub-divisions, then, do not help us much. They have only served to show the existence of a deeper duality which cuts across both of them, with a third element remaining stubbornly apart. Both breaches of custom and of morality may evoke either liberation from restraint or the god's-eye view, and, whichever they evoke, the primary sense of contrast with normal or 'fitting' behaviour will still remain as part of our enjoyment.

Moreover, it is obvious that these elements are by no means confined to comic vice. There is indeed such a thing as comic virtue. Consider Mr. Pickwick, or the Vicar of Wakefield. Both are thoroughly good men. That is why we laugh at them. They have something of Bergson's comic rigidity; their virtues crop up with the same consistency as other people's vices, and with as little regard for appropriateness. We know that Mr. Pickwick will always be benevolent and sympathetic, even towards a rascal and a cheat. Does this mean that Dickens is satirizing goodness? Not at all. We continue to respect and admire Mr. Pickwick; but we feel that we understand him, and that makes us at home with him. We see through him just as we see through the liar, the glutton, or the hypocrite. We look down on him; but not in the sense of despising him, only in the sense of enjoying the god's-eye view. To understand everything is to pardon everything, and maybe to applaud a good deal. It is also very good fun, and makes us feel at home with ourselves and the universe. To look up to somebody, on the other hand, means to contemplate qualities which we admire in the original sense of wonder at: that is, we feel that they are beyond our mental grasp. This may also be a pleasurable sensation, and is necessary to some temperaments. It all depends on whether you want a cosy little world or a vast, heroic and inspiring one. Hero-worship and laughter are necessarily opposites. We may laugh at good men, but not at great men.

5

FINDING CONNECTIONS

HUMOUR, we have just said, is incompatible with hero-worship. No doubt this explains why a good deal of humour consists in destroying hero-worship. It deliberately breaks down the atmosphere of mystery and sanctity on which hero-worship depends. Debunking is one of the surest sources of laughter. Our most famous modern humorists have made a speciality of it. Lytton Strachey debunks the heroes of history, and Bernard Shaw debunks the whole heroic attitude to life. They do not do this merely to raise a laugh. Shaw's attitude is made explicit in the preface to his *Pleasant Plays*.

... I can no longer be satisfied with fictitious morals and fictitious good conduct, shedding fictitious glory on robbery, starvation, disease, crime, drink, war, cruelty, cupidity and all the other commonplaces of civilisation which drive men to the theatre to make foolish pretences that such things are progress, science, morals, religion, patriotism, imperial supremacy, national greatness and all the other names the newspapers call them. On the other hand, I see plenty of good in the world working itself out as fast as the idealists will allow it; and if they would only let it alone and learn to respect reality ..., we should all get along much better and faster. At all events, I do not see moral chaos and anarchy as the alternative to romantic convention; and I am not going to pretend I do merely to please the people who are convinced that the world is only held together by the force of unanimous, strenuous, eloquent, trumpet-tongued lying. To me the tragedy and comedy of life lie in the consequences, sometimes terrible, sometimes ludicrous, of our persistent attempts to found our institutions on the ideals suggested to our imaginations by our half-satisfied passions, instead of on a genuinely scientific natural history.

This is the creed of a social reformer, not of a humorist. Why then does its application make for humour? So far I have suggested that it is because the attitude of the natural historian is also the god's-eye view. But is this all? The special meaning of debunking is not merely that we gaze coolly, impersonally, and with unblinkered eyes at the antics of men and women, but that we direct this gaze toward people who are generally regarded with quite other emotions. We are familiar enough with the god's-eye view as applied to people who do not normally claim veneration. This is merely the comedy of low life, which has been the mainstay of English humour from Chaucer to W. W. Jacobs. The convention which regards one social class as somehow intrinsically superior to another provides an obvious point of vantage for the god's-eye view. We simply look at the lower classes from the angle of the upper classes. Debunking is low-life comedy applied to high life. It is done by pointing out that the motives and the behaviour of the upper classes are not essentially different from those of the lower classes. And precisely the same technique can be applied to military, political, or religious heroes. If it is funny for a duke to behave like a dustman, it is also funny for Julius Cæsar or Abraham Lincoln or even General Gordon to behave like a mere mortal.

But this is more than a fresh application of a familiar type of humour. A new ingredient has been added; as well as the familiar amused contemplation of human antics, we have the contrast with the customary attitude to these heroes. And this immensely heightens the joke.

We have here, in short, the imparting into one sphere of something belonging to another. This special form of it we have already described as universe-changing. We all of us build up special attitudes of mind toward particular persons and institutions. Some of these are private and peculiar to ourselves; the vast majority are common property, standardized in the community, and deliberately inculcated in children. You will find these attitudes epitomized and collected in the copy-books; or, rather more emotionally expressed, in the works of Ella Wheeler Wilcox or Mr. Edgar Guest. And, indeed, in other more reputable poets.

East, west, home's best.
God could not be everywhere and so he made mothers.
The world's well lost for love.
Breathes there the man, with soul so dead, who never to himself has said, 'This is my own my native land'?
It is a sweet and fitting thing to die for the fatherland.
Let whining Indians cringe and kneel, an English lad must die.

Here we have typical expressions of the dominant attitudes to family life and to patriotism. The point here is not whether

these propositions are true or false. They express certain sentiments which are automatically evoked by the institutions they
refer to. The word sentiment is used here in the technical sense
given it by McDougall: a complex of emotions centring round
a particular object. Whenever the object crops up, the emotional attitude is there, ready-made.

But suppose we contrive to present the object in a light which
evokes a different, incompatible attitude? We can do this
simply by denying that it has the qualities attributed to it; but
this will probably evoke disbelief and indignation. It is far
more telling to set one stock response to catch another: to show
that there is a connection between the object of veneration,
and some other object conventionally evoking contempt. This
may also cause disbelief and righteous indignation but, unless
our emotions are too deeply involved, it may instead cause
laughter. Finding ingenious connections between objects
usually held to be poles apart, and entitled to utterly different
emotional attitudes, is a large part of the stock-in-trade of Bernard Shaw. Here is an example from *Getting Married*:

THE GENERAL: Is Leo to be encouraged to be a polygamist?
THE BISHOP: Remember the British Empire, Boxer. Youre a
British General, you know.
THE GENERAL: What has that to do with polygamy?
THE BISHOP: Well, the great majority of our fellow-subjects
are polygamists. I cant as a British Bishop insult them by
speaking disrespectfully of polygamy.

Here we have two institutions which call forth well defined
emotional attitudes: the British Empire and polygamy. To
suggest that respect for one implies respect for the other brings
the two attitudes into violent conflict.

Our attitudes are not, of course, confined to objects of deep
emotional import. We feel that certain attitudes are appropriate to all sorts of objects, most of them of no great importance. Comparatively few of us are stirred deeply by antiques:
but the conventional attitude to collectors is one of respect, as
part of the mystical aura that surrounds Culture and Art. We
also have a very definite attitude to clocks that won't go.
Stephen Leacock brings the two attitudes into conflict by suggesting that an antique is, after all, only a clock that won't go.

This clock in the hall? An antique? Oh yes, indeed. Isn't it just marvellous? It's a Salvolatile. Does it keep good time? Gracious! What an idea! Of course not! [etc.]

It would be easy to multiply examples. Attitude mixing, universe-changing, is one of the stock techniques of humour. Mark Twain used one simple form of it in his *Connecticut Yankee in the Court of King Arthur*. There is an aura of romance and splendour surrounding the remote past. By mixing it indissolubly with the prosaic present, as we must do whenever we try to think of historic figures really living their everyday lives and not merely striking picturesque attitudes, we get an obvious formula for laughter.

Mock-heroic verse is another application of the same general principle. The poetic convention is that certain topics deserve high-sounding epithets and noble rhythms. The mock-heroic poet proves to us that these apply equally well to commonplace topics.

O Beer! O Hodgson, Guinness, Allsopp, Bass!
Names that should be on every infant's tongue!
Shall days and months and years and centuries pass,
And still your merits be unrecked, unsung?

C. S. CALVERLEY

Universe-changing, then, has a very wide application. In a word, we may say it consists simply of the inappropriate. Any inappropriate comment on any situation is likely to call forth a laugh. But the comment cannot be wholly inappropriate. It must fit some element in the situation. Otherwise it would be simply nonsensical. The inappropriate calls attention to some fact which is usually ignored, or which is regarded as unimportant.

I had written to Aunt Maud
Who was on a trip abroad
When I heard she'd died of cramp,
Just too late to save the stamp!

HARRY GRAHAM

Here we have a question of values. The loss of a stamp is usually regarded as insignificant compared with the loss of a relative. No one is likely to question this seriously; but it is amusing to reverse the scale of values. The inappropriate always involves such a reversal, and there are times when it may be meant seriously. Shaw calls himself a writer of immoral plays: in the sense that it is his set purpose to lead people to question the accepted values and conventions. It is not surprising that despite this seriousness of purpose, his plays are very amusing, because (apart from Shaw's special skill as a humorist) reversal of values is in itself a formula for humour.

What, then, does incongruity in humour really amount to? Let us distinguish, by way of summary, the main elements we have detected in it:

(a) To begin with, we have the simple contrast between what is expected by convention and what we see before us. We have already noted this as an element in comic vice.

(b) But since there must be some appropriateness concealed in the inappropriate, the incongruous calls attention to neglected elements in the situation.

(c) The inappropriate behaviour thus links the situation in question to other situations to which the behaviour would be appropriate.

Incongruity, then, may range from the simplest types of comic contrast to the subtlest satire. In skilful hands, it can raise fundamental questions about the whole system of moral values. When Shaw coined his phrase about 'the trade unionism of married women' he did more than trace an ingenious connection between two institutions normally kept in different compartments of our minds, and evoking utterly different emotional responses. He is drawing attention to a real aspect of marital morality which is conventionally ignored.

The neatness, the suddenness, the directness with which the two universes can be linked is an essential part of the joke. There must be an immediate contrast which shocks the mind. In his poem 'The Bubble', Gerald Bullett tells us that his hero

> Offered his budding manhood to the Lord:
> Lord Kitchener, who took a proper pride
> In teaching youth the joys of homicide.

Here the connection between the conventionally heroic view of war and its harsh reality is effected through the single word —Lord. This is a verbal trick; but the duplicity of meaning serves to bring out a real duplicity in the situation. The distinction between serving the Lord and serving the war lords has never been very clear, either to individuals or to nations. But does the humour lie in the verbal trick or in the underlying meaning?

On the face of it, the verbal trick is all that is necessary. We laugh at plays upon words even when they are not accompanied by satire; we are not amused by denunciations of war unless they are accompanied by verbal play or some similar tricking of the mind. The joke, it may be said, lies wholly in tracing a connection between two dissimilar things: the implication may or may not be present that the two are after all really similar.

But this is not the whole story. For if the connection turns out to be purely verbal, we feel dissatisfied with the joke. The pun *qua* pun is the weakest form of wit. Plays upon words are felt to be merely puerile unless they are accompanied by some play upon meaning. We do not merely feel that the couplet above is more penetrating than the average music-hall gag; we feel that it is actually funnier.

Can plays upon words all be reduced to this formula? Is a pun merely a means of finding an arbitrary connection between two dissimilar things? If so, we have found a very satisfactory means of accounting for a peculiarly troublesome form of humour. I believe that this element is present in most puns and near puns. Consider the account given by Groucho Marx of a hunting trip in Africa:

We shot two bucks, and lost. That was all I had in my pocket . . . . We took some pictures of the native girls. Of course they were undeveloped. But we hope to be back next trip . . . . One morning I woke up and found a big rhinoceros staring right into my tent.

And what did you do?

What could I do? I had to marry his daughter.

The puns here lead the listener to suppose that the narrator is talking about one thing, when in reality his words turn out to apply to something quite different. But there is not, I think, any real suggestion that the connection is other than verbal; that hunting is really a crap game, or that explorers are more interested in pretty girls than in anthropological records. But of course I may be wrong. James Feibleman, from whose book on humour I take these examples, apparently disagrees. He thinks that all humour is at bottom satirical, and that the Marx Brothers give us here a criticism of romanticism. Now it is true that hunting is usually considered heroic and manly, while gambling and sex call forth different attitudes. 'I woke up and found a big rhinoceros staring right into my tent' is on the face of it a heroic situation. The secondary meaning behind the phrase 'big rhinoceros' leaves the narrator in a guise that is anything but heroic. Even here, then, there may be a trace of attitude mixing, of universe-changing. But the connections traced between the 'universes' are superficial and arbitrary; they depend on words alone. If these puns strike us as slightly above the average, it is not because of any satiric intent; it is because the verbal ambiguity enables Groucho Marx to smuggle in a number of references to the forbidden subject of sex.

This does not, however, destroy our original contention that puns are essentially a device for tracing connections, even though superficial and arbitrary, between dissimilar things. It would be convenient if we could regard this as disposing of all verbal play. Unhappily, plays on words have a further appeal, which does not link so neatly and easily with other types of humour. Long before he has learnt to appreciate a pun, a child will delight in jingles like

A noisy noise annoys an oyster.

The appeal of rhyme, of assonance, of word rhythm, goes far beyond the field of humour. But there are amusing combinations of words and sounds just as there are beautiful ones. There are even merry and jocular tunes. In the 'Everyman' anthology of humour there is a poem by Edith Sitwell which depends almost entirely on this type of word play:

When
Sir
Beelzebub called for his syllabub in the hotel in Hell
    Where Proserpine first fell
Blue as the gendarmerie were the waves of the sea
    (Rocking and shocking the barmaid).

In the poem as a whole there are one or two common or garden puns; but most of it is word-play of an entirely different kind. Nor can you dismiss this as a high-brow aberration. Nursery rhymes have the same appeal. All comic verse depends on it in part. Why is a double rhyme, and still more a triple rhyme, automatically comic? Why will a simple, pedestrian statement have a certain amusing charm if expressed in verse that is neat and smooth?

In lone Glenartney's thickets lies couched the lordly stag,
The dreaming terrier's tale forgets its customary wag.

C. S. CALVERLEY

I have no answer to these questions. I do not quite see how these considerations fit into any theory of humour. But I do not think that we should ignore them entirely. Most plays upon words can be satisfactorily explained as the exploiting of verbal ambiguities so as to connect things normally unconnected. This may be done for its own sake; in which case the joke is usually weak. It may be done in order to show real, and unfamiliar, connections that are present in the things themselves. It may be a means of providing the veiling required by indecency or by veiled insults. But in addition there is a certain humorous effect which comes from juggling with words as sounds.

6

NONSENSE

NONSENSE of the Edward Lear type seems to have some affinity with the element in word-play we have just been discussing. Words like 'bibboned' and 'runcible' have an appeal which can hardly be explained by any theory of humour. They belong with Miss Sitwell's poem and with nursery rhyme phrases like 'hickory dickory dock'. But not all humorous nonsense is of this type.

Lewis Carroll is usually linked with Edward Lear; but his nonsense is more intellectual and less æsthetic in its appeal.

'Would you—be good enough,' Alice panted out, after running a little further, 'to stop a minute—just to get—one's breath again.'

'I'm *good* enough,' the King said, 'only I'm not *strong* enough. You see, a minute goes by so fearfully quick. You might as well try to stop a Bandersnatch!'

This too is a play upon words; but there is no universe-changing. The technique is to take some well-worn, trite form of words, and explore it for unexpected and impossible meanings. The method is precisely the method of serious intellectual endeavour—of logic or mathematics. But the object is different. We are no longer concerned to find truth and order and new meaning. We are looking for fantasy and disorder and nonsense.

Why? The most obvious explanation lies in the word escape. 'It is diverting,' says Schopenhauer, 'to see that strict, untiring, troublesome, governess, the reason, for once convicted of inadequacy.' Chesterton elaborates the theme, taking Lewis Carroll as his text:

His strange double life in earth and dreamland emphasises the idea that lies at the back of nonsense—the idea of *escape*, of escape into a world where things are not fixed horribly in an eternal appropriateness, where apples grow on pear trees, and any odd man you meet may have three legs. Lewis Carroll, living one life in which he would have thundered morally against any one who walked on the wrong plot of grass, and another life in which he would cheerfully call the sun green and the moon blue, was, by his very divided nature, his one foot on both worlds, a perfect type of the position of modern nonsense. His Wonderland is a country populated by insane mathematicians. We feel the whole is an escape into a world of masquerade; we feel that if we could pierce their disguises, we might discover that Humpty Dumpty and the March Hare were Professors and Doctors of Divinity enjoying a mental holiday.

The point is not, as Eastman has supposed, that the logic is false logic, the mathematics inaccurate. There must, of course, be some fallacy involved, or the conclusions would not be absurd. But the point lies in the absurdity of the conclusion, not in the errors in the reasoning. If these are too glaring, the joke becomes weak. What amuses us is that an apparently water-tight argument can lead to such a palpable absurdity. There is the familiar element of contrast here; but what is more important is the suggestion of revolt which Schopenhauer emphasizes.

As an example, consider Robert Lynd on the counting of fishes' eggs. He quotes a sentence from the *Encyclopædia Britannica*:—'The sturgeon lays about 7,000,000; the herring 50,000, the turbot 14,300,000, the sole 134,000, the perch 280,000', and comments:

This is the sort of sentence I always read over to myself several times. And when I come to 'the turbot 14,300,000,' I pause, and try to picture to myself the man who counted them. How does one count 14,300,000? How long does it take? If one lay awake all night, trying to count turbots' eggs instead of sheep, one would hardly have done more than make a fair start by the time the maid came in to draw the curtains and let the sun in on one's exhausted temples. A person like myself, ignorant of mathematics, could not easily count more than 10,000 in an hour. This would mean that, even if one lay in bed for ten hours, which one never does except on one's birthday, one would have counted only 100,000 out of the 14,300,000 eggs by the time one had to get up for breakfast. This would leave 14,200,000 still to be counted. At this point most of us, I think, would give up in despair. After one horrible night's experience, we would jump into a hot bath, muttering 'Never again! Never again!' like a statesman who can't think of anything to say, and sends for a quinine-and-iron tonic. Our friends, meeting us later in the day, would say with concern: 'Hullo! You're looking rather cheap. What have you been doing?' And when we answered bitterly, 'Counting turbots' eggs,' they would hurry off with an apprehensive look on their faces. The naturalist, it is clear, must be capable of a persistence that is beyond the reach of most of us. I calculate that, if he were able to work for fourteen hours a day, counting at the rate of 10,000 an hour, even then it would take him 122,214 days to count the eggs of a single turbot. After that it would take a chartered accountant at least 122,214 days to check his figures. One can gather from this some idea of the enormous industry of men of science.

Here the argument follows logically enough from a single false premise: that naturalists calculate the number of fishes' eggs by simple enumeration. Grant this, which is a natural enough assumption for the uninitiated to make, and all Mr. Lynd's ludicrous conclusions are justified.

Precisely the same technique occurs in Whately's *Historic Doubts relative to Napoleon Buonaparte,* or in Ronald Knox's proof (complete with cryptograms), that Queen Victoria wrote *In Memoriam.* But here the fallacy in the reasoning is important; because these are parodies and satires. They are aimed (respectively) at the higher critics and at the Baconians. Nevertheless, they can be enjoyed purely for their own sake, as ingenious pieces of nonsense, by readers who are not interested in the satire. In the same way, you can enjoy Butler's account of the evolution of the machines without concerning yourself with either its implications as a criticism of evolutionary theory generally, or as a half-serious discussion of the real dangers inherent in a machine age. In other parts of *Erewhon* the satire and the moral are more inextricably part of the always reasonable but always ridiculous argument, but nevertheless the book is an excellent example of this type of intellectual, dialectical nonsense.

But it is not only logic that can be exploited in this way. The other methods of persuasion, the more rhetorical devices of metaphor and analogy, can also be twisted or exaggerated into nonsense. Consider G. K. Chesterton on the game of croquet:

. . . how far you really are from the pure love of the sport— you who can play. It is only we who play badly who love the game itself. You love glory; you love applause; you love the earthquake voice of victory; you do not love croquet. You do not love croquet until you love being beaten at croquet. It is we, the bunglers, who adore the occupation in the abstract. It is we to whom it is art for art's sake. If we may see the face of

Croquet herself (if I may so express myself) we are content to see her face turned upon us in anger. Our play is called amateurish; and we wear proudly the name of amateur, for amateurs is but the French for lovers. We accept all adventures from our Lady, the most disastrous or the most dreary. We wait outside her iron gates (I allude to the hoops) vainly essaying to enter. Our devoted balls, impetuous and full of chivalry, will not be confined within the pedantic boundaries of the mere croquet ground. Our balls seek honour in the ends of the earth; they turn up in the flower beds and the conservatory; they are to be found in the front garden and the next street.

Here is argument reinforced by rhetoric; the whole is an admirable piece of fooling. It is not, of course, wholly fooling; and it might be objected that I should not cite this passage in a discussion of nonsense, since it contains a serious argument, however playfully treated. But one of Chesterton's main characteristics is that he can seldom resist the added touch which tumbles him over the edge into absurdity. He does this to his own detriment, since it leaves the reader dubious about his more serious passages. The essay on nonsense from which I have already quoted begins with a characteristic appeal for freshness of outlook, for a sense that the world is just beginning:

That it is good for a man to realize that he is 'the heir to all the ages' is pretty commonly admitted; it is a less popular but equally important point that it is good for him sometimes to realize that he is not only an ancestor, but an ancestor of primal antiquity; it is good for him to wonder whether he is not a hero, and to experience ennobling doubts as to whether he is not a solar myth.

This sentence is certainly mainly serious; it is almost the chief tenet in the Chesterton creed. Yet the final touch about the solar myth definitely tumbles it over the edge. Chesterton does this so continually and exuberantly that one can only suppose that he does it for the fun of the thing, because he cannot resist this peculiar type of nonsense. And this is precisely the phenomenon we are considering: why such nonsense should be, at least to some minds, irresistible. For this reason Chesterton seems an admirable example, even though he continually deviates into sense, and so makes analysis more difficult.

In the croquet passage there is, of course, more than a touch of the mock-heroic, and so of universe-changing: this highfalutin' poetic attitude, we feel, does not belong in the same compartment of our minds as croquet. But this is only incidental. In both these passages Chesterton begins an analogy, at least half-seriously, and deliberately carries it to such lengths that it becomes absurd. And this is the same technique as Whately's or Butler's. It is also the technique of exaggeration and parody, both of which loom large in most theories of humour.

Even if we leave on one side the intrusion of the mock-heroic, or of satire, or of parody, it is obvious that there are still two elements in all these examples. A good deal of our pleasure comes from the sheer ingenuity of it all. That is why Eastman's explanation is so inadequate. We delight in Whately's skill as a logician; we know, of course, that the argument must have a flaw; but we are delighted because we cannot detect it, not because we can.

It is tempting to regard this ingenuity as the real source of all our pleasure in this type of humour. The nonsense would then be merely an incidental part of the procedure, not its end-product. The absurdity of the conclusion would show us that the performer really had pulled off a clever trick, just as our knowledge that rabbits seldom flourish in top-hats guarantees the skill of the conjuror.

The obvious objection to this view is that we do not laugh at dialectic skill when it is applied to serious ends. We gain pleasure from it, but not amusement. But, apart from this, we can find examples of pure nonsense where this element of ingenuity is absent. There is a Charles Addams drawing of a man on skis descending a slope. We can see the parallel trails left by his course through the snow. And in the middle, between the track made by his left foot and the one made by his right, there is a tall tree! We can only suppose that his body has passed through the tree: no other explanation is possible.

Here is pure absurdity with no distracting secondary feature; strictly analogous to apples growing on pear-trees, and any odd man you meet having three legs. If people laugh at this sort of thing (and they do) it can only be because sheer absurdity, for its own sake, delights them. And it is difficult to explain this except as an escape from 'that strict, untiring, troublesome governess, the reason'.

The type of funny story christened by a writer in *Esquire* 'the shaggy dog story', seems another example of sheer, undiluted absurdity. One of them relates how a man entered a baker's shop and asked if he could buy a cake baked in the shape of the letter S. The baker replied that he would need to have a special cake-tin made, and that this would cost money. 'Expense is no object,' replied the customer. Thereupon the baker promised to have the cake ready in a few days. On the appointed day, the customer called, and examined the cake. 'This won't do,' he said. 'This is a script S, and I wanted a capital S.' The baker agreed to have another tin made in the desired shape, and arranged for the customer to call again. This time he expressed approval. 'Excellent! Exactly what I wanted.' 'I'm glad of that,' said the baker. 'Will you take it with you, or would you like me to deliver it to your address?' 'Oh, don't bother,' said the customer, 'I'll eat it here!'

Various explanations have been advanced of shaggy dog stories by Freud, Eastman, and others, and we shall be concerned with some of these later. Kant's formula, 'frustrated expectation', applies fairly well: the raconteur has for once exploited the peculiarities of his own art to fool his listener. Trained by long experience of funny stories to expect them to work up to a point, he finds himself suddenly presented with an entirely pointless one. The shock of surprise expends itself in laughter.

There may be some truth in this theory; though if it were true, one would expect the trick to work only once or twice. Yet there is a cult of the shaggy dog story: and a devotee will preface his narration by saying: 'Here is a new shaggy dog I just heard.' On Kant's theory this should defeat the narrator's purpose, by telling the listener to expect pointlessness. But the formula does not, in fact, seem to prevent the joke from meeting with success. One could argue, of course, that the expectation engendered is partly beyond the listener's conscious control; that he cannot in a moment rid himself of long instilled preconceptions about the nature of stories, and so is still able to enjoy deviation from the pattern, even when he has been prepared for it. But this does not seem very different from the less pretentious statement that we enjoy any sort of absurdity for its own sake, just because it is a release from the 'eternal appropriateness' we normally expect. Kant's formula may of course explain this fact: at the moment we are merely concerned to note that it is a fact.

Summarizing, we may say that there are three types of humorous nonsense:

(a) Any fantastic departure from possibility, as in the shaggy dog story, or the drawing of the man on skis. If this is enough to make us laugh, it may be asked, why isn't any fantasy or fairy tale funny? The answer is that the fairy tale is at special pains to create an atmosphere in which its fantasies seem natural, or at least plausible. It is when absurdity is presented abruptly, without any sort of apology or plausibility, that we laugh.

(b) The twisting of familiar material, by means of argument, rhetoric, or exaggeration, so as to obtain an absurd conclusion.

(c) This twisting may be done, not for its own sake, but as a means of parody or satire, to point the conclusion that such-and-such is really nonsense, after all.

7

MISFORTUNES

HITHERTO we have found connections between all our classes. We have not indeed reduced them to a single all-embracing formula: we have on the contrary been concerned to stress differences. But although we might find it difficult to state the resemblance precisely, we can, I think, feel some similarity between them. But misfortunes and want of knowledge or skill seem completely apart from the rest.

Small misfortunes do cause a good deal of laughter. 'Just try this experiment,' says Gelett Burgess. 'Tell several persons the story of an accident you have had. Ninety per cent of the hearers laugh. If you see the accident and it is grave, laughter is inhibited. But the mention of it, somehow, is comic.'

There is plenty of evidence to support this. Kimmins found that children delight in this kind of humour, especially young children. Thus a boy of five, asked for the funniest sight he had seen, told of a fat man running for a bus who fell in the mud. A girl of six described a duck with its head caught in a jam-pot. A girl of ten recounted the adventures of her aunt when bathing: 'Auntie came up covered with sea-weed, and she had several crabs biting her . . . . She looked so comical that we laughed till the tears came out of our eyes.'

Kimmins found this delight in the misfortunes of others less frequent at the age of nine or ten, and almost negligible in older children. But it continues to be at least one element in a good many of the stories he quotes from children of all ages. And slapstick is so popular in comic films, that it is obvious that adults also enjoy the sight of a fat man covered with mud, or a middle-aged woman bitten by crabs.

Not without qualms of conscience, however. Even the children seem somewhat on the defensive in this matter. A seven-year-old told with glee how his mother fell out of a hammock, but hastened to add: 'She didn't hurt herself much.' Girls often go further, and persuade themselves that their laughter has a sound moral basis. 'I saw a boy chasing a poor cat. He fell, and burst the seat of his trousers, so instead of hurting the cat he'll get hurt himself when he sees his mother.'

This may explain why 'the biter bit' is a sure formula for laughter. It is not, of course, always necessary to appease our consciences in this way: we laugh when we see a stranger slip on a banana-skin, or hit his thumb with a hammer, and we do not pause to ask whether he deserved this fate or not. But our laughter is certainly heightened if the misfortune comes from the victim's own misguided efforts. Suppose, for example, that he has impatiently wrested the hammer from someone else, saying: 'Let me show you how to do it!' Most of us would agree that this makes the joke much better.

The same is true of jokes depending on lack of knowledge or skill. A piece of stupidity may be funny *per se*. The malapropism or the schoolboy howler will raise a laugh simply because it is 'wrong'. But such jokes nearly always have an added element—the downfall of pretentiousness. The schoolboy's mistake may make us smile; it is the schoolmaster's mistake that makes us roar with laughter. So do the moral lapses of parsons. It serves them right, we feel, for claiming to be infallible.

We have been speaking of all these refinements on the simple themes of misfortune and stupidity as salves to our consciences. But there are other possible explanations. Some would claim that we enjoy the downfall of the pretentious simply because they irritate us. Their claims make us feel inferior, and we are therefore especially glad to enlarge our egos a little at their expense. We will have to discuss this later. But there can be little doubt that some sop to the moral sense is also necessary. When we laugh at physical misfortunes particularly, we like to feel that the victim after all 'did not hurt herself much'.

Apart from the pride that comes before a fall, other factors in the situation may enhance our enjoyment of misfortune. Take the story of the shopkeeper who was asked by a child for a pennyworth of aniseed balls. He had to mount a ladder and drag the tin down from a high shelf. The child departed, and he returned the tin to its place. Immediately another child entered with the same request, and he had to mount the ladder again. As he was about to put the tin back again, a third child entered. The shopkeeper paused half-way up the ladder, the tin in his hand. 'I suppose you want a pennyworth of aniseed balls, too?' 'No,' said the child. So the shopkeeper continued mounting the ladder, and replaced the tin. Back on the floor again, he turned to the child. 'Well, what is it you do want?' 'A ha'p'orth of aniseed balls.'

Why do we laugh here? Not merely at the shopkeeper's misfortune. This is of course part of the joke, and an important part. In a play or a film, the audience would laugh at the mere sight of the shopkeeper mounting the ladder again and again as successive children streamed in. But obviously, the real point of the joke is in the conversation with the third child. Yet it is not 'frustrated expectation': we know that the shopkeeper will inevitably have to go up that ladder again; the story can end in no other way. What amuses us is the fact that the shopkeeper's question, intended to avoid this catastrophe, is answered truthfully and in perfect good faith, and yet results in his being utterly misled.

This element is often present in jokes about the misfortunes of others. We often laugh because the victim 'brings it on himself' not in the sense that he deserves the misfortune, but in the sense that his very efforts to avoid it land him more deeply in the mire. This is a favourite formula with professional humorists. A good many of W. W. Jacobs' stories, for example, conform roughly to this pattern.

As another example, consider the story of the prince who was offered three wishes by a good fairy. Shrewdly, he stipulates as his third wish that any future wish he may have will also come true. The fairy considers this sharp practice; but, though annoyed, feels bound to keep her word. She does, however, contrive to grant his wishes in such a way as to cause him more discomfort than pleasure. The story gives several examples of this: the denouement comes when the prince is sitting in his palace playing a difficult game of patience. For once he gets the game out: this pleases him so much that he is moved to exclaim at the end of it: 'I wish I could have that half-hour again.' Immediately his wish is granted, right up to the moment when he says: 'I wish I could have that half-hour again.' Immediately this too is granted, and so on endlessly. The result is that the prince ends his days locked up in a room in his palace, endlessly repeating a half-hour's game of patience.

It would be a mistake to regard this story as purely an example of just retribution. What pleases us is the neat symmetry by which the prince's very efforts to secure happiness result in the most extreme misery.

All this is not to deny that the misfortunes of others, purely in themselves, often cause laughter. But it is well to remember that this element is often fused with others; and that these others are not always sops to our consciences or added reasons for wishing to feel superior to the victim of misfortune.

We have now considered all the classes on our list except masquerades, veiled insults, and indecency. But these have been given some attention in our preliminary discussion, and all are fairly straightforward. In any case, they will have to be discussed in the following section, and to treat them further now might involve tedious repetition.

Part 2

THEORIES OF HUMOUR

8

SUPERIORITY THEORIES

I. Hobbes and Bain

S ULLY regards all theories of humour as variants of two main ones: the moral or degradation theory and the intellectual or incongruity theory. I think there are two more: the release from restraint theory and the ambivalence theory. Most writers on humour can be brought within one of these groups.

The degradation theory springs from Hobbes: or, less certainly, from Aristotle. Aristotle, in this as in other contentious matters, is found to have uttered a few fragmentary opinions which have been interpreted to the advantage of either contending party. We laugh, he says, at what is ugly but not painful. Further, comedy deals with characters of a low type, who are nevertheless not bad in the full sense of the word. This certainly sounds like a patriarchal blessing on the theory that laughter springs from our feeling of superiority at people less fortunate than we. W. S. Lilly, however, claims this blessing for the incongruity theory, citing in support Butcher's edition of the 'Poetics'. The argument is that Aristotle's idea goes far beyond the narrowly æsthetic. Ugliness includes 'incongruities, absurdities, the cross purposes of life, its imperfect correspondences or adjustments, and that in matters intellectual as well as moral.'

There can be no doubt about the claim of Hobbes to be the chief and most vigorous exponent of the superiority theory; and no doubt, either, about the extent of his influence. Laughter, in his famous phrase, is 'a kind of sudden glory' and 'glory', of course, is used in the sense of 'vainglory', or self-esteem. How do we attain this happy state? Mainly by contemplating the infirmities of others; we must suppose 'thank God that I am not as this publican' to be the commonest sentiment behind laughter. But Hobbes does not say that this is the only sentiment behind it. We may also laugh at our own follies, provided that they are in the past and we are conscious of having surmounted them. This is, of course, only a variant of the first type: our past selves take the place of other people in order to inflate our present self-esteem. And there is yet another possibility: we may laugh at 'our own actions performed beyond our expectations'. Here we have the glory without the degradation of others: though it is of course still arguable that even here we have at the back of our minds the thought of keeping up with the Joneses.

Ludovici makes much of the subjective side of Hobbes' phrase:

Laughter is self-glory. So we can now understand why a person can laugh apparently at nothing . . . unprovoked by any external stimulus . . . We can now also understand all those laughs in which there is definite outside provocation; for, although Hobbes quite unnecessarily limits the series of these external stimuli, those externally provoked laughs not mentioned by him are . . . implicit in his two words self-glory.

In other words, Hobbes explains the laugh of sheer joy: the young girl conscious of being well-dressed, the schoolboy exulting in life as he stands stripped on a sunny beach, and so on. Other theories, claims Ludovici, cannot account for this.

But not all the emphasis, he continues, should be placed on the second word in Hobbes' formula. He also stresses the adjective 'sudden'. The new and unexpected are the only occasions of laughter. It is a sudden access of self-esteem that causes us to burst into laughter: not a steady sense of superiority. This is obviously an attempt to explain the elements in laughter which were to give rise to the main rival theory: Kant's 'frustrated expectation'.

The obvious criticism of Hobbes is that this saving adjective is not enough. The advocates of 'frustrated expectation' find more in humour than a mere unexpectedness. To them the essence of it is a 'tricking of the mind', a sudden switching from well-worn mental paths to new and surprising ones. This too may be a kind of sudden glory; but not in the sense of self-glory.

More specifically, how many of our types of humour can Hobbes account for?

(a) Any Breach of the Usual Order of Events

On the face of it, mere novelty and oddity does not seem sufficient reason for thinking well of ourselves. But we have already suggested that anything out of the ordinary is felt to be wrong.

To laugh at the newfangled may be an indirect expression of satisfaction with the old-established order of which we feel ourselves part. On this view we laugh at oddities of costume because they reassure us about the correctness of our own dress, at strange idioms because they reassure us about the correctness of our own speech.

This seems reasonable enough, and is certainly often true. But is it always true? The film version of J. B. Priestley's *Good Companions* was an immensely successful comedy. At the screening which I saw, the biggest laugh of the evening was provoked by a single line. The Yorkshireman is examining a broken-down car. He delivers a terse verdict: 'Moocky ploogs.' Did the audience really enjoy this because its members were pleased to reflect that they pronounced muck to rhyme with buck and not with book? It is, of course, impossible to disprove this theory, but it does not seem psychologically right. It does not, that is to say, reflect the attitude one sensed in the audience at the time, an attitude which was not in the least derisive. It is true that it is not easy to say why this simple phrase should have struck its hearers as screamingly funny. But simple surprise, together with the jingle contained in the phrase, seems the most obvious explanation.

Too much, however, can be made of the absence of obvious derision in laughter. Eastman, who opposes the Hobbes theory with great force and fury, cites a child's version of a well-known hymn:

> Shall a mother's tender care
> Fail toward the child she-bear?

We feel, he says, affection rather than scorn for the child who made this very natural mistake. The point of the story is not that children are stupid, but that they are 'infinitely dear'.

This is true enough, but it can be retorted that scorn (though the term is too harsh) is an element in affection. It is not really scorn, of course, but a comfortable appreciation of the human foibles of the object of our affection. And who will say that our own self-esteem is not directly increased thereby? We talk about 'lovable human weaknesses', meaning that we feel at ease with the person concerned, able to relax in his presence without worrying about our own inferiority. For the same reason we feel at ease with children: and something of all this may be involved in their 'infinite dearness'.

But Eastman is certainly right when he insists that this couplet is funny, not because of any good-humoured condescension in our attitude to children, but because of 'the child she-bear'. The condescension can at most be only one element in our attitude to children in general and childish mistakes in particular. It may reinforce our laughter: it can hardly be the main cause of it. That lies in the fact that a form of words, meant to convey one meaning, has somehow succeeded in conveying a startlingly different one. The child is only introduced to make the misinterpretation plausible. And it is this essential part of the joke that the Hobbes theory simply does not explain.

All this is relevant to the *Good Companions* example. Here again the audience, though by no means derisive towards Jess Oakroyd, regard him with good-humoured condescension: he is a 'lovable old Yorkshireman'. They laugh at any 'characteristic' remark he makes: characteristic of his lovableness, characteristic of his Yorkshire origin, characteristic, in short, of the qualities which make the audience at ease with him and satisfied with themselves. 'Moocky ploogs' can be explained in this way much more completely than 'the child she-bear'. But even here there is still an unexplained element: the neatness of the phrase, and its jingling sound, which help to make it amusing, and which Hobbes can hardly explain.

Sully's example of novelty, the burst of fireworks which made a child laugh, also sets a problem for Hobbes. Ludovici shows him the way out when he insists that subjective laughter, joy or 'feeling good', is an important part of his formula. If we enlarge self-glory to include this, the fireworks will fit in well enough.

Notice, however, that we have already had to stretch Hobbes' formula a good deal. Contempt for others has to include every kind of pleasant condescension, affectionate as well as scornful; and self-glory has to include 'feeling good' even when there is no contempt for others at all. With these provisos, most examples of laughable oddity will probably fit the formula fairly well.

(b) Any Forbidden Breach of the Usual Order of Events

Here Hobbes would seem to come into his own. Comic vice seems the perfect example of laughter caused by self-glory. But we have already found that comic villains are of two kinds:

those we laugh at and those we laugh with. Hobbes accounts for the first, but what of the second? When we laugh at Malvolio, we are no doubt deriding him, praising God that we are not like him; but what happens when we laugh at Falstaff?

Or take indecency. When we laugh at a smutty joke, are we deriding indecency? Are we not rather condoning it? We can say, of course, that we condone it in order to increase our own self-esteem. We are laughing off our sense of guilt at our own guilty desires. And this, it may be said, is behind all our enjoyment of this second type of comic vice, the kind we sympathize with. To glory in wrong-doing is after all a common enough form of self-glory. The young tough who brags about his misdeeds is likely to revel in the very vices which excite sympathetic laughter—drinking, whoring, and the like.

But notice what a shift we have made here. Self-esteem based on others' shortcomings has been replaced by self-esteem based on others' achievements. This is the very reverse of Hobbes' own account of the causes of laughter: our own achievements or the failures of others. Furthermore, the achievements of others we are considering are after all an odd kind of achievement — vices which we condemn openly and secretly admire. Obviously we are dealing with a very complex sort of self-esteem indeed. We are, in fact, in the realm of Freud rather than Hobbes, and perhaps it would be as well to abandon the attempt to reconcile them.

Hobbes himself was almost certainly thinking of only one kind of comic villainy—the sort that is laughed at, not with. His theory became a stock argument with which to refute the Puritans' objections to stage comedy. Comedy, it was argued, held vice and folly to ridicule, and so enhanced virtue.

Notice, however, that the god's-eye view, which we found in comic vice and in much other humour besides, fits Hobbes' theory quite well. Here we have a kind of self-esteem based not indeed on the sharp derision of others, but on a very lively, if tolerant, appreciation of their weaknesses. This is essentially the attitude of amused tolerance which we suggested was often an element in affection.

(c) Importing into One Situation What Belongs to Another

The weak point in the Hobbes theory is that it cannot account for this very important type of humour. We have already discussed one example in 'the child she-bear', and seen that it cannot be explained solely as a child's blunder. But there is another line of defence open to Hobbes. 'The child she bare' is a phrase heavy with emotional associations. The solemn rhythm, the archaic language, the subject, all combine to rouse the familiar stock response to the idea of mother and infant child. The 'child she-bear' belongs to a different mental compartment altogether. And the transition, it can be said, does involve degradation. The incongruity is, in Spencer's phrase, a descending incongruity.

How far is this true of all attitude-changing? The joke, it may be said, lies in the destruction of an attitude of pious reverence: in the debunking of the whole complex of solemn clap-trap which builds up such attitudes. Laughter is the antidote to rhetoric; and rhetoric requires us to lose ourselves in an emotional orgy, to abase ourselves before some object of veneration. In freeing ourselves from the rhetorician's spell, we are surely increasing our self-esteem.

There is much truth in all this. Once again, we have had to twist Hobbes a little. It is unlikely that he had in mind the more subtle type of self-esteem engendered by revolt against hackneyed shibboleths. But nevertheless this fits his general concept well enough. But there still remains an element in the joke, and an important element, which lies outside Hobbes' sphere.

This is the pure intellectual pleasure we take in finding that a form of words meant to convey one meaning can bear a totally different one. This may be present even when there is no attitude-changing or debunking; though it is true that such jokes tend to be unsatisfying. But on the whole Hobbes can account for incongruity rather better than one would at first suppose.

(d) Word-play

It is with word-play, however, that his inadequacies become apparent. We have seen that word-play often involves attitude-changing; that it may be a device for connecting two different universes of discourse. In so far as this is true, what we have said in the last paragraph applies, and may be a sufficient defence for Hobbes. 'The child she-bear' is indeed a good example of word-play.

But we have also seen that, over and above this, there is a

pleasure in manipulating words for its own sake which it is not easy to explain away. This has been fully discussed: we need only say here that Hobbes does not seem able to account for it. Some of his followers have tried, but we shall deal with their theories separately.

(e) Nonsense

And precisely the same may be said of nonsense. We have seen that nonsense is sometimes a means of universe-changing, an instrument of satire or parody. Here the Hobbes formula applies fairly well.

But we have also found two other elements in nonsense. The first is an intellectual pleasure in the skill with which apparent sense is suddenly revealed as nonsense: we cited Whately's *Historic Doubts* as an example of this. This is, of course, also a feature of incongruity, as we have just seen.

Secondly, there seems an unquestioned delight in nonsense for its own sake, just as there is a delight in word-play for its own sake. And it seems most reasonable to suppose that this is some form of release from restraint, rather than self-esteem.

Nonsense, then, contains both of the factors in humour which are most troublesome to the Hobbes theory.

(f) Small Misfortunes; Want of Knowledge and Skill

Hobbes has no difficulty here. Indeed it is commonly said that his formula takes into account only this type of humour. Our survey shows this to be unjust; but nevertheless, it is true that with every other type we have felt some strain in applying the formula. Only here does it fit easily and obviously. The strength of Hobbes' theory is that this is a common and universal type of humour. His followers claim that it is the basic type, and that others are refinements on it.

We could have mentioned other classes of humour; but none of them raise any fresh points of importance. There is the class comprised in the formula: anything masquerading as something it is not, which includes pretences, mimicry, peeping behind the mask. Where the humour springs from unmasking a hypocrite, the Hobbes formula obviously applies. Where it is a form of attitude-changing, it is covered by what has been said under that heading. Indecency has been touched on. Veiled insults afford Hobbes little trouble, though he can explain the insult better than the veiling.

Summarizing, the Hobbes formula is a completely satisfactory explanation of many important types of humour. It will apply fairly well to others, provided (a) that we soften the notion of contempt to cover the god's-eye view, i.e. an attitude of urbane, clear-sighted, amused tolerance; and (b) that we include in self-esteem the more subtle methods of inflating the ego which involve revolt against oppressive morals or conventions. But there still remain two elements which he cannot explain: a purely intellectual pleasure in neatness and skill, and, on the other hand, a pure irrationalism which delights in word associations, rhythms, and sheer absurdity.

Of all the attempts to modify and extend Hobbes' theory so as to meet these objections, the most convincing is still Alexander Bain's. Bain expands Hobbes in two main directions. First, he does not demand direct consciousness of our own superiority. We may, for example, laugh sympathetically with another who scores off his adversary. Secondly, he does not demand a person as the object of derision: it may be an idea, a political institution, or even 'inanimate things that by personification have contracted associations of dignity, of which last the couplet of Hudibras upon sunrise is a sufficient example'.

When this has been said, Bain feels that the single word 'degradation' is a sufficient formula for humour. 'The occasion of the ludicrous is the degradation of some person or interest possessing dignity, in circumstances that excite no other strong emotion.'

Bain realizes, of course, that he must explain away the claims of both incongruity and relief from restraint. He begins with a frontal attack on incongruity in a much-quoted catalogue of incongruities which, he says, do not cause laughter:

A decrepit man under a heavy burden, five loaves and two fishes among a multitude, and all unfitness and gross disproportion; an instrument out of tune, a fly in ointment, snow in May, Archimedes studying geometry in a siege, and all discordant things; a wolf in sheep's clothing, a breach of bargain, and falsehood in general; the multitude taking the law into their own hands, and everything of the nature of disorder; a corpse

at a feast, parental cruelty, filial ingratitude, and whatever is
unnatural; the entire catalogue of vanities given by Solomon—
are all incongruous, but they cause feelings of pain, anger, sad-
ness, loathing, rather than mirth.

Many of these actually do cause laughter when there are no
other emotions to inhibit it. Some of them indeed (the man
staggering under a heavy load, the instrument out of tune) are
stock devices of motion picture slapstick. Others (the fly in
ointment, snow in May) are not incongruous in the sense of
rousing two sharply contrasted attitudes. It would probably
be just as easy to compile a companion list of degradations
which do not cause laughter: Bain's own definition, it will be
remembered, contains the saving clause: 'in circumstances that
excite no other strong emotion.'

But his main argument against incongruity is simply to assert
that degradation is always present. In reply to Herbert Spencer

It does not apply to the many instances in which no-one's dignity is implicated, as when we laugh at a good pun

he says flatly:

I very much wish he had produced such a pun, as I have never
yet met with one of the sort . . . I quite understand the laugh
of pleasure and admiration at a felicitous stroke of mere wit;
but no one confounds this with the genuinely ludicrous. Wit,
with all its brilliance and ingenuity, is sadly wanting in unction
if it takes no-one down.

As an example, he takes Butler's couplet:

> For rhyme the rudder is of verses,
> With which like ships, they steer their courses

which Campbell had quoted in an attempt to refute Hobbes.
But here, says Bain, there is an obvious degradation of the
poetic art: 'Instead of working under the mysterious and lofty
inspiration of the Muses, the poet is made to compose by means
of a vulgar and mechanical process.'

Now we have suggested that the essence of incongruity is
'universe-changing', the sudden collision of ideas normally kept
in different compartments of the mind. And it is true enough
that this usually means that some noble, lofty, venerated idea
is brought into contact with something trivial or disreputable.

Is Bain right, then, in saying that incongruity is really degradation?

It is not easy to prove the case either way. If there are puns in which nothing is degraded, they are usually very weak ones. But the real point is psychological: it is a question of what a joke *feels* like. Are we conscious of triumphing over some hallowed idea, or is it simply that we feel an exhilarating sense of enlarged mental horizons? If both feelings are present, can we say that either is primary?

There is a *New Yorker* drawing of an artist in his studio. The room is full of nude studies, all of the same girl. But in every picture there intrudes, somewhere, the set, determined face of a middle-aged woman, staring with implacable suspicion and vigilance. The caption reads: 'She was a good model, but I could never get her mother to trust me.'

Now, Bain would find degradation here easily enough. The artist's aloof, æsthetic appraisal of the feminine form has been brought into shattering contact with the mother's much more prosaic attitude. No doubt it is a degrading contact. Or, if you like, it is the mother who is degraded by her own inflexibility of mind. But neither of these explanations seems quite adequate. There is an odd, ironic pleasure to be obtained simply from viewing this conflict of attitudes—a conflict which somehow epitomizes the whole human comedy. We are not, I think, triumphing over either of the protagonists. But there is this to be said for Bain: the detached attitude which views the human scene as a comedy of cross-purposes is itself a degradation of the opposite, romantic attitude to life.

Nevertheless, one cannot help feeling that formulas like 'degradation' ignore the part played in humour by the sense of freshness, the exploring of new mental avenues. And Bain himself does not deny that there is a pleasure to be had from wit (which he defines as an unexpected and ingenious play upon words) quite apart from degradation. Indeed, he says that wit is often a means of making degradation acceptable. 'It being not always permissible to degrade a person or thing by open vituperation or depreciating adjuncts, some disguise or redeeming is sought out and the forms of wit are well adapted for this purpose.' But the obvious question here is: would the vituperation be funny at all without the wit? Probably Bain would say that the wit is necessary merely to allay those inhibiting emotions which dispel laughter.

Bain is quite conscious of the part which release from restraint plays in laughter.

The posture of artificial and constrained seriousness demanded by the grave necessities of life, and occasionally imposed without any great necessity, is, as it seems to me, one point of departure in the production of the ludicrous. Our struggles, difficulties and dangers, screw us up into an attitude of earnest attention as well as of laborious effort, and the remission of both the one and the other is a joyful relief. A man is grave in the prospect of misfortune or death; in disposing of weighty interests, as legislator, judge or military commander, in setting out on a difficult enterprise or taking up a responsible position. Those that are merely witnesses of such transactions are enjoined to assume a grave demeanour.

But in all this we are conscious of strain, and are more or less deliberately seeking relief.

The serious and the mirthful are in perpetual contrast in human life; in the characters, and in the occasions and incidents of our everyday experience. The mirthful is the one aspect of ease, freedom, *abandon*, and animal spirits. The serious is constituted by labour, difficulty, hardship . . . . It is always a gratifying deliverance to pass from the severe to the easy side of affairs; and the comic conjunction is one form of the transition.

How does the comic conjunction cause relief? It consists, says Bain, in the degradation of those serious interests which impose these restraints upon us. One proof of this is that we always laugh most readily when our attitude of respect is forced and reluctant:

The sincere worshipper at church is shocked by a profane incident which makes the irreverent or unwilling laugh . . . . False or faded deities and dignities; splendour and show without meaning; the unworthy occupants of high office; hollow pretensions, affectation, assumption and self-importance, vanity, airs and coxcombry; all the windings of the hypocrisy that aims at seeming greater than the reality; painful strivings to gain glittering positions—are among the things that commonly induce laughter, when brought into the embrace of meanness and degrading inferiorities. It is true that, for the sake of the mirthful pleasure, we are occasionally disposed to waive even our serious feelings of respect, and to hail the descent of true dignity with a lively countenance, but it is against our better nature to do so, and we are glad when the case is of the other sort.

Here, as in Bain's treatment of incongruity, there are two questions. Does relief from restraint always entail degradation? Is nonsense, for example, merely a means of scoring off that implacable taskmaster, the reason? And, if we grant this, is the degradation primary or secondary? Bain puts a good deal on the restraint which the serious business of life continually imposes upon us. Why should relief, then, not be sufficient in itself to cause laughter? On the face of it, doesn't it look as if degradation is merely the means to relief, and not the end-product?

It is over these questions, and the corresponding ones about incongruity, that the whole controversy about humour really rages.

9

SUPERIORITY THEORIES

II. LEACOCK AND LUDOVICI

THE FOLLOWERS OF HOBBES have, of course, been aware of his defects, and have tried to alter his theory so as to avoid them. The last chapter has, indeed, dealt less with Hobbes himself than with the general superiority theory which he founded. Now we must consider in more detail some of the versions of his theory as they occur in contemporary writers.

Stephen Leacock has written two books on humour but it is doubtful if he makes much original contribution to the theory of humour. He has some valuable observations to make on technique; but his explanations of the underlying basis of humour tend to be scanty and unsatisfying. He does, indeed, express contempt for the whole academic approach to the subject; the hair-splitting philosophers, he says in effect, cannot hope to have the root of the matter in them. He then proceeds to accept uncritically one of the earliest academic theories of humour, without answering the criticisms that have since been brought against it, or even making any detailed attempt to apply it to his own examples and observations.

The result is nevertheless illuminating. For, since Leacock's knowledge of technique is considerable, the gap between his theory and his practical examples do reveal the inadequacy of the formula. This is obscured by most writers on humour, who begin with their theory and hunt for examples to fit it.

Laughter, says Leacock, begins as a primitive shout of triumph. 'The merry ha-ha' is the oldest and most primitive type of humour, and he regards this as a mere rejoicing in the misfortunes of others, whether caused by our own superior prowess or not. He cites Bret Harte:

> And he smiled a kind of sickly smile, and curled up
> on the floor,
> And the subsequent proceedings interested him
> no more.

and Harry Graham's *Ruthless Rhymes* as examples.

Laughter has, however, evolved from this primitive beginning: it has become kinder, more humane. We now laugh only at minor misfortunes: at 'pins and needles', but not at a broken leg. The clown at the circus is the modern, humane version of the Roman spectacle. But, through its primitive origin, humour came to 'turn on the contrast between the thing as it is, or ought to be, and the thing smashed out of shape and as it ought not to be'.

Having thus introduced the notion of contrast, Leacock seems to think that he has bridged the gap between the degradation and the incongruity theories: though he is far too scornful of academic hair-splitting to mention either. Henceforth he speaks cheerfully of 'incongruity' and 'contrast' without relating either to superiority.

For example, when discussing exaggeration, he quotes a remark of Bill Nye's: 'There must be at least five hundred million rats in the United States; of course I am speaking only from memory.' Here, says Leacock, the humour depends on the 'incongruity between the familiar form of words "speaking only from memory", and the queer purpose to which it is put—counting all the American rats . . . . It is not the number of rats that is exaggerated, it is the power of consecutive human observation'.

This account is not quite adequate. It is more than the mere oddity of counting rats that is in question. The joke depends on the deprecating way in which Nye apologizes for not doing something he could not possibly have done anyway. It is, in short, a simple example of an inappropriate attitude. The familiar form of words has something to do with the building up of this effect, certainly, and is important: though it is doubtful if this is really an example of exaggeration at all.

But all this is incidental. The point is, what has been 'smashed out of shape' here? Leacock is using this notion to cover any kind of inappropriateness, any 'frustration' of the most general expectation. The link with degradation depends entirely on the phrase—'smashed out of shape'. The normal pattern of expectation has been distorted: we get a destructive pleasure out of this just as we would out of smashing in the faces of our enemies. That is apparently the argument: it seems very thin indeed.

For apparently any deviation from the normal comes under the formula. Leacock gives no other reason for exaggeration and understatement, both of which he regards as important humorous techniques. He also speaks of 'face value technique', or the contrast between the face value of the words as generally understood and their logical significance. For instance:

'My old nurse! Can I ever forget her?'
'Yes, I think so, if you get a young one.'

Here, says Leacock, a rhetorical question has been answered.

Again, this seems hardly adequate. He has given us a very good example of attitude-mixing. One attitude is insincere, sententious, rhetorical; the other prosaic, and slightly disreputable. With great neatness, a form of words meant to convey one attitude has been made to convey the other.

No doubt something has been smashed out of shape: the insincere rhetoric. But oddly Leacock does not mention this. For him it is the hack phrase that has been degraded, not the attitude behind it.

As a practical humorist, interested in technique, Leacock naturally stresses word-play; and his explanation, as in the last example, is that it is the words which are degraded, or smashed out of shape. Puns, he says, are a form of triumph over words. So is mis-spelling, as practised for humorous effect by nineteenth century American humorists like Josh Billings and Artemus Ward.

Most followers of Hobbes are reduced to this explanation of word-play. On the face of it, it is singularly unconvincing. Perhaps Leacock feels this: at any rate, he has an interesting comment to make. The vogue for mis-spelling, he suggests, largely peculiar as it was to the United States, may have been due to the emphasis placed on spelling in the little red schoolhouse that meant so much to pioneer America. Even among adults, spelling bees were popular: it was proudly recorded of Abraham Lincoln that he could spell down any other adult in the settlement.

This is by far the most convincing argument yet advanced in support of the degradation of words theory. Once again, it brings in the notion of revolt from repression which we found indispensable to the degradation theory: it tells in favour of Freud rather than Hobbes. But it is doubtful if it can be applied to all verbal play. Certainly Leacock does not so apply it: indeed he lays no stress on the idea at all, merely mentioning it as an aside. For the most part, he seems satisfied if he can show that words have been in some sense smashed out of shape.

Leacock does admit the existence of the two elements in humour which we found hardest to reconcile with Hobbes. He speaks of the 'incongruity' whereby a sentence can have two sharply contrasted meanings, and also of the 'sheer ingenuity' of some puns. 'The thing is not exactly funny, but as smart as a clever conundrum.' And he gives us two excellent examples of nonsense.

The first is the series of mock critical studies of Sherlock Holmes. These take all the inconsistencies which occur in the Sherlock Holmes stories, which were written over a period of years, and treat them with great solemnity in the best academic manner as evidence of interpolations and the like. Leacock praises these very highly, but he does not analyse their appeal. He discusses them, however, under the general head of parody; and possibly he regards them as parodies of the higher criticism. It is true that Belloc has written something similar, with the avowed intention of burlesquing Biblical critics. After a detailed examination of his own book, *The Path to Rome,* which he treats as if it were an ancient manuscript, detecting in it a variety of authors, a number of later interpolations, and so on, he concludes: '. . . and with brains of that standard, Germans ask me to deny my God!'

But even this essay of Belloc's can, like Whately's *Historic Doubts,* be enjoyed by readers who have no interest in the higher criticism. And it is more than doubtful whether even the writers of these Sherlock Holmes studies are interested in it. They owe their appeal largely to their misapplied ingenuity: a perfectly logical superstructure has been raised on a false premise. Leacock, in calling these studies a 'vast piece of cheerful and wholesome nonsense', more or less assumes this point of view without making it explicit, probably without fully realizing it.

The second is an even better example of pure absurdity. It is W. St. Leger's poem, *A Gallop of False Analogies.* Discovering a phrase of Izaak Walton's, 'the chavender or chub', he proceeds to speak of 'the pavender or pub', of sheets 'as sweet as lavender, as lavender or lub', and so on. 'This,' says Leacock, 'is purely and simply a matter of words and sounds. It has no discoverable meaning whatever. But it is delightful.'

Quite so. But how does it fit in with the degradation theory?

And why is this rather weak joke so much better in verse than it would be in prose? Leacock is silent on these points. We are left to suppose that we are still somehow exulting over the degradation of words.

In dealing with the humour of character, Leacock puts forward something not unlike our notion of 'the god's-eye view'.

Funny characters are made by presenting, whether we are conscious of it or not, the same destructive contrasts and incongruities which are at the basis of humour itself . . . . (Thus in Mr. Pickwick we have) the dignity and decorum of middle age contrasted with its physical limitations; a highly scientific desire for information contrasted with an utter inability to measure its truth; a chivalrous and unwearied courtesy which makes him an easy mark: expecting truth and finding deception; seeing the world through roseate spectacles which presently turn a bad world rosy. Mr. Pickwick walks through life conveying with him the contrast between life as it might be and life as it is . . . .

Similarly, Mr. Micawber, 'with a competent manner concealing the utter incompetence within', and Sairey Gamp, 'combining the tenderest and most sacred functions of human life with complete indifference to their meaning!'

In this passage we can see how 'the contrast between the thing as it is and the thing smashed out of shape' has come to cover almost any contrast. The emphasis is all on incongruity, on things which do not fit together. Leacock says nothing of the other kind of comic character, the stereotype who is perfectly consistent but perfectly one-sided. But, apart from that, is it Mr. Pickwick or the rest of the world that is out of shape? Or is the point that the world, with all its disharmony, is always out of shape, as compared with some perfect state where everything always fits together?

Something like this may be in Leacock's mind, and if so, we have something approximating to the god's-eye view which sees men and women as well-meaning but stupid, perverse but lovable children. But while this is vaguely hinted at here, later on the conception becomes even vaguer.

'Humour, in its highest form, no longer excites our laughter, no longer appeals to our comic sense, no longer depends on wit.' Instead, it evokes an attitude not unlike the sentimental benevolence with which we look back on our schooldays, or the musical comedy version of history, which finds everything quaint and romantic. 'The fiercest anger cools: the bitterest of hate sleeps in the churchyard and over it all there spread Time's ivy and Time's roses, preserving nothing but what is fair to look upon.' This may be compared with an earlier comment on Sairey Gamp, that she could have been a repulsive character, but Dickens 'suffused her in a soft atmosphere of gin, and saved her'.

Here, surely, the god's-eye view has been exchanged for the 'roseate spectacles which presently turn a bad world rosy'. Surely some element of reality, some appreciation of the real good in these things, not a mere forgetting of the bad, is desirable?

Certainly this attitude is poles away from what we earlier described as the god's-eye view, the urbane, tolerant but clear-sighted attitude which pierces all shams and sees things exactly as they are. It is odd that Leacock should have plumped for the roseate spectacles, since they take him farther away than ever from degradation and the 'merry ha-ha'. But the truth is that he is always half-horrified at his own theory. He is anxious always to defend humour, to prove that it has risen above its cruel beginnings, that it is being constantly humanized. That is why he does not always make as good a case for degradation as he could: why he is anxious to show that humour often confines its cruelty to nothing more sentient than words.

There is none of this half-heartedness about Ludovici. Indeed, he enrols himself, with only a few reservations, in the ranks of the 'agelasts', the laughter-haters. Humour is for him one of the main causes of modern decadence.

No great creator, teacher, or world-builder has ever been a humorist in the modern sense . . . If a modern English or American humorist had been at the elbow of such a man, the usual exhortations to be humorous at all costs would have completely crippled all hope and desire to do anything epoch-making.

He tells us approvingly that there is not a joke in the whole of the New Testament; and, even though he does defend laughter in one passage, we may well think his defence more damning than his indictment:

I still feel able to defend laughter as a glorious pastime,

although I see in every laugh under the sun that element of self-glory which Hobbes' noble mind detected. But then, perhaps, I have not allowed myself to be convinced, either by modern legislation or modern clap-trap, that the highest object of every man's life is self-effacement, self-belittlement, self-abnegation, self-sacrifice. I see a higher purpose in life for the individual than that he should make himself his neighbour's servant or daily help, although I readily admit that there are millions of individuals whose one form of usefulness would vanish if they did not stand by their neighbours in this way . . . Therefore I see no objection to continuing our fidelity to laughter . . . I do but warn readers that, in our excessive longing to show teeth there may be neurotic compensation, in which case . . . . it is high time to think of other remedies than the exaltation of humour.

It is significant, in view of this passage, that Ludovici quotes his own (the authorized) translation of Nietzsche. Probably he is a Nietzschean; he is all in favour of the superman riding roughshod over his fellows. He does not, therefore, object to humour because it is cruel. Quite the contrary. But, unfortunately, it tends to be cruellest on the superman. It insists on debunking 'great men': moreover, it cultivates an attitude of detached tolerance which utterly destroys the ruthless bigotry which is necessary to the Napoleons. Cowardice and indolence, says Ludovici, hide in laughter: cowardice because to be earnest may excite derision, indolence because it is easier to be flippant than to face serious problems. There is certainly some truth in this; but it is noteworthy that cowardice and indolence are the opposite of strenuous heroism. And strenuous heroism is often, in practice, a synonym for ruthless bigotry.

Ludovici is a whole-hearted Hobbist, but like most modern Hobbists, he finds it necessary to modify and extend the famous formula. Indeed, he virtually replaces it with another, vaguer and easier to twist—superior adaptation.

To explain this phrase Ludovici quotes two familiar fables. One is the story of the mouse invited to pay a visit to a frog. He mounts the frog's back so as to be ferried across a stream. Half-way across something frightens the frog, and he dives under. The mouse is left to drown. 'From the moment the mouse mounts the frog's back,' says Ludovici, 'it is the frog who enjoys, as compared to the mouse, superior adaptation.'

Similarly in the fable of the fox and the stork. The fox invites the stork to dinner and offers him food on two platters, from which the fox alone can eat. The stork retaliates by inviting the fox to dinner and offering food in narrow-necked vases into which he alone can introduce his beak. At the first meal the fox, at the second the stork, enjoys superior adaptation.

When we laugh, then, we are glorying in a sense of being better adapted to a particular situation than someone else. So far, superior adaptation hardly seems to differ at all from self-glory. Perhaps we will grasp the shades of difference by considering Ludovici's examples.

He gives us a list of thirty-six. Many of these, however, are variations of the same type; some are merely comments or riders on previous examples. Thus No. 12 (or rather L, since he uses letters and not numbers) consists in the statement that misfortunes are more or less funny in proportion to the dignity of the victim. Including glosses of this kind, ten of the thirty-six deal with small misfortunes. Ludovici's case does, indeed, rest chiefly on this type of humour. No other class gets nearly such full treatment; some of the most important are slurred over with a bare mention.

Let us see first what he has to say about misfortunes. Three of the ten are straightforward examples, all of them familiar: the laughter of the gods on Olympus at the lame Hephaestos hobbling from one to another offering nectar; Harlequin belabouring the clown; and a man chasing his hat. It is not difficult to show that in each case the laugher enjoys superior adaptation to the victims. The gods are not lame; the child at the pantomime is not being hit; and the crowd in the street have their own hats firmly on their heads.

But it is sometimes the victim who laughs. Three of the examples deal with this:— the man who laughs when chasing his own hat, at the same time looking anxiously at those near him; a smartly dressed woman who slipped on a muddy London pavement, soiling her gloves, skirt, stockings, etc., and laughed heartily; and a child being teased. These, says Ludovici, are all cases of bluff. The victim is conscious of inferior adaptation, but, out of vanity, tries to pass it off by making the sign of superior adaptation. But this is exceptional; yet another example deals with the more usual reaction, resentment at being laughed at when we slip or suffer some other small mishap in front of a crowd.

The theory is borne out, Ludovici says, by three further observations. The first is that we laugh more heartily when the victim is a person of dignity, that is, a person to whom we normally feel inferior. Similarly, we laugh at mishaps to a performer on the stage: Voltaire said that an audience never laughs so loudly as when an actor in a heroic part trips over his long sword, or in some other way comes to grief. The reason, says Ludovici, is that he is placed in a doubly inferior position: he ceases to be master of the character he is acting, and also of himself simply as a man. Finally, there is Sydney Smith's statement that we never laugh at a horse, a child, or an old woman when they slip in the street. Because, says Ludovici, we do not feel inferior to them, and are not interested in asserting our superior adaptation. Children, however, will laugh at another child.

There seems to be a slight confusion here. The last statement seems tantamount to asserting that we only laugh when we have formerly felt our superiority to be in some way challenged. Ludovici's general attitude, however, seems to be that while this intensifies laughter, any case of superior adaptation, whether we have formerly felt inferior or not, is good enough for a laugh. On this theory, we should laugh at horses, old women and children all the time, whether they fall down or remain upright. Sydney Smith himself seems to have been thinking rather of conflict of emotions, of pity inhibiting laughter; and this certainly seems a likelier explanation.

The mishap on the stage can also be explained more satisfactorily. Isn't it the abrupt shattering of the illusion that amuses us rather than any sense of triumphing over the actor?

On the whole, however, Ludovici makes out a good case so long as he is dealing with misfortunes. Stupidity, or lack of knowledge, also fits his theory well. Here he cites the schoolboy howlers; adding that we must be able to recognize them as howlers by our own unaided knowledge. They are not funny if they have to be explained to us. Our superior adaptation is obviously undermined if we have to confess our own lack of knowledge.

Ludovici does not, however, quote any actual examples of schoolboy howlers. He seems to assume that any display of ignorance, any schoolboy's mistake, is a howler. Actually there is nearly always another element. The typical howler shows us a confusion, often verbal, between two widely differing things, which have become inextricably mingled in the child's mind. The child she-bear, already discussed, is an example. Eastman is on strong ground when he points out that often the same joke may be cited as an intentional witticism, or an unintentional blunder.

However, there are certainly some times when we do laugh at ignorance or stupidity merely in itself; so we need not press Ludovici too hard on the point. At most, he has merely chosen a doubtful example.

Contests, in the various forms in which they cause laughter, play into Ludovici's hands, because it is easy to say that we laugh at the triumph of the victor. Thus, he says, we laugh at a good ruse, a good trick, a good case of diamond cut diamond, or at a witticism, 'because we side with the stronger party and feel vicarious superior adaptation'. He also notes that a child will laugh when, after being chased, it reaches the safety of its mother's dress; and that, when one disputant in a public debate cracks a joke against his opponent, the audience often regards this as winning the argument. The reason here, he says, is that we cannot help feeling that the person who is laughed at must be inferior.

But what, we may well ask, is meant by a *good* trick, or a *good* ruse? Merely one that utterly defeats the victim? Must there not also be an element of skill, of ingenuity, of neatness, which provokes admiration, quite apart from any exultation over the fallen? Isn't it one point of the phrase—'diamond cut diamond'—that there should be skill on both sides, so that extreme ingenuity is necessary? And it is surely prejudging the whole case to treat a witticism as *merely* a remark made at someone else's expense. A witticism may well be a veiled insult: Ludovici can explain the insult, but not the veiling.

The difficulty, on Ludovici's thesis, is to explain why every contest, every instance of one man beating another, is not uproariously funny. Perhaps he would say it is: after all, we do laugh at the simple case of Harlequin belabouring the clown. Yet we have already noted that football matches or exhibitions of chess are not comic spectacles.

Usually some deception is necessary before the contest becomes comic. The comic hero *outwits* his rivals: if he got the better of them by straightforward methods, we would no doubt triumph with him, we would probably share his sense of superior adaptation, but I doubt if we would laugh with him.

Ludovici's instance of novelty is one that fits his formula very easily: laughter at hearing a foreign language spoken, or one's own language oddly pronounced. This is due, he says, to the parochial belief that one's own customs are 'right', so that one feels superior when confronted with other people's. Ludovici does not attempt to classify his examples: he no doubt regards his thirty-six as typical, but he does not himself apply labels like 'misfortune' or 'novelty'. It is not therefore necessary for him to prove explicitly that all comic novelty is felt as 'wrong'. Probably, however, his case does depend on this assumption. But laughter at novelty is not always derisive: there are the examples of a child laughing at a new word, or at a burst of fireworks, where he is exulting in the wonders of a new and glorious universe, not triumphing over their pettiness. Ludovici would no doubt claim that this too is superior adaptation, of a different kind. But delight in one's environment is not the same thing as feeling superior to others.

Yet Ludovici does not hesitate to stretch his formula in this way when hard pressed. Superior adaptation can apparently mean mere joy, without any explicit comparison with the position of others. This is no doubt permissible, so long as the comparison remains implicit. Thus we are told that a young woman, knowing herself to be well-dressed, 'smiles constantly and laughs at the slightest provocation'. This is probably legitimate enough: we can readily grant that she is, at least unconsciously, influenced by the thought of her dowdier sisters or of herself on less happy occasions. We may still ask why any 'provocation' however slight, should be necessary: it would seem that being well-dressed is a predisposition to laughter, rather than its cause. But that is another point, and one that we have already discussed. We are concerned here with the stretching of superior adaptation to mean joy or exultation in general, without even an unconscious comparison with others.

From the legitimate instance of the well-dressed girl Ludovici goes to the laugh of pleasure at meeting a friend, and here the formula is stretched a little more, and a little less plausibly. Every friend, he says, means an access of support, of strength, and so good adaptation. On the other hand, when an enemy passes and we are in company, we take care to smile or laugh, to indicate that we are none the worse off for his absence from our circle.

The argument here seems to be that our emotional life is always dominated by a basic feeling of insecurity. Hence all pleasure can be traced to the dispelling of insecurity. Hence it is only necessary to show that laughter is accompanied by pleasure for the formula 'superior adaptation' to be applicable. Ludovici makes this final transition when discussing laughing gas. Investigations show, he says, that inhaling the gas causes pleasant sensations, and 'pleasure has from the beginning of time been rooted in feelings of superior adaptation'.

This is surely Ludovici's weakest explanation. We may grant that part of our pleasure at meeting a friend is due to a sense of having an ally against a hostile world; although most of us probably feel that this is not the whole of friendship. But to assert, without further proof, that even the physically pleasurable sensations caused by inhaling a gas must be somehow equivalent to superior adaptation, is to widen and weaken the whole formula until it becomes worthless.

Ludovici also falls back on another type of widening, more defensible, but still suspect. He cheerfully includes relief from restraint in his formula, without any apology whatsoever. All nonsense, he tells us, can be regarded as liberation from the rigid laws of reason and logic, and this too is superior adaptation. He even finds authority for this in his master Hobbes, who tells us that 'laughter without offence must be at absurdities and infirmities abstracted from persons'. It seems likely, however, that by absurdities Hobbes meant eccentricities rather than nonsense of the Lewis Carroll type. He was still thinking of personal failings, not of false logic indulged in for its own sake.

The same explanation goes for indecency, for incongruity (which Ludovici interprets as the equivalent of nonsense), and for laughter in church or law-court. We have pretty obviously passed from Hobbes to Freud here. Liberation from restraint is no doubt superior adaptation in a sense; but it is different from triumphing over our inferiors. The question is whether Ludovici has succeeded in linking the two concepts by anything more than an ambiguous verbal formula.

Perhaps he has. The argument is, once again, that a haunting sense of inferiority is the obsession, conscious or unconscious, of us all. Anything that enables us to throw this off, if only for a moment, makes us laugh. Conspicuous evidence of our own superior prowess is one means of throwing it off; liberation from the restraints which impress our inferiority upon us is another.

So far, so good; though even here we will get some rather odd results. We will have to say, for instance, that laughter *at* comic vice and laughter *with* it, is essentially the same; though in the first we laugh because we do not share the failing of the comic villain, and in the second because we do share it, and are exulting in being freed from guilt because we share it. But after all any theory of laughter must reconcile these apparent opposites somehow. The real trouble is that Ludovici has proved too much. For him all pleasure must be rooted in the shedding of inferiority, and there .seems no valid reason why some pleasure should be 'funny', and some merely pleasant.

Superior adaptation has still, of course, to embrace the third main type of humour: the sudden mingling of two topics, or attitudes, normally kept in different mental compartments. Ludovici tends to evade this. He interprets incongruity as mere absurdity, or nonsense; it is just another instance of freedom from 'the mental and physical bondage of logic, reason and scientific method'. Kant's formula, he tells us, expectation that ends in nothing, is equivalent to surprise; and 'for millions of years surprise has meant possible danger'. We are therefore relieved when it comes to nothing.

This is obviously inadequate. Much humour consists in leading the reader or listener to expect one thing, and then suddenly presenting him with another thing. But it is seldom indeed that the first thing is any way dangerous. 'We took some photographs of the native girls,' says Groucho Marx. 'Of course they were undeveloped, but we hope to be back next trip.' We thought he was talking about photographs, and he turns out to be talking about girls; but is there any sense in which a danger has been averted? After all, girls are generally much more dangerous than photographs.

Ludovici probably intends to argue that he is speaking here of some atavistic survival. Surprise has become unconsciously associated with danger, and this association lingers even when we are surprised about some quite harmless matter. But there is a confusion here. It is not the surprise that comes to nothing:

it is the expectation that comes to nothing, thus causing surprise. On Ludovici's argument, this should be the reverse of pleasant: it should awaken some deep-rooted atavistic sensation of fear.

He is face to face with the same difficulty when he comes to discuss puns. It is perhaps a sign of uneasiness that he gives us three explanations, one from Bergson, and two from Bain. These are:—

(1) Repetition of similar sounding words is sometimes unintentional, and thus a sign of absent-mindedness and so of inferior adaptation.

(2) We feel superior adaptation at our cleverness at noticing the play upon words.

(3) We feel triumph at the degradation of a noble word.

The first two are not very convincing; and, when he comes to examples, Ludovici, like most Hobbists, leans heavily on the third. He gives us two puns:—

(a) 'We row in the same boat, you know,' said an obscure comic writer to his famous colleague, Douglas Jerrold. 'Yes,' replied Jerrold, 'but with different skulls.'

The degradation here, we are told, 'is obviously the reduction of the noble human cranium to the level of an oar for propelling a boat.' Quite obviously it is nothing of the sort. The point is that the metaphor by which the writer sought to establish his equality with Jerrold has been used to snub him. There is degradation here, certainly, but not of words. But Ludovici could hardly use this explanation, because he is not prepared to argue that all puns are veiled insults. If we concentrate on the verbal aspect of this joke, we can only say that the point lies in the neatness by which one form of words is made to convey two meanings. But it is safe to say that the degradation of the noble human cranium never even remotely enters our thoughts.

(b) The second example is happier. A schoolboy was asked: 'What does sick of the palsy mean?' He replied: 'Having the palsy so long you are sick of it.' Here there is degradation in the sense that a scriptural phrase, with all its hallowed associations, is suddenly reduced to modern slang. But even this is incidental to the anticlimax, which is the real reason for laughter—or such laughter as this feeble jest may be lucky enough to evoke.

We have not exhausted all of Ludovici's thirty-six examples, but enough has been said to show that our general comments on degradation theories apply to him. To summarize, he has a fairly good case while dealing with misfortunes, stupidity, contests and the like; he can, by stretching his formula, account more or less for nonsense and indecency; and he fails almost completely when confronted by incongruity in its broad sense.

The strength of his theory is that it does, as he points out forcefully, explain the sting of laughter. Derisive laughter is undoubtedly a fact: and there is undoubtedly such a thing as 'laughing off' real or fancied inferiority. But this is not the whole of laughter.

So far we have omitted what is perhaps Ludovici's most distinctive contribution: his theory of the physical origin of laughter. It seems only fair to deal with this separately as he himself insists that his general theory could still stand without it.

To say that, because laughter is the expression of superior adaptation, therefore it offends, would be to argue in a circle and to assume too much. It would amount to assuming that every creature, including some of our more intelligent domestic animals, is aware that laughter is the expression of superior adaptation and therefore, by implication, that it makes the object laughed at appear inferiorly adapted. But how could human beings and domestic animals immediately and instinctively know that laughter is the expression of superior adaptation?

Can it be possible that in the facial signals themselves there is some signal, some instinctively recognisable message, the precise burden of which has been forgotten by man, but which he unconsciously, and animals instinctively, read as a sign of superior adaptation, and therefore a menace to their own adaptation?

Ludovici goes on to argue that the essence of laughter is the baring of the teeth. Throughout the book he uses 'show teeth' as a synonym for 'laugh': the phrase is a happy one for his purpose, as it does suggest the hostility and suspicion which he finds lurking in all laughter.

He continues:

Teeth gleam. They are visible to the attacking or merely threatening foe. They are the animal's arsenal of weapons, its equipment for war, for survival in the struggle for existence.

But weapons and equipment for war and for survival are, in the jungle at least, the chief concrete factor in the claim of superior adaptation. To display teeth, therefore, is to make a claim of superior adaptation. It may be only bluff, as when the terrified kitten displays her teeth to a collie dog ... but at least the desperate claim she makes to superior adaptation frequently enables her to accomplish her object, which is to warn off the enemy without the danger of an actual trial of strength ...

Now, if we have really descended from the animals, is it not difficult to suppose that this habit of millions of years, so deeply ingrained, so useful, so intimately associated with success and survival, should have passed entirely out of our gamut of emotions, should have been utterly lost? ... Is it not much more likely that ... the expression of superior adaptation should have become volatilised, spiritualised, and been transferred to all those manifold and complex situations in society in which gregarious animals either find or feel themselves superiorly adapted, or merely lay a false claim to such a position by means of bluff?

We may agree with Ludovici that we have not lost the habit of baring our fangs, or snarling. But it hardly seems necessary to look for it in the smile.

Why, after all, should a facial expression more readily stir racial memories than anything else? All theories assume that some recognition of the basic factor in the laughable occurs in all persons who laugh. Ludovici is on better ground when he refers to the dislike of animals for laughter, but this is in any case doubtful. Moreover, the animal does not react to laughter as he would to the baring of fangs. Probably its dislike of any sudden unexplained sound is a sufficient explanation.

Consider Ludovici's original definition of superior adaptation, in which he quotes the story of the mouse and the frog, and of the stork and the fox. Would the frog bare its fangs (or whatever the frog equivalent may be) as he watched the mouse struggling in the water? Would either the fox or the stork bare theirs as they saw the other unable to get at his food? If either did, it would surely be the one who was victimized, not the triumphant host. True, the host might, if capable of it, laugh. But he would not 'show teeth' in the original, animal sense. In fact, showing teeth is not done by animals when better adapted, but when worse adapted. The kitten might well show her teeth to a collie, but it is doubtful if she would bother to show them to a mouse. It is chiefly when afraid that animals make the most terrifying displays of fangs. Ludovici gets over this by talking about bluff, which is sound enough; but his theory demands that this shall be secondary, derivative; it seems to be primary. Perhaps the theory would be better if the attempt to laugh off inferior adaptation were made its whole basis. But he would not then be able to explain joyous laughter.

10

BERGSON

SUPERIORITY theories of humour have also been called 'moral theories'. The laugher looks down on whatever he laughs at, judges it inferior by some standard, whether of morals or of *mores*.

It is obvious that an infinite number of variations are possible here, according to the particular theory of ethics you care to adopt. If the *summum bonum* is, for example, 'integration', then anything not integrated will be an object of disapproval, and hence of laughter.

Bergson's is both the clearest and most famous instance of such a variation on the superiority theory. His ideal is elasticity, adaptability, the *élan vital*. The opposite is of course inelasticity or rigidity. Hence the laughable is for him 'something mechanical encrusted upon the living'.

Can this formula explain all our types of humour? (Bergson, by the way, being opposed to all formulae on principle, denies that this is one: it is rather a leitmotiv capable of infinite variations', etc., etc. But that is by the way.) Bergson's book consists largely of an analysis of various types of humour so as to find inelasticity in them all. His classification is not the same as ours; we may nevertheless consider our main classes in turn and see what, if anything, he has to say about them. If he has added other important types outside our list, we may consider them separately.

(a) Any Breach of the Usual Order of Events

At first sight, novelty, oddity and eccentricity would seem to be the opposite of rigidity. We usally think of the social code as rigid: the eccentric who invites derision is laughed at because he cannot attain this desirable rigidity. Here is obviously a problem for Bergson. He does not state it quite explicitly, but his answer is quite clear.

In the first place, he would say that the departure from custom is often a means of revealing some intrinsic absurdity. Many things are comic *de jure*, but not *de facto*, because custom has deadened us to their comic nature. Thus all clothes are intrinsically ridiculous, because they are an awkward attempt to counterfeit the suppleness of life. But when we are used to a garment, we do not separate the garment from the wearer in our imagination. It is only out-of-date or eccentric costumes that make us look at them, as it were for the first time, and realize their comic side.

This is ingenious, but not wholly convincing. It is true that we see the funny side of foreigners' customs, and they see the funny side of ours; and often there may be something intrinsically funny in both. But may it not also be that the mere breach of custom is comic? It is not only funny to see a man in unusual clothes; it is also funny, very often, to see him without clothes at all. And this is so even apart from the added factor of indecency. For instance, if it is the custom to wear shoes, bare feet are funny. And this completely contradicts Bergson's explanation.

Secondly, Bergson suggests that every oddity will, when analysed, be found to suggest something mechanical. Physical deformities are funny if they can be successfully imitated by a normally-built person. Thus a hunchback suggests a person who holds himself badly. A negro suggests a man with his face covered with soot, a red nose appears painted, and so on.

Many of us will doubt whether this can be established in every case. After all, we laugh at a big nose, and at long ears, which are not easy to imitate, while we do not laugh at a one-legged or one-armed man, whom we can imitate very easily.

Finally, Bergson, like most other writers on humour, sees this distrust of eccentricity as a proof of the social function of laughter. Society continually fears that the individual will cease to aim at the increasingly delicate adjustment of wills necessary if men are to live together without friction. Therefore society is suspicious of inelasticity of character, mind and even body, because it is a possible sign of separatist activity. 'Any individual is comic who goes his own way without troubling himself to get into touch with the rest of his fellow beings. It is the part of laughter to reprove his absent-mindedness and wake him out of his dream.'

Here we have one of Bergson's main points: that absence of mind, in one form or other, is one of the chief causes of laughter. It is perhaps the clearest case of failure to adjust oneself to the constant flux of life. And it leads to some of the most richly comic types. Don Quixote, for example, is adjusting himself, not to the world he sees round him, but to the romances of chivalry in which he is steeped. 'How profound is the comic element in the Utopian, romantic bent of mind! Yet if you introduce the idea of absent-mindedness, which acts as a go-between, you will see this profound comic element uniting with the most superficial type.'

No doubt much eccentricity is of this type. The individual, preoccupied with his own obsessions, fails to adjust himself to the society in which he lives. We talk of society moulding the individual; and you need to be fluid if you are to fit into a mould. But the mould itself must have rigidity; and the moulded object will eventually harden into the same rigid outlines. All of which suggests that it is not rigidity itself, but only the wrong kind of rigidity, that we laugh at.

Quite so, says Bergson; but you forget my other point, that our own customs are often intrinsically funny, and would appear so but for the blinkers of custom. If we laugh at the stubborn individual who will not fit the mould, foreigners laugh at the mould itself. And in the same way small groups within society often have customs that seem ridiculous to society at large. Thus we have jokes about the oddities of doctors, lawyers, and other professional groups. All rigidity is comic, if only we can stand outside it and see it clearly.

This is plausible, but again not quite convincing. For the social function of laughter is surely two-fold. It does help to eradicate the stubborn nonconformity of odd individuals. But, when it takes the form of laughter at foreign groups, it also helps to build the *esprit de corps* which resists alien influences. That is to say, its function is to preserve rigidity as much as to check it. Excessive rigidity or excessive fluidity will alike lead to nonconformity. Both invite derision. Obviously, then, it is nonconformity itself, not rigidity, that leads to laughter.

Bergson is here up against a problem that all moral theories encounter. Granted that we laugh at any departure from a standard, is the standard merely conventional, or is it rooted in reason rather than custom? The unthinking, it is often said, will laugh at anything strange; true humour will laugh only if the novelty is really unreasonable, and it will laugh just as loudly at the accepted thing, if that is unreasonable. 'Punch' laughs at the foreigner who shoots a fox; more subtle minds see the absurdity of the whole elaborate code of fox-hunting.

Bergson may say, in defence, that his position is precisely this. The subtle mind detects any inelasticity, any failure to adjust oneself to the universal flow. But most men are only sensitive to those rigidities which conflict with pet rigidities of their own. But the difficulty here is whether any standard, however good, does not involve some rigidity. Most of us will agree with Feibleman's criticism. Bergson, he says, errs in putting all the stress on the inadequacy of forms as contrasted with flux. This is one function of comedy, but the end is not unmitigated flux, but better forms.

(b) Any Forbidden Breach of the Usual Order of Events

Bergson's treatment of comic vice is interesting and suggestive; we have already drawn upon it in our own general discussion. The basic type of comic character, we found, was the animated mannerism. 'Vices,' says Bergson, 'lend us their own rigidity instead of borrowing from us our flexibility. A vice simplifies us. There are vices into which the soul plunges deeply, so as to give the vice its own flexibility, but these are tragic vices. The comic vice is, as it were, a frame.'

The obsession, the *idée fixe*, the 'humour', is certainly one great source of the comedy of character. But we saw earlier that the most satisfying comic character departs from this simple rigidity. An animated mannerism is amusing up to a point, but the greatest comic characters are many-sided, complete human beings. This led us to the concept of the god's-eye view. The essential point, we decided, was that we should feel that we understood the character thoroughly. This does imply a certain rigidity. The character is, as it were, a datum, which reacts to a situation, not an unknown entity which changes with events. We may agree, then, with many of Bergson's conclusions: that comedy deals with types, tragedy with individuals; and that the spectator of comedy must be detached, remote, not emotionally involved in the predicament that he is watching. But our point would be that rigidity is the means, rather than the end. Provided only that we can continue to preserve the god's-eye view, the more flexible and whole a comic character can be, the better.

We may think, too, that Bergson goes too far in excluding sympathy altogether. He regards the comic spirit as a stern parent or magistrate ceaselessly curbing all faults which society finds harmful. 'Unsociability in the performer and insensibility in the spectator are two essential conditions of comedy.' And again: 'Laughter is above all a corrective . . . intended to humiliate. By laughter, society avenges itself for the liberties taken with it. It would fail in its object if it bore the stamp of sympathy or kindness.'

This leads him to the rather startling conclusion that it is impossible to laugh at oneself. Whereas the tragic writer, he says, directs his attention inwards, so that his characters are men he might have been himself, the comic writer looks only outwards. 'However interested a dramatist may be in the comic features of human nature, he will hardly be so, I imagine, to the extent of trying to discover his own. Besides, he would not find them, for we are never ridiculous except at some point that remains hidden from our own consciousness.'

This is, to say the least, highly questionable. It is interesting to notice what a complete contrast we have here with Leacock's view, that humour presents us with 'rose-tinted spectacles which presently turn a bad world rosy'. We found reason to doubt this view also; but perhaps the one extreme will correct the other. The explanation is probably that Bergson was thinking of Molière, and Leacock of Dickens. French comedy is no doubt more pitiless than English. At any rate, we may have no difficulty in finding comic characters in English literature who are presented sympathetically. We may even guess that some of them display faults the author was aware of in himself. Goldsmith, for example, delighted in ridiculing feckless Irishmen. And not only sentimental Victorians like Dickens, but modern writers like Wells or Sinclair Lewis, do not hesitate to rouse our sympathy for their Kippses and their Babbitts while we laugh at them.

All this tells against the rigidity theory. Bergson's argument applies best to the stereotype, the animated mannerism; the comic poet, he says, isolates the fault in his character, does not show its organic relation to the man's whole make-up. This is essential; otherwise our feelings would be roused.

The god's-eye view, however, demands that we see the character steadily and see him whole. We see him, it is true, as from a great height, so that his pretensions are dwarfed, and his aspirations unimportant, like a child's. Provided only that we are able to maintain this distance, it is an advantage that we should see his whole make-up, and even that we should 'sympathize with his emotions.

As before, we have found it convenient to consider comic vice as part of the wider field of comic character. But even so, we have considered only one type of comic vice. What of the Falstaff type, the man we laugh with, and not at?

Bergson should find it easier to allow for this than Hobbes and his more immediate followers. For escape from moral repression is, after all, escape from the rigidity of a moral code. Morals are no doubt necessary; but like all abstractions, they are somewhat inadequate to the essential individuality of things. Morality is yet another mould: it is fitting to laugh at those not fluid enough to conform to it; but it is as well to stand off occasionally and observe the rigidity of the mould itself.

All this would seem the obvious answer for Bergson. Yet he does not in fact make it. He does not indeed consider the problem at all. Nowhere, so far as I know, does he say much about laughter as a means of escape from repression. Where he does touch on it, he seems to confuse these two notions of laughing at and laughing with, the butt and the wit. In the course of his comparison between humour and dreams, he says:

When the comic character automatically follows up his idea, he ultimately thinks, speaks and acts as if he were dreaming. Now, a dream is a relaxation ... To break away from logic and yet continue to string together ideas is to indulge in play ... So comic absurdity gives us the impression of playing with ideas. Our first impulse is to join in the game. This relieves us of the strain of thinking. Now, the same might be said of other forms of the laughable. Deep-rooted in the comic, there is always a tendency ... to take the line of least resistance, generally that of habit. The comic character no longer tries to be ceaselessly adapting and readapting himself to the society of which he is a member ... Here too our first impulse is to accept the invitation to take it easy. For a short time ... we join in the game ... But we rest only for a short time. The sympathy that is capable of entering into the impression of the comic is a very fleeting one. Thus a stern father may at times forget himself and join in some prank his child is playing, only to check himself at once in order to correct it.

Here the distinction between the butt and the wit is entirely blurred. Playing with ideas is the same thing as the easy automatism of habit that leads to comic vice. There is no essential difference between Lewis Carroll and the stage miser—we laugh at both in order to correct them. And any feeling of delight we may have in the ingenuities of Carroll is only fleeting; our dominant feeling is of disgust and scorn. It is impossible to accept this view; and since Bergson had another available which fits his theory perfectly, it is difficult to understand how he came to adopt this one. It is a pity that he does not deal with indecency, which would raise the escape from repression theory in its clearest form. Probably, however, he would regard indecency as merely a special instance of the physical (matter, rigidity) impinging upon the spiritual (soul, fluidity). As we shall see, this is one of his formulæ for laughter.

(c) Anything Masquerading as Something it is Not

Bergson has a clear explanation of mimicry. Since every individual is different, true personality cannot be imitated. In proportion as our mannerisms are imitable then, they fail to express our essential selves. Thus the gestures of a public speaker should faithfully reflect the subtle nuances of speech. If they do this, they should be infinitely variable. But a gesture which occurs with automatic regularity has obviously failed in its purpose; and these are precisely the gestures which are easily imitated. Similarly our mannerisms should reflect the infinite variety of our mental states. If they did this, exact imitations could never occur. Hence any imitation reflects a lack of subtlety, of adaptability. That is why it causes laughter.

Hence Pascal's saying: 'Two faces that are alike, neither comic in itself, excite laughter when together through their likeness.' This explanation assumes that our laughter is aimed at the person imitated. This is true enough of most mimicry, and is especially true of parody. But it does not apply to comic hypocrisy, to the peculiar joy of peeping behind the mask, where we laugh at the pretensions of the imitator. Here Bergson has to change his ground slightly: he would say that we laugh here at the clumsy attempts of the mechanical to simulate the infinite suppleness of life.

Using the term 'disguise', he does, indeed, make much of this explanation. He begins by making the point, already mentioned, that odd clothes are funny because they shock us into realizing the intrinsic absurdity of all clothes. Surprise, he tells us, is not the essence of the joke, as some have supposed; surprise merely performs the incidental function of dissolving our prepossessions. This is also the function of disguise; and a person wearing odd clothes is in effect disguising himself.

Having thus introduced the notion of disguise, Bergson goes on to say that disguises of the individual, of nature, and of society, are all comic. A dog half-clipped, a wood plastered with election notices, are disguises of nature. They suggest a masquerade in which nature has been mechanically tampered with. Similarly, anything inert or stereotyped on the surface of society suggests society disguising itself. All ceremonies have their latent comic element. They are, as it were, the clothing of society—serious only when identified with their object. They are comic as soon as we neglect the matter and think only of the form.

There is a good deal to be disentangled here. In the first place, Bergson should say, not that a person wearing odd clothes is disguising himself, but that he is disguising his clothes. For on his view, it is the clothes that we laugh at, not the person; and we laugh at them just because they are clothes— lifeless cloth having the audacity to simulate the infinite suppleness of the human body. The wearer, on the other hand, is presumably an object of respectful admiration. In contrast to the ridiculously rigid garments he wears, he shines forth as the infinitely lissom representative of the *élan vital* on earth.

One doubts, somehow, if this is an adequate analysis of our feelings when we laugh at a film funny man in baggy trousers and an outsize hat. The whole connection between odd clothes and disguise seems rather slender.

Bergson's main point is, however, clear enough. In every masquerade, we have the mechanical imitating the living, and revealing its own inadequacy. Now it is true enough that comic hypocrisy, as distinct from mimicry, reveals the inadequacy of the imitator. But is this inadequacy necessarily rigidity? For instance, a stock device of comedy is to disguise a man as a woman, or vice versa. Now it may well be that some of the comic effects come from the relative clumsiness of men as compared with feminine gracefulness. But, if this were all, it would not be funny to reverse the process.

It is of course open to say that any masquerade shows that it is impossible for any one thing to counterfeit another perfectly. And this, of course, is rigidity of a kind. Thus a successful imitation is comic because it is made possible by some lack of flexibility in the thing imitated; and an unsuccessful one is comic because its failure shows a lack of flexibility in the imitator. But actually Bergson goes further than this. By flexibility he means something more positive than mere lack of adaptability. He speaks always of the mechanical aping the animate: cloth imitating the body, art imitating nature, ceremony imitating the social flux.

It is clear, however, that this does not cover every case. When we laugh at Mr. Pecksniff, it is because he describes his selfish and ignoble motives in the terms proper to exalted virtue. Our amusement has nothing to do with the rigidity of vice or the flexibility of virtue. We laugh because what is proper to one thing has been twisted so as to apply to its direct opposite. Masquerade, in short, leads us to inappropriateness, to our next main class:

(d) Importing into One Situation What Belongs to Another

Here again, Bergson claims that comic inappropriateness is always caused by the mechanical impinging upon life. Thus he tells us that it is comic to call our attention to the physical in a person when the moral side is concerned, as when a speaker sneezes at a pathetic part of his speech. Stoutness, he thinks, is probably comic because it suggests a person embarrassed by his body. And we may broaden this general concept to include any case of the manner seeking to outdo the matter, the letter ousting the spirit. Thus it is funny for a lawyer, a magistrate, or a doctor to speak as if justice or health are of less importance than the formalities of their professions.

Again, we laugh every time a person gives us the impression of being a thing, as when Sancho Panza is tossed in a blanket like a football, or Baron Munchausen turned into a cannon-ball travelling through space. Another example is M. Perrichon counting his parcels before getting into a railway carriage: 'Four, five, six, my wife seven, my daughter eight, myself nine.'

Bergson is here calling attention to a very important point about comic incongruity. The humour often does depend on a reversal of values. We commonly regard our wives and our suitcases as being on different levels of value; and it becomes comic to mix them.

Many of Bergson's examples will be found to involve this reversal of values. For example, as an illustration of the hardening of social institutions into mere forms, persisting after their purpose has vanished, he cites the story of the customs officers who went bravely to the rescue of the crew of a wrecked ship. The first thing the officers said when they finally got the sailors ashore was: 'Have you anything to declare?'

It is true enough that we have here an official carrying out his customary duties like an automaton, regardless of altered circumstances. But why have the circumstances altered? Only because we regard human lives as infinitely more important than tariffs. This seems to be the core of the joke. The automatic persistence of the official is incidental only; it is the machinery, the means rather than the end.

Bergson's philosophy demands that values shall depend on elasticity. The inanimate, the completely rigid, is at one end of the scale: the soul, the completely fluid, is at the other end. It would take us far afield to examine this system of ethics. We need only note that, as Bergson applies it, it all seems plausible enough. We certainly do regard the body as lower in the scale than the spirit, the thing as below the person. But the real point is that any system of values will do, provided only that it is accepted. For instance, it is funny for a keen amateur gardener to lavish unceasing care on a weed under the impression that he is nurturing a choice bloom. And I do not suppose than even Bergson could demonstrate that the horticultural code of values has much to do with flexibility. Indeed, weeds adapt themselves to the eternal flux of garden life much more readily than prize flowers.

Bergson has a second approach to the importing into one situation of what belongs to another. He calls it 'reciprocal interference of series'. But in order to follow his argument, we had better depart from our own classification a little, and consider his.

Bergson lists three comic devices which he regards as of great importance. The essence of life, he says, is that it is continually changing: the order of phenomena is irreversible, and every self-contained series is perfectly individual. Reversing these principles, we get *repetition, inversion,* and *reciprocal interference of series.* 'These are the methods of light comedy, and no others are possible.'

By repetition Bergson means a situation which recurs several times, and thus contrasts with the changing stream of life. For

example, you meet a friend whom you have not seen for a long
time; then you keep on running into him all day. This is a very
simple case. In comedy the same scene is introduced in varying circumstances, as when one group, of masters, have their
actions reproduced by a second group, of servants.

Inversion occurs in every instance of comic topsy-turvydom.
The prisoner lecturing the magistrate, the child teaching his
parents, are examples. The cheater cheated, or the biter bit, is
a special case.

Reciprocal interference of series:— 'A situation,' says Bergson,
'is invariably comic when it belongs to two independent series
of events and is capable of being interpreted in two entirely
different meanings at the same time.' Thus we have the stage-
made misunderstanding, in which the actors put one interpretation on events, while the audience know the real one. Another
instance is the repetition of events belonging to different periods.
Thus Tartarin de Tarascon is imprisoned in the castle of Chillon, like the heroic Bonivard before him, manacled in the very
chain used to secure Bonivard, and so on. The mock-heroic
generally can be analysed in the same way. And as a final instance Bergson cites the interlocking plots of comedy.

Summarizing, Bergson says:

Whether we find reciprocal interference of series, inversion,
or repetition, we see the objective is the same — to obtain
mechanisation of life. You take a set of actions and repeat it as
it is, or turn it upside down, or transfer it bodily to another set
with which it partially coincides — all these being processes that
consist in looking at life as a repeating mechanism with rever-
sible action and interchangeable parts.

Further:

The ludicrous in events may be defined as absent-mindedness
in things, just as the ludicrous in individual character always
results from some fundamental absent-mindedness of the person . . . Light comedy bears the same relation to actual life as
does a jointed dancing doll to a man walking — an artificial
exaggeration of the natural rigidity in things.

It is not hard to pick holes in most of this. With the parallel
scenes of masters and servants, more is involved than simple
repetition. The fact that the groups are of different classes is
important. Sometimes, as often in Shakespeare, we are invited
to laugh at the presumption of the servant who apes his master.

Sometimes we are invited to take pleasure in the demonstration that Judy O'Grady and the colonel's lady are sisters under the skin. In the first case we have unsuccessful imitation: in the second a subtle reversal of accepted values. But repetition is no more than the machinery in either case. The sense that life is a repeating mechanism hardly enters into our calculations.

As for inversion, Bergson's examples seem the very reverse of mechanical rigidity. The prisoner lecturing the magistrate, the child teaching his parents, both stubbornly refuse to be confined within the role which society expects them to play. So far from subordinating life to a formula, they show life overriding the formula. In the infinite flux of reality, there are occasions when the prisoner has moral supremacy over the magistrate, when the child has knowledge not revealed to his parents.

Further, we may doubt whether history is necessarily funny whenever it repeats itself. The point of Tartarin's exploits in the castle of Chillon is that a prosaic little nineteenth century bourgeois does not strike us as belonging in the same category as a romantic figure out of the Middle Ages. The same is true of the mock-heroic in general.

We may of course describe this as 'reciprocal interference of series' if we like. It is true enough that we have here two figures each of which rouses an entirely different set of emotions. Bringing them together involves a collision of values. And this is the essence of the joke, and not the mere repetition of events. It is not funny that modern armies should fight at Thermopylae, provided that we invest these warriors with the same heroic qualities as cling to their classical predecessors. Political orators, indeed, when they talk about the embattled legions of freedom defending once more the sacred shrines of our civilization, and so forth, use the coincidence to rouse emotions which would be quickly punctured by laughter. The repetition only becomes funny if we focus attention on those aspects of a modern army (tin hats, bully beef, etc.) which seem to us unworthy of the romantic aura which surrounds classical Greece.

It is, then, not merely the sense that life is a mechanism with interlocking parts, but the conflict of values that amuses us. And often enough, as with inversion, the conflict reveals that life is less mechanical than our own attitudes. Life is not a series of closed circles, each to be ticketed with its appropriate emotional response. There are overlapping elements everywhere, and we only arrive at our neat evaluations by ignoring them or formalizing them. There is prose in the mediaeval hero, and poetry in the black-coated modern bourgeois. Bergson seems to have inverted this notion.

These are real defects in Bergson's analysis. But what truth is there in his argument? It is true enough that we obtain pleasure, though not necessarily laughter, out of symmetry in events. Ingenious interlocking plots may not strike us as revealing any particular 'absent-mindedness' in things. But we do get a peculiar intellectual enjoyment out of seeing how everything fits in. And we do feel that real life is a good deal less neat and orderly. The story of the prince doomed to an endless repetition of his game of patience is an excellent example of this kind of humorous symmetry.

But do we deride this symmetry because we feel it reveals the rigidity that makes it impossible to adapt oneself to real life? Isn't it rather that we feel we can cope with life when it is reduced to a formula? This would link up with the view that our pleasure in many comic characters comes from the pleasant sense of seeing through them, following their reactions perfectly.

On the other hand, we have continually noticed an entirely opposite source of humorous pleasure. Again and again it is the shattering of the formula that we delight in: the revelation that it is not, after all, adequate to life. What we have called universe-changing is the supreme example.

It is odd that Bergson should have ignored this, for it would seem to fit his theory well enough.

(e) Word-play

There is no essential difference, according to Bergson, between word-play and other forms of humour. All we need do is transpose the types of humour already described to the sphere of words. Bergson thus obtains five main classes of word-humour:

(1) Inadvertently to say or do what we have no intention of saying or doing, as a result of inelasticity. In language we find this rigidity in catch-phrases, clichés. An absurd idea fitted into these phrases makes them comic. Examples: 'I don't like working between meals.' 'Only God has the right to kill his fellow-creatures.'

The weakness in this explanation lies in the phrase 'an absurd idea'. On Bergson's premises, it is hard to see why this should be necessary. Humour springs from rigidity. With words, clichés are the embodiment of rigidity. So far, so good. But why should we need to go farther? The conclusion would seem to be that clichés are in themselves funny. So they are, no doubt, to discerning minds. But most of us feel, with Bergson himself, that some addition is necessary. Perhaps he would say that this addition, this absurd idea, helps to remove the blinkers of custom and awaken us to the innate absurdity of the cliché.

But this seems hardly adequate. What really happens is that the familiar form of words momentarily traps us into accepting, as a familiar and respectable platitude, an idea which actually contradicts the dearest beliefs of platitudinous respectability. We have here, in short, another example of a stock response being transferred to an inappropriate stimulus. Sometimes, reinforcing the joke, there is the sly suggestion that perhaps the response is really more appropriate to the new stimulus than the old. Perhaps the gospel of industry really is a lie, and it is better not to work between meals. Perhaps the divine code really is more cruel and capricious than the human one.

How does this differ from Bergson's view? The rigidity of the cliché obviously is an important part of the joke, or at any rate of the machinery of the joke. But the real point lies less in this than in the abrupt reversal of familiar values. It is true that this is itself a shattering of moral formulæ, an exposure of another kind of rigidity. But here, as before, Bergson does not seem to have this in mind at all. He is satisfied once he has shown that reliance on a rigid form of words has trapped us into accepting something we did not mean to accept.

(2) The diversion of attention from the moral to the physical becomes, with words, taking a figurative expression literally, fixing our attention on the material aspect of a metaphor. *Example*: 'He's always running after a joke',—'I'll back the joke!'

Bergson comments on this that 'he won't catch it' would be less witty because 'catch' is also figurative; it does not compel us to form the image of two runners, one close on the other's heels.

But, we may ask, do we laugh at this image at all? Hasn't Bergson missed the real point of this joke, which is the implied insult it contains? It is true that the speaker has taken advan-

tage of the literal and the figurative meanings of running after
to make his point. But is this at all analogous to the physical
obtruding upon the moral? We do not feel that running after
(figurative) is somehow sublime, while running after (literal)
is gross and material.

The point is rather that a form of words meant to convey a
complimentary, or at least a neutral meaning, has been twisted
so that it becomes an insult. And there are two points here: the
twisting and the insult. Each makes us laugh. It is immaterial
that the twisting happens to be achieved by taking a metaphor
literally. Any kind of twisting would do, provided that it is neat
and plausible.

Bergson does not entirely ignore this, because he goes on to
say that wit often consists in trapping an interlocutor in his own
words, making him say the opposite of what he thinks. This,
he claims, is done by turning the concrete aspect of the metaphor against him. And he gives a further example:

'Gambling in stocks is very risky. You win one day and lose
the next.' 'Then I'll gamble only every other day.'

He adds that a variant of this device is to expand a symbol
on the concrete side, and to pretend that the expansion holds
good for the symbolic side. Examples are:

A Monte Carlo official was asked why his breast was covered
with medals, when he had been awarded only one. He explained that he had staked his medal on a number at roulette,
and won.

A bride of forty was criticized for wearing orange blossoms,
like a young girl. 'Why,' someone interposed, 'she's entitled to
oranges, let alone blossoms!'

The first of these two stories does support Bergson fairly well.
This joke does depend, at least in part, on the confusion between the medal, as a circle of metal, and the heroism it sym-
bolizes. But the second is a particularly good example of an
apparent defence being really an even more damning insult.
And in general we can hardly agree that the substitution of the
literal for the figurative is comparable to the intrusion of the
physical upon the moral.

Bergson seems to have in mind a second explanation: he
stresses the trapping of the interlocutor in his own words. How
is this meant to fit his theory? Is it that the speaker is convicted
of rigidity in that his words are not a perfect expression of his

ideas? Or is it, as Bergson suggests a little later, that the words
themselves are convicted of a kind of absent-mindedness?

Either theory seems more promising than the original one.
But against the first it may be said that the mere twisting of
meaning, 'playing with words' in the expressive common phrase,
seems enough to cause laughter even when no-one has been
trapped. In the story about the stock exchange, for instance,
the gag line might easily be represented as stupidity rather
than wit. As Bergson advances the second theory more explicitly when discussing puns, we will leave it for the moment.

(3) Inversion of words, or phrases, is, says Bergson, a stock
type of joke.

'What do you mean by emptying your pipe on my terrace?'

'What do you mean by putting your terrace under my pipe?'

Here again we may ask whether this is really explained by
saying that words are here treated as 'a mechanism with rever-
sible parts'. It is true that we may sometimes turn words inside
out, and raise a laugh in the process, for no reason at all. A
comedian may call a daffodil a dillydaffy. A schoolboy may
amuse himself by reversing his mate's name, so that Jack Wil-
son becomes Will Jackson. Crude facetiousness of this kind
might be plausibly explained in Bergson's terms. And no doubt
this remains as one element in such jokes as the one he quotes.
But it has pretty obviously been swamped by another and much
more important element. There is here, once again, a reversal
of values. The difference in phrasing reflects a real difference
in the point of view. Each speaker regards his own possession
as the important one; and this in itself epitomizes a good deal
of human nature.

Are we reading too much into a not very profound joke? Any
explanation of a joke is likely to seem over elaborate, since it
must put into precise terms what the joke itself only hints at.
But I think it will be admitted that any explanation of this one
will have to take into account the attitude revealed by the
second speaker. We might be content to say that it is 'amusingly
impudent', or 'blindly perverse', or something of the sort; but
the impudence or the perverseness can hardly be analysed except on the above lines.

Speaking generally, inversion of this type is merely a device
by which two differing viewpoints can be put side by side in
sharp contrast. The same contrast, less neatly exhibited, would

be less amusing; but on the other hand a mere inversion, like 'dillydaffy', which did not reveal any such contrast, would also be less amusing.

(4) Reciprocal interference, in the sphere of words, becomes the pun, where the same word appears to offer two inconsistent meanings. The double meaning may be only apparent, breaking down on examination, or it may express two differing ideas. Often a pun differs only slightly from a poetic metaphor; but whereas the metaphor reveals close harmony between language and nature, the pun makes us think of negligence on the part of language, which seems to have forgotten its function and claims to accommodate things to itself rather than vice versa. Plays upon words, then, reveal a momentary lapse of attention, a kind of absent-mindedness in words.

This is Bergson's equivalent of the explanation of puns used by most superiority theories. The punster is being superior at the expense of words: in Leacock's terms, he is maliciously glorying in a word crushed out of shape. Bergson undoubtedly makes this explanation seem more plausible than usual. But does the pun, or word-juggling in general, really reveal any rigidity in words? Isn't it rather their elasticity we revel in? Even simple inversion, like 'dillydaffy', seems more easily explained in this way. Are we really saying in effect: 'See how rigid, how like a machine, this word is; it can be turned upside down?' Aren't we rather saying: 'See how variable words are; the syllables may be transposed, and it still seems to make a kind of sense?' It is the child who chiefly delights in this kind of word-juggling; and he does so because he wants to explore all the possibilities of words, just as he wants to explore all the other possibilities of an infinitely varied world.

Undoubtedly the pun is, in Bergson's terms, a form of reciprocal interference of series. Two entirely disparate ideas, normally kept in separate compartments of our minds, are suddenly brought together. The connection may be only apparent, verbal; or it may be real. But in neither case does the connection seem to suggest a mechanical, rigid universe. On the contrary, it suggests that all things are inter-connected; that the gulf which seems to exist between the respectable and the unmentionable (to particularize one favourite type of pun) has after all many bridges; and that, if anything is rigid and inadequate to the infinitely variable flow of life, it is our own compartmentalism, our habit of putting different parts of life in different mental pigeon-holes.

(5) Transposition, in wit, corresponds to repetition in comedy. Repetition consists in arranging events so that the same scene is reproduced either between the same characters under fresh circumstances, or between fresh characters in the same circumstances, as when servants repeat the antics of their masters. Now, says Bergson, imagine an idea expressed in a suitable style and placed in a natural setting. If expressed in another style, and transposed to a different key, it becomes comic.

This device takes many forms. For example, we have the solemn transposed into the familiar, or parody. As an example Bergson quotes Butler's couplet:

> Like a lobster boiled, the morn
> From black to red began to turn.

Again, there is inverse transposition, or speaking of small things as if they were large. This gives us both exaggeration and the mock-heroic. Applying transposition to moral values, we get the expression in reputable language of some disreputable idea. Example: 'Your peculations are too extensive for an official of your rank.' This device, says Bergson, is much used by Dickens and Thackeray; but perhaps *Jonathan Wild* would be the best instance of what he has in mind.

Another common contrast is between the real and the ideal, what is and what ought to be. Here again transposition may be in either direction. Sometimes we state what ought to be done, and pretend to believe it is what is actually being done. This is irony. Sometimes we describe what is being done and pretend that this is what ought to be done. This is humour. And, as a final form of transposition, there is the use of professional jargon for ideas outside its sphere: 'Your kindness of the third ult.'

In all this Bergson has departed a fair way from his original contention. He would have us believe that the common characteristic of all these forms of humour is repetition: the recurrence with blind, piston-like regularity of a pet obsession, an *idée fixe*. This applies well enough to the last example, where the persistence of commercial phraseology can be regarded as evidence of a rigid habit. But when Jonathan Wild appears before us as a great man, does this mean that habits of thought proper to kings and generals have blindly attached themselves to a highwayman? To say this is to miss the whole point of Fielding's satire.

We might replace Bergson's 'transposition' by another word: inappropriateness. But the inappropriate is not just a mechanical repetition, a cropping up of ideas in spheres where they do not fit. It may equally be an upsetting of values, of proprieties which are themselves rigid. Bergson claims that 'degradation' and 'exaggeration', both of which have been put forward as comprehensive explanations of all humour, are only single forms of transposition, which is itself only one form of the comic. But it can equally be claimed that the persistence of a fixed idea is itself only one form of the inappropriate. Parody, or the mock-heroic, is not merely inept metaphor. Irony is not merely a blind confusion of the real and the ideal.

(f) Small Misfortunes

We have called Bergson's a superiority theory; and most superiority theories find their chief support in small misfortunes and want of knowledge or skill. Bergson, however, pays little attention to this type of humour. Comic vice, the other stand-by of the Hobbists, can be convincingly represented as moral inelasticity; but what of custard pies and banana-skins?

The banana-skin, of course, is easy enough, and Bergson seizes on it. One of his earliest examples is a man stumbling in the street. This, he says, would not be comic if the passers-by supposed that a sudden whim had caused him to sit on the ground. Their laughter is caused by his clumsiness, his inability to adjust himself.

We may note, in passing, that this is a doubtful assumption. It might be even funnier if a stout business man were to be seized with a sudden whim for sitting on the pavement. One of Chesterton's characters, Auberon Quin, is meant to be a sort of incarnation of humour; and he behaves in precisely this way, standing on his head, for instance, in a crowded street, to the embarrassment and dismay of his respectable companions. But let us ignore this and allow Bergson to develop his argument.

Let us suppose, he says, a person who attends to the petty occupations of life with mathematical precision. His surroundings have been tampered with by a wag, so that when he dips his pen in the ink-stand, it comes out covered with mud, and so

on. This, Bergson concludes, is exactly analogous to the man
who stumbles in the street. Both are unable to adapt themselves to changing circumstances. The only difference is that
the one happens naturally, the other is the result of human
manipulation of the environment.

And from this Bergson goes on to absence of mind, which is
a chronic and temperamental inability to adjust oneself to environment. And so to the *idée fixe*, which is the same chronic
disability in another form; and to 'absent-mindedness' in events
and in words.

Now it is true enough that all misfortune does result from an
inability to adjust oneself to circumstances. But the formula is
so wide that one feels that some more precise demonstration of
rigidity is necessary before Bergson has proved his point. Perhaps he feels this himself, for here and there, as instances crop
up, he supplements this general explanation of misfortune. A
laughable expression of the face, he says, is one which makes
us think of something rigid, an ingrained twitching or a fixed
grimace. It is all the more comic if it suggests to us a simple
mechanical action, like eternally blowing an imaginary trumpet.
Stoutness suggests a person embarrassed by his body, the mental hampered by the physical. Apart from such special cases,
however, he seems content to identify comic mishaps with lack
of adaptability.

And this, as we have said, seems a little too vague. There is
truth in it, certainly. Eager human aspirations being continually
impeded by the demands of the human body, the limitations of
human foresight, the rigidity of human habits: all this is perhaps the essence of the human comedy. We have seen, too,
that we laugh more loudly when the victim of misfortune brings
it on himself, or when it comes in spite of his precautions against
it; and this supports Bergson's view. But, when all this has been
said, is there not, perhaps, some more immediate and less highfalutin' reason for a small boy's laughter when his brother slips
into a puddle, or his teacher sits down on a tack?

This is about all that Bergson has to say about our classes of
humour. We must remember, however, that he is not following
our classification. His account of humour does cover most of
our classes: and we may easily guess how he would deal with
one or two that are not there. Want of knowledge or skill, for
instance, would not worry him: it can be identified easily

enough with rigidity. The most serious omissions are indecency and nonsense. Both of these are most easily explained as relief from restraint. And Bergson does not seem to have a place for this kind of humour.

He does succeed, however, in uniting the incongruity and the superiority theories. Humour is for him essentially derision: it serves the social purpose of castigating unsocial behaviour. But unsocial behaviour is essentially inflexibility—the inability to adjust oneself. And incongruity can also be regarded as a form of flexibility: it occurs whenever an idea, appropriate enough in one context, insists on thrusting itself forward where it is not wanted.

It is really a very impressive case. The formula 'something mechanical encrusted upon the living', which did not seem very promising at first sight, has turned out to contribute a good deal to our understanding of humour. In particular, it casts much light on comedy in character. The animated mannerism, the man with the fixed idea, does provide a clue to much of our laughter at human antics. What we have called the god's-eye view can be represented well enough as the spectacle of men fumbling with clumsy fingers, blinkered eyes, and inadequate ideas, to grasp an infinitely varied and subtle universe.

But even to say this is to read something into Bergson. He himself keeps rather closer to the more narrowly moral view. Laughter is society's defence against eccentrics. Flexibility is, for him, adapting oneself to social conventions. As we have seen, he does not develop the more promising theme, equally open to him, of the final inadequacy of these conventions themselves.

It is for this reason that Bergson tends to confuse the butt and the wit; it is for this reason that he avoids the laughter of release, or relief from restraint. When we laugh, we must always be deriding something mechanical which impedes the evolutionary undulations of society towards a still greater affinity with the cosmic flux. It is difficult to see why he does not allow that society may also stand off and laugh at itself; that it may occasionally find its own proprieties more comically inadequate than violation of them could ever be.

Perhaps Bergson would say that he does mean to imply this. But if so he certainly misses many opportunities of illustrating it. For then he would see the mock-heroic, not as a mere mech-

anical repetition of the same scene in different settings, but as
a criticism of the romantic attitude that puts different parts of
life on different levels of value. He would see in the criminal
rebuking the judge, not an absurd attempt to invert the sensitive fabric of society, as if it were a mere machine which works
equally well in reverse, but the innuendo that our code of justice might be closer to reality if it were turned upside down.

Much the same can be said of Bergson's treatment of incongruity. His point seems to be that 'everything is what it is and
not another thing'. We do damage to this divine individuality
whenever we so much as find a resemblance between two things.
Hence mimicry. Incongruity sins against the nature of the
universe by forcibly bringing together two things which should
remain aloof each in its supreme singularity.

Now we would agree that much humour consists in finding
unexpected connections between ideas usually kept apart. But
it does not seem true that we laugh at this in order to deride
the connection, to affirm our belief in the real incompatibility
of these ideas. Our laughter expresses, often enough, the simple
joy of exploration. It pleases us to find, or to play at finding,
these unexpected links between apparent disparates. It is
pleasant to find new attributes in something we have always
thought of as dully familiar. This explains much playing with
words or with ideas. If contempt enters into our laughter at
all, it is contempt for our former belief that these connections
did not exist, that these two ideas must always remain poles
apart, or in a fixed relation that cannot be upset. Often enough,
too, we may feel some relief at having escaped from what now
seems a cramping view of reality.

All this implies a shattering of formulæ, an escape from too
rigid conventions, whether social, moral, or artistic. And, we
have asked, since rigid formulæ are anathema to Bergson, why
does he avoid this explanation? Why do we have instead the
spectacle of this apostle of flexibility endorsing the view that
different parts of experience should be kept in different compartments of our minds, each carefully ticketed with its appropriate emotion?

Two reasons suggest themselves. In the first place, although
the theory we have outlined can be made to fit Bergson's general
philosophy, it does rather dilute his central concept of rigidity.
It is only in a remote, metaphorical sense that rigidity becomes

the essence of the ludicrous. Consider, for instance, the drawing of two children talking together in the street. Their background sums up the modern world rather neatly. It comprises newspaper billboards shrieking headlines. about the current world war. One of the children is saying to the other: 'What are you going to be if you grow up?'

There is no very obvious rigidity here. The slight change in the conventional utterance does reflect perfectly the tremendous change in the contemporary world. Clearly, too, it is not the persistence of old habits of thought, the preoccupation with careers in the presence of imminent catastrophe, that amuses us here. There is, it is true, a suggestion of inappropriate emotion, of a calm acceptance of something so monstrous that it should be impossible to accept it calmly. And what gives the joke point is the reflection that all of us do exhibit just this acceptance, this taking for granted of the wildest insanity. And that, perhaps, is rigidity of thought, in a sense. But it is rather a strained sense. We could equally argue that we have here too much flexibility; the flexibility that enables human beings to adapt themselves to any tyranny, however senseless.

Now, although Bergson is occasionally driven to interpret rigidity in just this dubious, metaphorical sense, it is not surprising that he should prefer to seek it nearer at hand. Accordingly he tends to ignore these questions of value, and to concentrate on the machinery of the joke. That is why he relates his formula to details of technique, like repetition or inversion, and ignores attitude-mixing. Otherwise he would be open to the criticism that we have in fact made of his treatment of small mishaps, that his formula, while indeed applicable, is too broad to be quite adequate.

The second reason may go deeper. We have seen that this shattering of formulæ involves a reversal of values. Now when values are found inadequate, it is by appeal to another code of values. If we find war monstrous, it can only be because we have definite ideas about the value of human lives and the evil of human suffering. And this is precisely the point Feibleman makes when he urges against Bergson that, when forms are criticized, it is in the interest of better forms, not unmitigated flux.

All codes of values involve a certain rigidity, just because they are codes. To discard one code in favour of another, then, is not to escape from rigidity. When humour reverses values, it may well be that it exposes some ready-made generalization as inapplicable in a given case; but there will always be some other generalization lurking in the background. We have seen that humour is sometimes aimed at the eccentric who will not conform to a code, and sometimes at the code itself. In either case the appeal is to some code of values; either the standard which the code represents, or another which transcends it. Probably it is because Bergson realises this that he is prepared to convict the eccentric of rigidity, but not the code. For ultimately humour appeals to a code of values even when it escapes from one.

11

FEIBLEMAN AND McDOUGALL

ANOTHER, recent, variant of the moral theory is James Feibleman's. At first sight, his formula gives us the moral theory in its broadest possible form:—'the world as it is contrasted with the world as it ought to be.' This implies that all humour is satire, and at once raises all the problems we found confronting Hobbes.

Like Bergson, however, Feibleman develops his theory of humour from his metaphysic, though in his case the metaphysic is Platonic realism or something like it. There are, he tells us, two orders of existence: the possible and the actual. The possible is fixed and unchanging: it enters into actuality as the truths of logic and mathematics, and as something more diaphanous which Feibleman calls 'the intrinsic vividity of feeling'. The actual, on the other hand, is imperfect, ever-changing and incomplete. But it is seeking always to become perfect, fixed and complete. It is 'a fluxing, half-blind, dialectic approximation toward a perfect exemplification of the ideal conditions of the logical order'.

Any thing, then, or in Feibleman's terms, any 'organization', is a compromise between the perfect, ideal order and the imperfect, actual order. Obviously then we may regard it in two ways: we may admire it for its approximation to the ideal, or we may criticize it for falling short. Tragedy adopts the first viewpoint, comedy the second. Comedy ignores the value of an organization, and points to its limitations. It always denies and never affirms, always rejects and never accepts.

Psychologically, however, comedy is felt as an acceptance of the comic aspect of things, not as a rejection. And at this point Feibleman works in the compensation theory. 'Laughter is sometimes the reaction to insuperable obstacles in the way of a goal, by which we are reconciled to defeat. For there are many contradictions and disvalues inherent in the human situation which we can never hope to surmount.'

We may notice in passing that it is a little odd to regard tragedy as an acceptance of what value there is in an imperfect world. Most people would say that tragedy involves a vivid sense of the limitations of the actual. Why else should it be linked with sorrow, and comedy with joy? On Feibleman's premises, one would expect the reverse. His proviso about the psychology of comedy is perhaps an attempt to escape this difficulty. But even if a malicious pleasure in the defects of the world enables us to laugh off our despair at the hopelessness of finally achieving the ideal, he has still to explain why tragedy should bring us tears. And incidentally, what is the explanation of this malicious pleasure? Hobbes can explain it as vanity at our own superiority; but Feibleman, who does not seem to adopt this view, leaves it unexplained.

Let us, however, see how Feibleman applies his theory. Comedy, he tells us, has two main methods. It may proceed, first, by direct ridicule of the 'categories of actuality'. As an example, he cites Hemingway's story, *Torrents of Spring*, where the ultra-'literary' girl says to her man: 'Do come home, dear. There's a new Mercury with a wonderful editorial by Mencken on chiropractors.' This, says Feibleman, is direct criticism of the values of the contemporary literary generation.

Secondly, comedy may proceed by 'confusing the categories of actuality as an indication of their ultimate unimportance'. In Lawrence's preface to *The Seven Pillars of Wisdom* he explains why he has not adopted any consistent system of transliteration from the Arabic: 'I spell my names anyhow, to show what rot the systems are.' This is the explanation of all comic nonsense and absurdity; it is meant to show, by implication, what rot the systems are. Puns and word-play generally have the same basis. They imply: Why take words seriously?

Two favourite comic devices, exaggeration and understatement, are developments of this method. Understatement refuses to take current values seriously. Exaggeration ridicules current values by pushing them to 'their ultimate apogees'. Examples are the caricature, Charlie Chaplin's shoes, the cascade of knives which flow from Harpo Marx's pockets, the grammatical errors of Ring Lardner's characters.

In all this Feibleman has made an ingenious attempt to overcome the main stumbling-blocks of the moral theory: incongruity and absurdity. He can do this because his system of ethics, like Bergson's, is in a sense, an intellectual one. For him the good is the logical. The eternal verities, in which the ideal enters absolutely into the actual, are the propositions of logic and mathematics. Now humour, it has often been noted, must always be plausible. Absurdities and incongruities must always appear to have some connection with the world of fact. It can therefore be regarded as a criticism of the world of fact, an exposure of the irrational elements which always do lurk there. It represents the farthest possible departure from the stern logic of the universe which constitutes the ideal. Thus nonsense is satire, just as comic vice is satire. For the irrational is the immoral.

It all sounds reasonable enough when argued like this. The difficulty comes when we apply it. Consider Feibleman on Groucho Marx, for instance:

Told he cannot stay in a closet, Groucho says: 'If there weren't any closets there wouldn't be any hooks, and if there weren't any hooks there wouldn't be any fish, and that would suit me fine.' This, says Feibleman, is an attack on the form of the syllogism. It is an effort to set forth an illogical chain of deductive reasoning. It is also a criticism of the psychological order of reasoning. The order in which ideas occur to us is seldom the logical order. Groucho, by showing the psychological order as absurd, affirms the logical order indirectly.

In his anxiety to find satire everywhere, Feibleman is here betrayed into saying that this Marxian rigmarole is both a defence of the syllogism and an attack on it. But leaving this aside altogether, can we say that these considerations are present, even subconsciously, to the audiences who laugh delightedly at Groucho's antics?

This joke (such as it is) follows a familiar pattern. It consists in linking together two unconnected things (closets and fish) by means of an ambiguous word (hook). It is true enough that this involves the psychological mechanism of association of ideas. But it is hardly a criticism of that process. It is much more plausible to say that in the real world we do suffer, more or less consciously, from the need to concentrate on the precise connection between ideas, and that this type of fooling is welcomed as an escape from that necessity. Even this seems pedantic and far-fetched when applied to the happy trivialities of the Marx Brothers, but it does fit the mood of exuberance, of 'loosening up,' which those trivialities engender.

Feibleman himself adopts this explanation of absurdity when discussing Walt Disney. Disney, he says, shows us what ought to be and pretends that he is showing us what is. He creates a delightful dream world in which animals speak, trees come alive, and so on. It is the kind of story-book world which adults have always created for children.

Here we have nonsense, then, presented not as an exaggeration of the irrational tendencies which are the bane of the real world, but as a direct picture of the ideal world. Apart from the inconsistency with Feibleman's earlier account of nonsense, it is a little odd to be told that 'the ideal order of existence', the harmonious, rational heaven from which logic and mathematics emanate, 'the logic toward which all creation is aimed and toward which events grope' is a fairyland of talking horses and cricket-playing ducks. One feels that this is going altogether too far. Pleasant as it may be to escape momentarily into this world, would we really like to live in it permanently?

We have already noted that Feibleman does not adopt Hobbes' self-glory theory. He cannot therefore explain small misfortunes as due to our own sense of superiority. He has to explain them rather as due to the limitations of the fleeting world of actuality. When a clown falls down he is satirizing 'the dignity of man and the awkwardness of walking with the gingerly balance of the upright position'. We may accept this as applying fairly well to falling off ladders, slipping on banana-skins, and custard pie comedy generally. No doubt all these are part of 'the human predicament', the pitfalls which beset imperfect man in an imperfect world. Certainly Feibleman is on fairly safe ground when he cites Charlie Chaplin as an example of 'the little man pitting his tiny might against the emptiness and discouragement of the actual world'.

Feibleman has an interesting account of non-humorous laughter, though he would not admit that it is non-humorous. Man, he says, exists at the following levels (given in ascending order):—physical, chemical, physiological, psychological, sociological. Comedy may exist at each level as follows:—

> Physical: slipping on a banana-skin, hitting
>   one's thumb with a hammer.
> Chemical: laughing gas.
> Physiological: tickling.
> Psychological: hysteria.

All the more familiar, higher types of comedy are sociological.

This neat *schema* hardly bears analysis. The examples of 'physical' comedy seem rather to be physiological: they reveal the shortcomings of man as a physiological organism, not as a physical entity having mass, density, etc. More important is the fact that only these first examples seem to fit Feibleman's general theory. It is hard to see how tickling or laughing gas can be regarded as 'the indirect affirmation of the ideal logical order by means of the derogation of the limited orders of actuality', which is Feibleman's definition of comedy. Nor does he attempt to show how this is possible, though he refers to them all as 'perspectives of comedy'. Obviously his best line would be to say that these are instances of laughter occurring below the level at which comedy is perceived.

Feibleman has another schematic classification of the kinds of comedy which is rather more fruitful. Comedy, he says, ranges through: 'Joy, Divine Comedy, Humour, Irony, Satire, Sarcasm, Wit, Scorn.' This is in descending order. Reading upwards, each genre increases in the breadth of its field of criticism, but lessens in the intensity of criticism. Joy contains almost no criticism at all, and so marks the upper limit of comedy. Scorn is intense criticism, very limited in its objective.

Obviously, careful definition and close argument would be needed to defend all these categories. Feibleman hardly attempts this, though he gives one or two examples. But there is, I think, much of interest in the general thesis that the upper reaches of humour are marked by a broadening of application and a lessening of derision. In particular, Feibleman's 'divine comedy' seems to be much the same as our own 'god's-eye view'.

'Divine comedy,' he says, 'is directed against the "whole finite predicament".' It is a humorous, dispassionate, objective view of the whole human situation.

This is a precise and penetrating description of what is perhaps the essence of comedy. And Feibleman's theory does explain it much better than Hobbes'. We have already seen that the notion of superiority, of flattered vanity, hardly fits the tolerant, sympathetic yet keen-eyed, keen-witted, penetrating quality of the 'god's-eye view'. But the 'derogation of the limited orders of actuality' does fit it well enough. Men are fumbling children, likeable but limited: that is the key-note of humour in its higher reaches.

If we accept this broader view of satire, Feibleman's treatment of incongruity becomes much more convincing. The linking of two normally unrelated concepts, 'attitude-mixing', often became, we found, 'universe-changing'. That is to say, it often reveals the inadequacy of the water-tight compartments in which we normally try to confine different parts of reality. And what is this but 'the derogation of the limited orders of actuality'?

Let us take some of Lewis Carroll's nonsense verse.

> The music of Midsummer madness
>   Shall sting him with many a bite
> Till, in rapture of rollicking sadness,
>   He shall groan with a gloomy delight:
> He shall swathe him. like mists of the morning,
>   In platitudes luscious and limp,
> Such as deck, with a deathless adorning,
>   The Song of the Shrimp!

This can hardly be called satire; but it has more than a touch of parody. The author is exploiting familiar Swinburnian phrases and cadences, well-worn 'attitudes', and mingling with them ideas that do not belong there. Consider, for example, the air of mock profundity with which the metre weights the last line.

Even here, then, in this skilful inconsequence, there is a sense in which we have an attack on familiar sentiments, 'a derogation of the limited orders of actuality', a demonstration of 'what rot the systems are'.

It is true that the suggestion of parody is not always as obvious as this; but it is certainly there in refrains like

> Sing Flies, sing Frogs, sing Fiddle-strings!

and possibly even (though attenuated almost to vanishing-point) in verses like

> He thought he saw an Argument
>   That proved he was the Pope:
> He looked again, and found it was
>   A Bar of Mottled Soap.

Can we, then, restate Feibleman's thesis as follows? All humour is satire; but there are two types of satire. There is the familiar type, in which we take our stand on some familiar code of values, and point out how our object falls short. And there is another type, in which we ridicule these codes themselves by applying them to something which they simply do not fit. In this second type we are exposing the inadequacy of familiar concepts, 'spelling our words anyhow to show what rot the systems are'.

In this form, there is much to be said for the theory. Here we have at its strongest the case for regarding all humour as satire. But notice, first, that we have had to read something into Feibleman: though not, I think, more than he meant. And, secondly, the case is still not quite proven. There are still some elements in humour not accounted for. We have seen that incongruity does imply, often enough, a debunking of stock attitudes and familiar codes; but we have also seen that there seems to be some quite independent pleasure in the linking of disparate ideas for its own sake. And we have seen, too, that nonsense seems to be a momentary escape from disciplines which we embrace readily enough once the holiday is over. It is not, or at least not always, a permanent criticism of those disciplines and an indirect affirmation of better ones.

The best proof of these points is the feeling of inadequacy which seizes us when we read Feibleman's explanations of Disney or the Marx Brothers. Somehow we cannot help feeling that he has missed the point, the thing, whatever it is, that makes these fancies funny.

Something similar may be said of Feibleman's classification of humour. When scorn becomes satire, we may ask, is it merely that the intensity of derision lessens and its field of application widens? Isn't it rather that scorn gives us disapproval pure and unadulterated, while satire gives us disapproval mixed with humour? We still do not know what the vital element is that makes the difference. But it seems certain that it is not merely a different type of disapproval.

Feibleman, then, makes out a strong case. He shows us that much humour undoubtedly is satirical, and that an element of satire enters even into the incongruous and the nonsensical. But he leaves us with the conviction that this is not the whole truth about humour.

Before leaving superiority theories, it may be as well to say something about the theory of laughter put forward by Professor William McDougall.

McDougall's is not a superiority theory; but he can be dealt with here because he, too, regards the misfortunes of others as the main cause of laughter. He does not, however, think that the pleasure in laughter comes from a glow of superiority. Laughter is pleasant merely because the physical processes involved, the oxygenation of the blood and so forth, are pleasant. For this reason we enjoy laughter and seek occasions of laughter. But laughter is not the expression of pleasure.

The things we laugh at are not pleasant in themselves; on the contrary, they are invariably unpleasant. The misfortunes of others, in particular, are unpleasant because of our natural sympathy for our fellows. Sympathy means simply that we tend to share the emotion of others. Fear in one member of a herd will cause fear in the rest. This is obviously a serviceable mechanism which makes, on balance, for the survival of the group.

But, in a world like ours, too much sympathy can obviously be a nuisance. Survival does not demand that we should feel discomfort every time our companions bark their shins or prick their fingers. Laughter is a natural, instinctive mechanism by which we convert pain, in such cases, into pleasure. It is essentially a disruption of our mental processes, a check to the flow of thought. It breaks up the train of mental activity, preventing us from dwelling on the distressful situation which is the occasion of laughter. And, since laughter is a pleasurable physical sensation, the sympathetic pain is transmuted into pleasure.

McDougall's theory does allow for the disruptive nature of laughter, its peculiar character of jolting us out of a particular mental 'set' or train of thought. But in so far as he regards it as merely an antidote to sympathy he does not seem to account for any of the objects of laughter except the misfortunes of others. He does, however, include our own minor misfortunes. Laughter then becomes a means of seeing ourselves objectively, of refusing to dwell unnecessarily on our own pain. This is why we laugh at tickling, since tickling is merely one instance of a minor personal discomfort.

Laughter, then, is the antidote not merely to sympathetic pain, but to pain in general. We must suppose that, when brought face to face with a painful situation, the organism always has a choice of two reactions. It may indulge in grief, thereby intensifying the pain, or it may bring into play the curious series of physical movements we call laughter, thereby gaining a positive physical pleasure. Whether it chooses one course or the other will presumably depend on habits acquired in the course of experience, either the experience of the individual or of the race. Thus we would have to suppose, on McDougall's account, that for some reason human beings, and even some animals, have evolved an instinctive tendency to respond to tickling with laughter. Why the response has not become linked, in the same unconscious, mechanical manner, with other minor discomforts (except the discomforts of others) he does not tell us.

But presumably he would say that we learn to laugh at those misfortunes where it will not serve any useful purpose to indulge in grief. It's no use crying over spilt milk. Consequently we laugh at it; because laughter is a physical mechanism which breaks up the train of our distressful thoughts, and also enables us to gain some physical pleasure from the wreck. All of us can say, with Byron: 'If I laugh, 'tis that I may not weep.'

We cannot dismiss this theory out of hand on the ground that it implies that the only objects of laughter are small misfortunes. McDougall often writes as if these were the sole objects of laughter; but he does also make the more general statement that laughter is always at 'some maladjustment, something inappropriate, which would displease us if we did not laugh at it'. This seems to be his only concession to the facts about laughter on which the incongruity theories rely.

But are laughable objects always, in themselves, unpleasant? It is true that laughter often occurs when we are jolted out of some train of thought, some attitude of mind. But it is by no means certain that the train of thought is always in the direction of grief. Indeed, it is only plausible to assert that all laughable objects are unpleasant (and in particular that the inappropriate is unpleasant) if we suppose that an innate conservatism makes it unpleasant to be jolted out of *any* frame of mind. But on this view McDougall's account of the disruptive function of laughter is obviously confused. If the disruption serves to wrench our minds away from a distressful train of thought, then obviously the disruption of our thoughts cannot itself be the cause of our distress.

But is there any other sense in which the inappropriate is unpleasant?· Apart from this innate conservatism, why should we be distressed at finding some new element in experience, some fact which does not fit in with life as we had imagined it?

Of course we may be mistaken in supposing that the disruption which McDougall finds in laughter is the same as the breaking up of old habits of thought which occurs when we encounter a new fact or situation which does not fit in. We would then have to suppose that there are two separate disruptions. One is the dissolution of preconceived mental habits, and is intrinsically painful. The other is a turning away from this pain (resulting, in some obscure way, from the physical movements involved in laughter) and is intrinsically pleasurable.

But this view is no longer plausible. Can we say that the child who laughs excitedly at a new physical sensation, like sliding down a hill, is simply refusing to cry over spilt milk? That the sensation would be painful if he did not laugh at it? McDougall has to distinguish sharply between joyful laughter of this sort and other kinds of laughter. Here, he tells us, laughter is merely an incidental result of the access of energy that comes with keen pleasure. This energy spills over into all kinds of purposeless movements, like shouting, singing, jumping, running, waving one's hands. Such movements are properly called gambolling. Occasionally gambolling may include laughter, but this is not typical laughter, and does not throw any light on its true function.

This may account for laughter at sliding down a hill. But the child may also laugh at a new word, or an old word turned upside down, or a new face, or a new feature on an old face, like a false nose. Laughter here is plainly not a mere spilling over of surplus energy. Is it, then, refusing to cry over spilt milk?

It seems more reasonable to suppose that there is a direct pleasure to be gained from 'exploring new avenues,' rearranging our experience in new mental patterns. Of course, it would be possible for such mental explorations to be painful, if we adopt the timorous attitude of mind which shrinks from all that is unfamiliar and untried. In this sense we may say, with McDougall, that the incongruous does present us with a choice. We can either regard it as painful or as pleasant. In the latter case we laugh at it. But obviously the pleasure is not a mere turning away from the pain. It is not that the situation is intrinsically painful, only we choose (perversely) to make it pleasurable. On the contrary, the situation is intrinsically pleasurable. It contains the pleasure of freedom, the pleasure which comes from enlarging mental horizons. And the freedom is freedom from old habits of mind, not freedom from the pain caused by breaking old habits of mind.

Putting all this more briefly, we may say that McDougall's theory depends on his assertion that all laughable objects are intrinsically painful. This is obviously true of small misfortunes, but not of all the laughable objects on our list. Masquerades, word play, and importing into one situation what belongs to another, for example, all seem to be intrinsically pleasurable.

Secondly, even if we were to grant this point, it would still be a little odd to suppose that any painful object can cause laughter simply by an act of choice. It would seem more likely (since we do not laugh at all pain) that some painful objects have some further characteristic which makes them laughable.

12

INCONGRUITY THEORIES

I. Kant, Schopenhauer and Spencer

KANT is generally regarded as the father of incongruity theories: though his contribution, like Aristotle's, consists of a few passing comments. But he has given us a formula which has proved enlightening, though few find it entirely adequate. Laughter, he says, is 'an affection arising from the sudden transformation of a strained expectation into nothing'.

At first sight, this puts all the emphasis on surprise; and while this is undoubtedly one element in humour, it is not everything. A joke is more than a surprise. Furthermore, surprise is not always present in humour. We laugh at some familiar eccentricity ('just like old so-and-so') precisely because it is familiar. Many comedians have what might be called 'signature gags', which their public learn to expect from them. And in the practical joke, it is the victim who is surprised. The spectators know what is going to happen, and are waiting eagerly for it. Yet it is they who laugh.

Kant's formula, however, implies more than surprise. Notice the phrase: 'a strained expectation'. In physical terms, we may think of this as the 'motor set' which often precedes action. The runner crouching with muscles tense waiting for the start of a race is one example. We may regard 'an attitude of mind' as somehow parallel to this. In the one case the body is prepared for certain definite movements; in the other the mind is prepared for definite thoughts, or at least for thought objects of a definite kind. The parallel should not be pressed too far; but when we talk of entering a cathedral reverently, or approaching some great man with feelings of awe, something like this seems to be in our minds.

Laughter, then, is the abrupt dissolution of such an attitude of mind. We can see how readily this fits many of the types of humour we have analysed. The mind is as it were wound up ready to proceed in a definite direction: it is suddenly wrenched off its path and turned in a different direction. Something like this seems to be in Kant's mind; and we have already described this process under the term 'attitude-mixing'.

It was left to Schopenhauer, however, to develop this idea fully. True, he dismisses Kant's theory with the brief statement that it is insufficient to explain most examples of humour. But his own theory is generally regarded as an expansion of Kant's. Perhaps, however, it would be truer to say that Kant's theory becomes intelligible when it is interpreted in the light of Schopenhauer's. At any rate it is Schopenhauer who makes explicit the incongruity theory of humour.

The source of the ludicrous, says Schopenhauer, is always the paradoxical and therefore unexpected subsumption of an object under a concept which in other respects is different from it. It is possible, he adds, to trace everything ludicrous to a syllogism in the first figure with an undisputed major and an unexpected minor, which to a certain extent is only sophistically valid.

This sounds very fearsome, remote and technical. We may perhaps feel its force if we apply it to one of the examples we have already quoted. Consider the Shaw dialogue between the General and the Bishop about polygamy. In the form of a syllogism this becomes:

Major Premise: All British institutions are to be respected.
  ('Remember the British Empire, Boxer. Youre a British General, you know.')
Minor Premise: Polygamy is a British institution.
  ('The great majority of our fellow-subjects are polygamists').
Conclusion: Polygamy is to be respected.
  ('I cant as a British Bishop speak disrespectfully of polygamy').

Here the major premise is, for the General and for most of Shaw's audience, undisputed; the minor is certainly unexpected and just as certainly 'only sophistically valid'. It is true in a sense, but hardly in the sense in which we generally interpret the term.

We have here, then, a general concept: the respectability of British institutions. And under that concept we have managed to subsume an object, polygamy, which, to quote Schopenhauer's definition further, 'in another and more predominating aspect, does not belong to it at all, but is strikingly different from everything else that can be thought through that conception'.

Schopenhauer himself gives us a number of examples, though not, it must be confessed, with very good grace.

In the first volume I regarded it as superfluous to illustrate this by examples, for everyone can do this for himself by a little reflection upon cases of the ludicrous which he remembers. Yet, in order to come to the assistance of the mental inertness of those readers who prefer always to remain in a passive condition, I will accommodate myself to them.

These examples Schopenhauer divides into two main groups. The first are witticisms. Here, he says, we begin with the object, the percept, and pass from it to the concept. The second class is the absurd; and here we pass from the concept to the percept.

As an example of wit we have the story of the king who laughed at a peasant because he was wearing light summer clothing in the depth of winter. 'If Your Majesty had put on what I have you would find it very warm.' 'What is that?' 'My whole wardrobe!'

Under this last concept, says Schopenhauer, we have to think both the unlimited wardrobe of a king and the single coat of a poor peasant.

Again, there is the couplet on a tedious preacher:—

> Bav is the true shepherd of whom the Bible spake,
> Though his flock be all asleep, he alone remains awake.

Or the epitaph on a doctor:—

> Here lies he like a hero, and those he has slain around him.

The pun is merely a special case of this: the ambiguous word enables us to subsume an inappropriate percept under some general concept. Thus in Mercutio's 'Ask for me to-morrow, and you shall find me a grave man', we are able to subsume the percept of death under the very different concept of seriousness.

Parody, and the mock heroic, is another special case. It substitutes for the incidents and characters of a serious poem or drama insignificant low persons or trifling motives or actions. Thus commonplace realities are subsumed under the lofty concepts given in the theme.

Similar is the application of serious quotations to trivial events. Thus a young man, in love with a friend's wife, quoted Schiller's lines:

> Let me be, I pray you,
> In your bond the third.

Under the concept through which Schiller presents to the mind a moral and noble relation, he has subsumed a forbidden and immoral relation.

As an example of absurdity we have the invitation to the man who said he was fond of walking alone. 'So am I. Let us go together.'

Here we start from the concept: A pleasure which two love they can enjoy in common, and subsume under it the very case which excludes companionship.

Again, there are the soldiers who were set to guard a prisoner. To while away the time they played cards with him until they found him cheating, when they indignantly turned him out of the guardhouse.

Here we start from the concept: 'Cheats should be turned out', and subsume under it the one case in which ejection is no punishment.

At first sight, this is an odd distinction to make between wit and absurdity. In the last story, for instance, would it really matter if we began with the particular case and led up to the generalization? We could do this easily enough by putting the story in this form:

Two soldiers, who had been set to guard a prisoner, ejected him from the guard-house. Asked why, they explained that they had found him cheating at cards..

Probably, however, Schopenhauer was thinking of logical priority. In the first group of examples, the emphasis is on the percept (e.g. the tedious preacher). By comparing him to a watchful shepherd, we bring out his real defects. Consequently, the subsumption strikes us as a criticism of the percept. In the second group it is the concept which is convicted of inadequacy. This is most clearly seen in the examples Schopenhauer quotes from Baron Munchausen, where, as he puts it:

The fact is so conceived that it is plausible when thought merely in the abstract and therefore *a priori*. When we come down to perception of the particular thing, its impossibility, and indeed the absurdity of the assumption, is brought into prominence. Examples are the melodies, frozen in the post-house, which are thawed out in the warm room; or when Munchausen, sitting on a tree in a hard frost, drops his knife and then draws it up again by the frozen jet of his own water.

Even if we accept this explanation, however, it seems obvious that Schopenhauer has not put enough emphasis on the element of criticism. In the first group, the most obvious common quality of all the stories is that someone is being ridiculed. It is not merely 'a percept, in most respects different', that is being 'subsumed under the concept': It is an insult that is being 'subsumed' under a complimentary form of words. Even in the story of the king and the peasant, the peasant has succeeded in turning a reproach against the critic who utters it.

Schopenhauer should really say, then, that in the one case we ridicule a particular thing by exposing its inadequacy when confronted with some general concept, and in the other case we ridicule a general concept by showing its inadequacy when applied to a particular thing.

In fact, he seems prepared to admit only the second.

In every suddenly appearing conflict between what is perceived and what is thought, what is perceived is always unquestionably right; for it is not subject to error at all, requires no confirmation from without, but answers for itself. Its conflict with what is thought springs ultimately from the fact that the latter, with its abstract conceptions, cannot get down to ... the fine shades of difference of the concrete. This victory of knowledge of perception over thought gives us pleasure. For perception is the original kind of knowledge inseparable from animal nature, in which everything that gives direct satisfaction to the will presents itself. It is the medium of the present, of enjoyment and gaiety; and moreover, it is attended with no exertion. With thinking the opposite is the case; it is the second power of knowledge, the exercise of which always demands some, and often considerable, exertion ... It must therefore be diverting to us to see this strict, untiring, troublesome governess, the reason, for once convicted of insufficiency.

Later writers on humour seem to have taken more than one hint from this passage. The whole notion of thought blundering in its attempts to get down to 'the fine shades of difference of the concrete' is very close to Bergson. But, oddly, Bergson steers away from some of the implications where Schopenhauer grasps them boldly. Only occasionally will Bergson admit that reason is at fault: usually, when a recalcitrant individual refuses to be subsumed under some general concept, he sees this as evidence of inelasticity in the individual. But Schopenhauer traces all the pleasure of laughter to our desire to escape from reason; and thus anticipates another of his successors, Freud.

If we are to take this passage as final, we will have to revise our interpretation of Schopenhauer's first group of examples. It is not, after all, the preacher who is at fault for being only partially subsumed under the concept 'true shepherd'; it is the concept itself which is convicted of inadequacy.

Absurd as this conclusion seems, there is something to be said for it. We have described this witticism as an insult masquerading as a compliment. According to Hobbes, the insult alone should be enough to cause laughter. It is true that insults sometimes do: among children, 'You're a monkey' is regarded as a scintillating flash of wit. But why do adults deny wit to this childish comment, while they allow it to the couplet under discussion? Isn't it the whole point that a complimentary form of words has been twisted to convey an insult? In this case Schopenhauer may well be right. The insult no doubt reinforces the joke by appealing to our malice, but the distinctively witty thing about it is precisely this twisting, this discrepancy between the concept and what is subsumed under it.

We may still doubt whether there is any real sense in which reason has been convicted of inadequacy here. But it is at least plausible to maintain that the essence of the joke lies in the twisting of the meaning. The intellect finds a distinctive pleasure in this quite apart from any derision involved.

It still seems paradoxical to leave out the element of derision altogether. It is difficult to believe that the only essential difference between wit and absurdity is the slight difference in technique to which Schopenhauer calls attention. And of course there are other types of humour, in which derision occurs even more strongly, which Schopenhauer does not discuss at all.

How, for instance, are we to apply Schopenhauer's formula to misfortunes? Schopenhauer merely tells us that

conceptions whose observed incongruity with percepts make us laugh are either those of others or our own. In the first case we laugh at others; in the second we feel surprise, often agreeable, at least amusing. Therefore children and uneducated people laugh at the most trifling things, even misfortunes, if they were unexpected and therefore convicted their preconceived conception of error.

Schopenhauer here seems to be falling back on the notion that unexpectedness is itself enough to cause laughter. On this view a man slipping on a banana-skin is funny because it runs counter to 'a general expectation' that men walking along a city street will remain upright. Misfortune thus becomes merely a special case of novelty. To say that we laugh 'even at misfortunes, if unexpected', is to overlook the fact that misfortunes often seem a main cause of laughter, whether unexpected, or, as in practical jokes, carefully prepared. Further, we have here the odd suggestion that we are laughing, not *at* the man who slips on the banana-skin, but at our own generalization about the uprightness of citizens, which has been convicted of inadequacy.

And this raises another difficulty. In an attempt to explain the sting of laughter, Schopenhauer suggests that the laughter of others at what we say or do offends us because 'it asserts that there is great incongruity between our conceptions and objective realities'. But when a man slips on a banana-skin, it is apparently not his concept that is at fault, but our own. Why then should we be pleased when we discover our own inadequacy, but annoyed when others discover it for us? Perhaps Schopenhauer would say that this is natural enough: even Hobbes allows us to laugh at our own past errors. But we would at least expect that the man who slipped on the banana-skin would laugh even more heartily; for after all it is he who has exposed the inadequacy of our reason for us. Yet somehow it never seems to occur to him that the joke is on us.

How does Schopenhauer's theory fit our other classes of humour? We have found difficulty in applying it to misfortunes. What of comic vice? Schopenhauer himself gives us no help here: he does not deal with comedy of character at all. But we found resemblances between his theory and Bergson's; and Bergson makes comedy of character one of his strongest points. Can we adapt his notion of comic stereotypes to Schopenhauer's formula?

When the miser, for example, obtrudes his passion for money into a situation where it is out of place, can we say that he is subsuming some percept under a concept which does not really include it? Scot or Jew stories may sometimes give instances of this. The Scot who escorted his fiancée into the theatre with 'The Woman Always Pays' in neon lights over the entrance was perhaps making an intellectual error of this kind. But this is not a simple instance: for we have here a kind of pun. Are we to say, then, that the Scot's meanness is merely incidental to the story: that its function is merely to make it plausible that he should misinterpret the play's title? Formally, this may be so, but most people would insist that the real point of the story lies in its exposure of Scottish meanness, just as they would insist that the real point of the story of the king and the peasant is that the peasant has scored off the king.

Let us take a less equivocal instance of meanness: Shylock's exclamation when he finds that Lorenzo has absconded with Jessica and a fortune: 'My daughter! O my ducats! O my daughter!' Here we have a reversal of values precisely equivalent to Harry Graham's quatrain about Aunt Maud. There we had the assertion that the loss of a stamp was more to be deplored than the loss of an aunt. Here we have a suggestion that the loss of a daughter and the loss of a substantial sum of money are equally to be deplored. Shylock's attitude is not, of course, as wildly farcical as Graham's, but it has its comic side.

No doubt it is possible to treat Shylock's ejaculation as equivalent to a dubious syllogism. All instances of loss are to be deplored. Jessica's departure and the theft of his ducats are equally instances of loss. Therefore they are equally to be deplored. Notice that we have here had to smuggle in the word 'equally': that is, the judgment of relative values which Schopenhauer hardly allows for. But nevertheless it can be claimed that Shylock's error is precisely that he has subsumed the loss of a daughter and the loss of a fortune under the same general concept; that he treats a spiritual loss as on all fours with a material one.

But suppose we have an actual reversal of values? In the musical comedy *Of Thee I Sing*, the question is propounded: 'Which is more important? Corn muffins or justice?' And the answer (given in unison by the nine Judges of the Supreme Court of the United States) is: 'Corn muffins!' Now here, as in Shylock's exclamation, we have two dissimilar things brought together. The mere fact that they are compared might perhaps be advanced as proof that they have been brought under a single concept, though I do not quite see what the concept is. But the answer amuses us simply because it is a blank reversal of common sense: there does not seem to be any way in which Schopenhauer's formula applies at all.

All these examples can be treated much more easily as

instances of frustrated expectation—Harry Graham's quatrain particularly, because here we have been tricked into believing that he was grieving for his aunt, when it turned out to be only for his stamp. And with the others we can say that there is a 'general expectation' that a man will regard his daughter as more important than his ducats, or justice as more important than corn muffins. Now the element of surprise certainly does enter into our amusement in every case. But does it explain it wholly? Are all these merely instances of novelty?

The objection both to 'frustrated expectation' and to Schopenhauer's fuller formula is that they stress the formal side of a joke to the exclusion of its content, or what any normal person would regard as its content. We suggested that the formula 'frustrated expectation' only takes on meaning if we consider it as the dissolution of an emotional attitude. But Schopenhauer hardly seems to admit that the emotions are involved at all. For him humour is purely a matter of finding connections where none exist. Formally, this is often so, as we saw in our own analysis. But what gives life to the joke is the presence of conflicting attitudes to the things thus united. Thus the passage from Shaw would hardly be funny if we did not presuppose a more than rational fervour for British institutions and a more than rational abhorrence of polygamy. It is not merely a matter of finding ingenious connections between one thing and another 'which in a more predominating aspect does not belong to it at all'. The real background of the joke is the whole complex of ideas and beliefs of a typical British General of the year 1908. Without this, we might get a mild pleasure from the ingenuity of the argument, but I doubt if we would get much more. But perhaps Schopenhauer would deny the relevance of this, just as he overlooks the element of malice in his examples of wit. For him, all humour is of the type of Whately's *Historic Doubts*. The essence of it lies in the ingenuity of the argument, underlined by the absurdity of the conclusion. If any derision creeps in, it is at the exposure of the inadequacy of this type of reasoning. All this applies perfectly to Whately, but not to all humour. Or at any rate it does not *fully* explain all humour.

Consider indecency, for example. It is true enough that most smutty stories consist of smuggling in a reference to sex or excrement under cover of something respectable. Here is frustrated expectation, if you like. We thought the subject was something innocuous, and it turned out to be sex. Or, as Schopenhauer would put it, the percept (sex) was subsumed under the innocuous concept. Most smutty stories can be analysed in this way. But you can hardly explain them without taking into account the whole complex of ideas, beliefs, inhibitions and fears which surround the subject of sex.

We can test this last assertion, because Max Eastman does try to do exactly this. He tells the story of the housewife and the iceman. The iceman is passing down the street, and the housewife calls out to him from an upstairs window:

'Have you the time?'

'Yes,' he replies, 'if you can get someone to hold the horses.'

Eastman explains this as purely 'frustrated expectation'. The essence of the jest is in the 'tricking of the mind', the fact that we thought the query was about the time of day, when it turned out to mean something rather different. Eastman admits that

It seems hardly possible in the excitement of the thought finally arrived at, that the failure to arrive at so pale a prospect as the time of day could be what makes it funny. You must remember, however, that you were giving your attention to the story... Your total conscious being... consisted of that enterprise of organisation. Its collapse was a collapse of your pattern of experience. Such a thing is not trivial no matter what the content of the pattern.

The difficulty here, of course, is that the 'collapse of the pattern' without the intrusion of sex, or of something else equally exciting, would not be funny, or at any rate not nearly so funny. Eastman's point seems to be that the sexual reference reinforces the joke, but is extraneous to its real essence. He does not hold this view quite consistently, as we shall see. But for the present it should be enough to say that any explanation of indecent jokes which leaves out the indecency can hardly be adequate.

At the same time, it may be retorted that the indecency by itself would not be funny without the tricking of the mind, 'the collapse of the pattern'. This point has often been overlooked, and the great merit of Kant and Schopenhauer is that they call attention to it. I do not believe that this is more than one element in humour; but I do believe that it is the most important single element.

Let us recapitulate for a moment, in order to bring this out.

(a) First of all, much humour does consist in tracing connections where none seem to exist. (This is, of course, not quite the way Kant and Schopenhauer describe it; but I believe it is the essential part of what they both, in their different terminology, have in mind.) And this tracing of connections does give a peculiar intellectual pleasure, just in itself. This explains puns and all word-play, and much nonsense and absurdity.

(b) As well as this intellectual pleasure, emotional attitudes are often involved. This occurs whenever the two ideas thus connected are normally kept in different compartments of our minds, and regarded as evoking utterly different responses. Connecting them thus compels us to revise our whole scale of values. But often we do this merely for the fun of it, for the pleasure of exploring new mental paths. We have here, then, only an extension of (a); but without this new element of 'attitude-mixing' humour generally strikes us as 'pointless' and rather irritating. That is why a pun, *per se*, is 'the weakest form of wit'. A good pun needs at least this added element, and so does satisfying nonsense. Indecency is a good example: it is precisely because the transition from asking the time to making an indecent proposal does involve a violent collision of emotional attitudes that Eastman's story strikes us as funny, and his explanation, which is solely in terms of (a), seems inadequate.

(c) But often this reversal of values is not wholly in fun. Our mental exploration may uncover a real connection between our mental compartments. Most satire depends on this. Parody is one obvious instance: the mock-heroic, when used light-heartedly without any implication of parody, comes under (b). Indecency, when it involves a real criticism of current morals, belongs here. It is important to notice that the satire may be of two kinds. It may be directed at the more exalted of the two ideas, which is degraded by being connected with the other one. Or it may be a debunking of the whole system of values which keeps the two ideas rigidly apart.

All this may be regarded as an extension of Kant and Schopenhauer. Its inclusiveness should demonstrate the great value of their contribution to our subject. But we must notice two things. First, we have had to recognize the existence of other elements besides the one they specify; and these other elements (codes of values, satirical intent, emotional attitudes) are precisely those stressed by the opposing school of Hobbists. Secondly, there are still some types of humour which are unaccounted for.

Small misfortunes, in particular, do not fit in here except in so far as they are instances of novelty.

Herbert Spencer's theory may be regarded as an attempt to supply at least one of these deficiencies. His formula is 'descending incongruity', and the adjective 'descending' implies a judgment of value. Not that Spencer himself makes any very definite criticism of preceding incongruity theories: he is largely prepared to accept Kant's formula, but he sets out to answer a question which had been generally overlooked. Why, he asks, should the perception of incongruity lead to the peculiar bodily actions we call laughter?

His answer is that laughter is an overflow of nervous energy. All nervous excitement will expend itself in one of three ways. It may produce muscular action: when you burn your finger, you will jump about, or screw up your face. Or the discharge may go into the viscera rather than the muscles: in which case the pulse beats more rapidly, the digestion is affected, and various other subtle changes may occur. Finally, the nervous excitement may be passed on to some other part of the nervous system. The energy, that is to say, may be used up, not in physical action, but in thought. 'Sensations excite ideas and emotions; these in their turn arouse other ideas and emotions; and so, continuously.'

These three channels are not mutually exclusive. Nervous energy, once roused, will generally discharge itself in all three directions at once. But there is only a limited quantity of energy to be divided among them. Where there is a strong discharge along one channel, the others will be only mildly affected. That is why weeping and wailing assuages grief. By using up our energy on physical action, we leave less available for melancholy thought.

Laughter is a display of muscular excitement, but it differs from most such displays in that its actions are purposeless. In fear we make incipient movements of flight, and in anger incipient movements of aggression; but the only object of the movements of laughter is to use up surplus energy. Hence the nervous energy simply flows into the most accustomed routes. Now the human animal most often expresses emotion through the organs of speech. Hence the muscles round the mouth are the first to be affected by laughter. Next come the organs of respiration; and, after that, if there is still energy to be used up, we may clap our hands or slap our knees, or throw back our heads.

What does this physiological explanation tell us about the psychology of laughter? Spencer makes his interpretation clear by an example:

You are sitting in a theatre, absorbed in the progress of an interesting drama. Some climax has been reached which has aroused your sympathies—say, a reconciliation between the hero and heroine, after a long and painful misunderstanding. The feelings excited by this scene are not of a kind from which you seek relief; but are, on the contrary, a grateful relief from the painful feelings with which you have witnessed the previous estrangement. Moreover, the sentiments these fictitious personages have for the moment inspired you with, are not such as would lead you to rejoice in any indignity offered to them; but rather such as would make you resent the indignity. And now, while you are contemplating the reconciliation with a pleasurable sympathy, there appears from behind the scenes a tame kid, which, having stared round at the audience, walks up to the lovers and sniffs at them. You cannot help joining in the roar which greets this contretemps. Inexplicable as is this irresistible burst on the hypothesis of a pleasure in escaping from mental restraint; or on the hypothesis of a pleasure from relative increase of self-importance, when witnessing the humiliation of others; it is readily explicable if we consider what in such a case, must become of the feeling that existed at the moment the incongruity arose. A large mass of emotion had been produced, or, to speak in physiological language, a large portion of the nervous system was in a state of tension. There was also great expectation with respect to the further evolution of the scene—a quantity of vague, nascent thought and emotion into which the existing quantity of thought and emotion was about to pass.

Had there been no interruption, the body of new ideas and feelings next excited would have sufficed to absorb the whole amount of the liberated nervous energy. But now this large amount of nervous energy, instead of being allowed to expend itself in producing an equivalent amount of the new thoughts and emotions which were nascent, is suddenly checked in its flow. The channels along which the discharge was about to take place are closed. The new channel opened—that afforded by the appearance and proceedings of the kid—is a small one; the ideas and feelings suggested are not numerous or massive enough to carry off the nervous energy to be expended. The excess must therefore discharge itself in some other direction; and in the way already explained, there results an efflux through the motor nerves to various classes of the muscles, producing the half-convulsive actions we term laughter.

From this analysis, Spencer infers that there are two conditions necessary for laughter. First, the nervous energy must not
flow into either of the two alternative channels: that is to say,
the laughter must not be inhibited by other emotions or by other
trains of thought. Secondly, the incongruity must be a descending one: that is to say, our attention must be suddenly transferred from great things to small.

Now we have seen that incongruity usually does involve the
dissolution of an emotional attitude; and we have seen, too, that
this is generally brought about by the linking of something respected with something disreputable. But it is doubtful whether
Spencer's explanation quite fits the facts. In the story of the iceman and the housewife, the incongruity is surely, on Spencer's
argument, an ascending one. We expend very little emotional
energy on the time of day, and a good deal on the substitute
that is offered in its place. It is true that the one is respectable,
if colourless, and the other decidedly disreputable; but this only
suggests that Spencer is wrong in reducing this distinction to
quantitative terms. Incongruity usually involves a transition
from something high in the scale of values, like the British
Empire, to something low in the scale, like polygamy; but it by
no means follows that the second generates less emotional
energy than the first. On the contrary, the most successful jokes
are those which suddenly plunge us into some subject highly
charged with emotional tension. That is why topical jokes are
popular: an oblique reference to a current scandal is always
good for a laugh.

The plunge, it may be objected, is still a plunge: still involves
a descent. But it is a moral descent, not a diminution of energy.
Spencer would seem to be misled by the double meaning of the
terms 'great' and 'small'; to have confused the qualitative sense
of the words with the quantitative. Even in his own example,
it is doubtful if the unimportance of the kid really contributes
much to our laughter. The point is rather that its appearance
abruptly shatters the illusion: brings us back from the world of
dramatic make-believe to the reality. Spencer, of course, makes
a point of this too; and, in so far as he stresses the shattering of
a state of nervous tension, we need not quarrel with him.

From this point of view, indeed, it is possible to defend the
greater part of his theory. Spencer is wrong when he suggests
that a joke never directs our attention into new and livelier

channels of interest; but he is right when he says that it involves the abrupt dissolution of an emotional attitude. And this can be said, reasonably enough, to liberate nervous energy. As a physiological explanation, however, this is probably too vague to be of much use: it has never been very clear what precisely nervous energy is. At the same time, Spencer's is almost the only physical explanation of laughter that has been advanced; and most later writers have been glad enough to adopt it, even when they disagree with his account of the psychology of laughter. And, although Spencer's general physiology is probably out of date, modern science does not appear to have much to say about the physical causes of laughter.

13

INCONGRUITY THEORIES

II. EASTMAN

MAX EASTMAN'S second book on humour, *Enjoyment of Laughter*, concludes with quotations from various other writers. One of them, Merrel D. Clubb, remarks on the great need for an eclectic theory of humour:

> The work of men like Aristotle, Hobbes, Schopenhauer, Richter, Darwin, Spencer, Lipps, Sully, Bergson, Freud, Dumas, Eastman and Fabre is all too useful to be waved aside. The only way to overcome the defects which are present in the writings of all of them is to attempt that which none of them have tried to do, namely, to build a harmony out of the surprisingly large number of true statements which have been made regarding the nature of humour.

Eastman seems a little annoyed at this:

> I feel honoured to see my name mentioned in such a row of dignitaries, but I must protest that my theory is not the proposal of a new word or ingenious phrase, but an attempt to make that higher generalization for which Mr. Clubb so rightly yearns.

In spite of this disclaimer, I think we may safely treat Eastman's as a development of the incongruity theories. It is true that he does go to some pains to make his theory a composite: there are at least three separate strands in it. But of these 'frustrated expectation' is certainly the most important. And, while he regards disagreeable things as the main subject-matter for laughter, Eastman denies that this implies derision.

What are the three strands? Eastman himself summarizes them very neatly in an ingenious illustration. All humour, he tells us, is epitomized in the technique of amusing a baby. First, he says, you must laugh or smile at him. That is to say, you must induce a playful mood. Nothing is funny unless it is taken 'in fun'. This is a fundamental fact about all humour—and, to the extent that he stresses this, Eastman's is a play theory.

Given this playful attitude, which is a first essential, we may proceed to amuse our baby by one of two methods. We may:

(a) make a face, or (b) offer him something he will want a little, and then reach out and jerk it smilingly away.

These two methods correspond, Eastman tells us, to the two main theories of humour. In (a) we have Aristotle: 'What is ugly but not painful'; and in (b) we have Kant: 'expectation dissolved into nothing'. These, he adds, are not incompatible: they merely define two types of unpleasantness, that which offends our sensibilities, and that which frustrates our impulses.

We laugh, then, at unpleasant things taken playfully. One proof of this is that all stock jokes are about unpleasant things—mothers-in-law, bills, drunks, taxes, tramps, excretion, vermin, bad taste, etc., etc. But all this unpleasantness falls into one or other of these two classes: the funny sight and the frustrated expectation, or, as Eastman also calls them, the ludicrous and the witty, or poetic and practical humour.

What is funny in both types is simply their unpleasantness, that is, the fact that, in some sense or other, they disappoint us. We may find it easier to laugh at other people's disappointments than at our own; but this does not mean that we are laughing at them out of superiority. There need be no derision in laughter: babies, for example, are incapable of feeling derision, and yet they laugh. When derision does creep in, it is an extraneous addition.

Only babies, apparently, can take their humour neat. Pulling a face will strike most adults as mere foolishness. Some jokes are still of this elemental, childish type, as when Groucho Marx says: 'I would horsewhip you if I had a horse.' But when he says: 'When I first came to this country I hadn't a nickel in my pocket; now I have', there is a difference. Formally, the humour depends on the same technique as the first joke. Its essence is 'the snatching away of meaning', the 'tricking of the mind'. But the first joke snatches away the meaning and gives us nothing in its place; the second does present us with something: a hint that America is not quite the glorious country of the success stories after all. This gives the joke 'point'. But, Eastman emphasizes, point is not essential to humour: it is merely an extraneous concession to adult lack of playfulness.

As a further example, Eastman quotes the story of the house-wife and the iceman, given in the last chapter. Again, there is the story of the slave held up to auction, for whom no-one would bid. He began to solicit a buyer himself, shouting his own qualifications: 'I can mop, wash dishes, take care of the children —if there are no children, I can take care of that.' Here, says Eastman,

a trick has been played upon us. We have been led on and fooled. We have been playfully deprived of what we were on the point of grasping. But also, and in the very place of it, we have been presented with a gift—with two gifts in fact, the opportunity to rejoice in a man bold enough when on the auction block to make the most insolent suggestion imaginable, and the opportunity to think about an illicit and exciting pleasure.

But, he adds, the humour lies in being fooled, not in the illicit suggestion or the insolence. We can prove this by telling the story in different words: 'A slave when on the auction block boasted jestingly that he could be used for purposes of propagation.' This is interesting, but not funny.

We have here, then, the startling claim that the best jokes have no point. Eastman embraces this paradox boldly, pointing to the 'shaggy dog' story as proof. This, he says, is pure humour, and actually funnier than a joke with a point.

We have already seen that this conclusion does seem to follow from Kant and Schopenhauer, and we have seen the arguments against it. Here it only seems necessary to add that Eastman himself is not able to sustain this point of view. When he comes to discuss puns, he has to admit that pointless puns are necessarily weak. He explains this by saying:

The punster does not lead us to expect one word, and then laughingly slip across another. He cannot do that, because it is not our habit to expect words. We expect meanings. Words are only containers of meaning. When one of these containers kicks back, therefore, or springs a leak, we do not experience a sudden coming to nothing of our expectations. We have to pull up first, to remind ourselves that these pulpy variables do exist, and only after that can we perceive that one of them has played us false.

This is hardly convincing. Of course we expect words. A whole series of jokes depend on just this.

> Mary ate cake and Mary ate jelly
> Mary went home with a pain in her head.

And there is a song which uses the same device:—

Up spake an aged pauper,
His face was bold as brass:
'You can take your Christmas pudden,
And throw it on the wall.'

In both these we know precisely what words we have been expecting. The author has done exactly what Eastman says is
impossible: he has led us to expect one word, and then laughingly slipped across another. It is true that the punster does
not do precisely this: but that is because we expect both words
and meaning. The pun gives us the word without the meaning,
which should be a very neat and plausible way of frustrating
our expectations. If it is not funny, or only mildly funny, it is
because Eastman is wrong in saying that pointless jokes are the
best.

As his treatise proceeds, and the examples multiply, Eastman
seems to accept this view himself. Again and again we find him
identifying wit with point. Compare, for example, his two
definitions of 'wit', one early and one late in *The Enjoyment of
Laughter*. On page 70 he says:—

A word or series of words which seems and pretends to be
heading toward a certain meaning, and which 'leads us on' in
the direction of that meaning, fails abruptly and with playful
intent to get us there at all . . . . In mature and pointed wit,
besides failing to arrive where we seemed to be going, we do
arrive somewhere else . . . But that . . . is incidental. Wit in its
comic essence, in so far as it is distinguished from presenting
ludicrous images to the imagination, consists in springing
practical jokes upon the mind of the person who is expected to
laugh.

But on page 315 he says:—

An atom of humour is an unpleasantness or a frustration
taken playfully. A witty joke is made by combining this unpleasantness or frustration with some idea or attitude of feeling
in which one can find momentary satisfaction.

Here wit has been definitely identified with point.

Again, when he comes to give us ten 'rules for good jokes,'
Eastman's rule nine reads:—

Give good measure of serious satisfaction . . . Jokes with no
point at all can be funny in an absurd way, but only if their
plausibility is deftly managed, their subject matter colourful, and
if surrounded with a good magnetic field of humour . . . A joke

... appeals to two interests ... one of which is disappointed, the other satisfied.

This is an important modification of Eastman's earlier position, that the 'satisfied interest' has nothing to do with the funniness of the joke, and may even detract from it. It appears that as he analysed example after example he found it difficult to avoid the common-sense view that the point is what makes the joke funny.

My second main criticism of Eastman centres on his distinction between 'poetic' and 'practical' humour. Practical humour is the 'snatching away of meaning'; poetic humour, or the ludicrous, is analogous to the funny face which amuses a baby. It is essentially a funny picture.

Now it is obvious that to talk about 'a funny picture' is to dodge the whole question. What makes it funny? Eastman never gives us any very satisfactory answer. To justify the term 'poetic humour' he compares Shelley's 'Ozymandias' with a speech of Mark Twain's on the futility of fame, in which he imagines the future historian's comments on President Grant: 'A popular poet of ancient times in the Aztec provinces of British North Africa,' and so on.

Both Twain and Shelley, Eastman tells us, 'make a general idea vivid by presenting a concrete instance'. He goes on to say that any joke which vividly rouses the imagination is poetic humour. ' "A man bit a dog" is so startling that you have to try at least to see *where* he bit him. That is the way words paint pictures in the mind.' And, as a further example, we have Wodehouse's 'He had the general demeanour of a saintly but timid codfish'.

The ludicrous, then, is humour which, by presenting a concrete instance, rouses a vivid visual image. But that is not all. 'Word-painting' and 'mental pictures', Eastman hastens to assure us, are inadequate terms. Poetry appeals to every sense; so must poetic humour. 'Not only sounds, smells, tastes and tactual sensations, but ideas, characters, emotions, even actions, can form the material of poetic humour.'

It is difficult to avoid the suspicion that Eastman is using 'poetic humour' as a convenient blanket term to cover all humour which does not fit his analysis of practical humour, or frustrated expectation. He uses the distinction to answer a problem put to him by W. C. Fields:

Fields plays the part of a . . . cocky person who has invented a burglar trap, a trick chair which releases a ball which hits the burglar on the head as soon as he sits down. The moment he goes towards the chair the audience knows he is going to sit on it himself. They laugh before it happens. The laugh is louder before it happens.

This seems to refute the whole frustrated expectation theory. Eastman explains that this is a funny percept, poetic, not practical.

A man who has invented a burglar trap and then goes and sits on it is funny. Merely to mention him is funny. He does not have to do the sitting down . . . The humour is perceptual rather than practical . . . If the laugh was at its peak before the blow fell, this proves I am correct—this was the humour of a ludicrous situation . . . not . . . a practical joke.

But why is it ludicrous? It is not a funny *sight* until the inventor sits on the chair. It is a funny idea, certainly, the biter bit idea, but why regard this as essentially a funny picture?

Incidentally, this is presumably Eastman's answer to Sully's point, urged against Kant, that a practical joke causes laughter in the person who knows what is going to happen, but not in the victim. If so we have the paradox that a practical joke, in the everyday sense, is not a practical joke in Eastman's sense, but is, on the contrary, a funny picture. Or, putting it another way, it is always the victim who laughs at the practical joke: for example, the baby when you snatch a plaything away from it. The laugh of the perpetrator is poetic humour.

This is perhaps not a very serious objection to Eastman, though it does suggest that his whole use of the term 'practical humour' is a little unfortunate, and that his statement that 'wit is a practical joke played on the mind' is due to hasty analysis. More serious is his continued vagueness about the precise meaning of poetic humour, which is not dissipated by his examples.

He tells us, for instance, that when Harpo Marx leaps into a wheeled garbage can, and rides away to war as in a chariot, we have a comic sight, whereas when Joe Cook goes to a telephone and takes down the receiver, and the whole instrument comes away in his hands, we have a frustrated expectation. The first is 'wrong as a perception—it is a violation of the pattern in which we contemplate the world'. Contemplate is an important word here, for Eastman insists that poetic humour is essentially contemplative, whereas wit is 'action of the mind'. That is, presumably, it is a frustrated 'motor set'.

But if a funny sight is a 'violation of pattern', how is it different from frustrated expectation? Poetic humour now becomes simply the odd, the uncustomary. If we do not expect a telephone to come away in the user's hands, neither do we expect a garbage can to be used as a war chariot. No doubt there is a difference between disappointing the particular, 'built up' expectation of a definite action, and a general expectation about how things normally behave. But if Eastman's distinction between the two types of humour merely reduces to the familiar argument about disappointing general expectations, it can hardly bear the weight he puts upon it.

Yet other incidental observations of Eastman's seem to support this interpretation. He makes much of the point that in practical humour the laugh occurs at a particular point of time, whereas in poetic humour it does not. This would be fully explained by the difference between a general expectation and a particular one. Again, he quotes with approval a saying of Charles Chaplin's that 'slapstick is a break in the monotony of normal conduct'.

And, in justification of his statement that poetic humour comprises not only funny pictures, but 'sounds, smells, tactile sensations, ideas, characters, emotions and actions', he quotes from Thurber and White: 'If any of you think you are going to find this use of the word confusing, I wish you would drop out. Get something else to read, or better yet, get some exercise.'

'What is ludicrous here,' Eastman explains, 'is an emotion. For an author to become irate to the point of driving a reader out of his book on the grounds offered is funny.'

It is hard to see any connection at all between this and the notion of funny pictures with which Eastman begins, unless it is that this behaviour, too, violates the general pattern of expected behaviour.

Poetic humour is extended in other directions, too, to include any unusual or startling comic trope. For instance, 'he gave her a look you could have poured on a waffle', from Ring Lardner, or: 'There isn't a parallel of latitude but thinks it would have been the equator if it had had its rights', from Mark Twain. The first of these might conceivably suggest a vivid image: it is hard to see how the second could. Both can be explained easily enough as a mild form of 'universe-changing': the bringing together of concepts usually kept well apart. Eastman does not help us to understand them by labelling them 'funny pictures', or poetic humour, and he does extend this concept until it becomes meaningless.

If we are right in regarding poetic humour as a rather vague portmanteau term which enables Eastman to dispose of those classes of humour which do not fit the frustrated expectation theory, we will not be surprised that he includes slap-stick under it. For he resolutely opposes all derision theories, and slapstick, which usually depends on small misfortunes, is obviously one of his biggest hurdles. He hardly surmounts it by dismissing a man slipping on a banana-skin as a funny sight.

Eastman's attempts to explain away all derisive laughter, though not entirely adequate, are interesting and often instructive. We have already quoted his comments on the child shebear story. It is true enough that the mere switching of ideas, in jokes of this sort, explains our laughter, and that we need not suppose that we are laughing at the stupidity of the child who made the mistake. It is probably his desire to maintain this position that makes Eastman insist that all humour depends entirely on the formal element in the joke, and that the point is irrelevant. He does not deny that the point—the 'serious satisfaction' introduced as a concession to adult lack of playfulness—may depend on malice. Consequently his reluctant admissions, already quoted, that point does play its part in humour after all, also weakens his denial of the derision theories.

Eastman's main position, however, is quite clear. He does not, of course, deny that satire is often involved in humour. But serious denunciation, he says, is hard work, a bore. Humour enables us to absorb it painlessly: it is the sugar round the pill. And this is only possible because they are two different things.

Where satire cannot be explained as an incidental 'serious satisfaction' grafted on to a 'tricking of the mind,' which is humour, Eastman turns to the play theory. He adopts the view that play is mimic combat, useful in training the young animal for the serious contests of later life. Laughter is a signal to the opponent not to take the attack seriously, like a puppy's tail-wagging when he is pretending to be fierce.

Repartee, then, is a manly sport conducted with words as

weapons. The pleasure is in the contest, not in the vanquishing of an opponent. We must distinguish between the pleasure of ascendancy—getting the better of another in a contest—and aggressiveness—delight in the misfortune of others.

It will be noticed that even here Eastman leaves a loop-hole for Hobbes. 'Ascendancy' suits the superiority theory just as well as 'aggressiveness', if not better.

One of Eastman's main tenets is that all humour deals with unpleasant things. This is necessary to link together poetic and practical humour. These, says Eastman, are merely two types of unpleasantness—that which offends our sensibililities and that which frustrates our impulses.

The link is never very strong. In the first place, why should we assume that a frustrated expectation is necessarily unpleasant? We may overlook the point that frustrated expectations, when they take the form of humour, are actually felt as pleasant. Eastman would no doubt say that this is begging the question. His point is that they would be unpleasant if they were not taken playfully, were not made into jokes. But is this true? It is possible, after all, to be pleasantly disappointed. It all depends on what we were expecting. Perhaps Eastman would argue that this, too, is irrelevant, and that frustrated expectation considered in the abstract, without regard to the content of the expectation, is unpleasant. But even this attenuated assumption is still doubtful. For if we often find comfort in the security of well-worn paths, we rebel, just as often, against monotony and routine. It would be just as plausible to argue that frustrated expectation, considered in the abstract, is pleasant *per se*, because, in Sully's words, it has a 'stimulating freshness' which 'rouses the feeling tone of the observer to joyous excitement'.

Secondly, we may also doubt whether a funny sight is unpleasant. Eastman's point seems to be that there is always some ugliness in the funny sight: it offends our æsthetic sense: it is 'ugly but not painful'. But he does not press this very far. And he does extend the notion of a funny sight until it includes any comic metaphor. He would have difficulty in showing that these still retain an element of ugliness.

Thirdly, even if we overlook these objections, and admit that both poetic and practical humour is 'unpleasant', it is obvious that at least they are very different kinds of unpleasantness. It is hard to see much connection between them; and one suspects once again that Eastman has been using a portmanteau term to give his theory a neatness and completeness which it really lacks.

His attempts to prove the unpleasantness of humour by examples are no more convincing. Bad grammar, for example, is funny, according to Eastman, simply because we have been taught it is wrong. This does not mean that we delight in it as a form of rebellion against our teachers. Still less does it mean that we delight in our own superiority over those who commit these solecisms. All it means is that bad grammar is unpleasant to us, and hence funny.

As an example, he gives us ambiguity. 'Mrs. S. was the last in the dirigible. Slowly, with her large nose pointed skyward, she headed for the distant horizon.' But it seems difficult to believe that we find this funny simply because we have been taught in school that ambiguity is wrong. We may take malicious pleasure in the imagined discomfiture of Mrs. S. The sentence may conjure up a vivid image, a 'funny picture' (whatever that may mean) in which a stout woman sails indomitably skywards. We may find pleasure in the accident that the same form of words is applicable both to Mrs. S. and to the dirigible. But the one thing we do not laugh at, surely, is the droll notion that a pronoun always relates to the nearest antecedent noun.

Again, Eastman remarks that Latinity ('hirsute adornment', 'succulent bivalve', and so on) is not very funny because it is not very wrong. But is Latinity felt as bad style by writers who use it for humorous effect? This type of humour is old-fashioned nowadays, and yet it is only fairly recently that the sin of Latinity has been insisted on in schools.

Finally, Eastman tells us that 'there is no sin of rhetoric more instinctively disliked than anti-climax, and none more naturally amusing'. But in actual fact children are taught about anti-climax by funny examples. They find them funny before they know they are wrong. This is also true of ambiguity.

As with bad grammar, so with bad versification. Ogden Nash, Eastman argues, exploits for humorous effect all the faults of the bad poet—strained rhymes, lengthy lines, artificial inversions, and so on. But this of course is a libel on Mr. Nash, who writes with great skill and resourcefulness. If he suddenly gives us a line three times the length of its predecessors, he somehow manages, against all the rules, to maintain the rhythm.

It is difficult to analyse the appeal of verse like this, but it is obviously inadequate to set it down simply as bad versification. And, even if this were true of Ogden Nash (and it is not) he would still be an exception to the general rule. For successful humorous verse in general demands meticulous accuracy in versification, just as any good joke demands perfect phrasing.

Our chief criticism of Eastman, then, centres round these three points:—

(1) He emphasizes the formal side of humour to the extent of making the point irrelevant, and even asserts that pointless jokes are the best. This is on the face of it a paradoxical position, and one that he cannot himself maintain.

(2) To provide for those types of humour which do not fit the 'frustrated expectation' formula, he uses the vague concept of 'poetic humour', which is never accurately analysed.

(3) He links these two parts of his theory together by the blanket term 'unpleasantness', which is only doubtfully applicable to either type of humour taken separately, and still more doubtfully applicable to both of them taken together.

We should not, however, allow these defects to blind us to Eastman's many merits. He does give us an excellent statement of the 'frustrated expectation' theory, and he does show us how far it is possible to carry that theory without relying on either derision or release from restraint. He does not pretend that the theory is all-inclusive; but he thinks he can allow for any other elements in humour by relying on Aristotle's formula and excluding Hobbes' altogether. And even here he seems to hanker after a completely Kantian theory: for, as we have seen, 'poetic humour', in so far as he does analyse it, seems to reduce to a frustrated 'general expectation'. But the fact that Eastman does not insist upon this may be taken as a tacit admission that this notion is inadequate to explain all the types of humour that are not cases of frustrated particular expectations.

We have insisted on Eastman's failure to sustain the view that the best jokes are pointless. It might be argued, however, that it would be fairer to disregard this and consider only his somewhat unwilling modification of this extreme position. Suppose him to grant, that is to say, that the point of a joke is not an extraneous addition, but is an essential part of its humour. His theory now amounts to this:—

Every joke, with the exception of (a) sheer nonsense, shaggy

dog stories and the like, and (b) poetic humour, has two elements: a formal element, which consists in 'a tricking of the
mind', a snatching away of meaning just within our grasp, and a
'point'. The point satisfies some interest of ours, and may consist in a malicious reference to people or institutions we dislike,
or in the release of some inhibition, (e.g., the mention of a forbidden topic, such as sex). Thus stated the theory becomes
surprisingly like Freud's, with whom Eastman is at some pains
to disagree. We should add, for Eastman stresses the point, that
malice and sex are by no means the only interests that a joke
may satisfy. The frank admission of cowardice, for instance,
will cause laughter as much as the frank admission of sexual
desire: for the current pretence that a man is infinitely brave
is as much a strain on human nature as the other pretence that
he is sexless. Indeed, Eastman suggests that almost all truth is
humorous, so complete are our pretences.

This extension of Freud need not, however, affect the theory.
The question is, how far can we regard this restatement of Eastman as an adequate theory of humour?

We have seen that there are some types of humour which
seem to rely entirely on aggressiveness or release from restraint.
Slapstick, that is to say small misfortunes, and comic vice are
examples. It is true that there is always an element of unexpectedness in these jokes, and that to that extent they frustrate
at least a general expectation. The mere fact that a particular
subject is taboo will mean that we do not expect it to be mentioned. This in itself is hardly enough to justify the view that
unexpectedness must always be present as well as the release
of an inhibition. More telling is the fact that insult or indecency
must usually be veiled before we admit it to be funny. But we
have still the practical joke, where everyone is well prepared
in advance for the discomfiture of the victim.

If we further modify Eastman to allow for this, we will find
that we have not one theory but a summary of most of the
existing theories. For we have these assertions:

(a) A joke may consist in frustrated expectation pure and
simple.
(b) It may consist in gratifying our desire for ascendancy
over others.
(c) It may consist in gratifying an impulse usually repressed
(e.g., sex or aggressiveness).
(d) It may consist in (a) combined with either (b) or (c).

There is one point of general importance that should be discussed before we leave incongruity theories, and that may conveniently be considered with reference to Eastman. Hitherto we have been more concerned with the resemblances between Kant and Schopenhauer than with their differences. But Eastman ignores Schopenhauer and relies entirely on Kant. How far, then, is 'frustrated expectation' an adequate description of the incongruity theory?

Let us consider one of Eastman's examples. He quotes B. L. Taylor's rhyme about the dinosaur who had two brains

> One in his head, the usual place
> The other at his spinal base
> And thus could reason a priori
> As well as a posteriori.

Now in what sense is this 'frustrated expectation'? It is true, of course, that we were not expecting an explanation of this zoological phenomenon in terms of a logical formula. But then we were not expecting anything in particular. Eastman would say, no doubt, that we think we are being presented with an explanation only to find that it does not really explain at all. We have been fooled. Meaning is snatched away from us just as we were about to grasp it.

But this does not seem to me to be psychologically true. It is always difficult to analyse mental processes of this type, but it seems hardly likely that anyone would be taken in, even momentarily, by the pretended explanation. It is far more likely that one would be struck first by the apparent *non sequitur*, and only secondly realize that the terms are after all verbally applicable. But this would not prevent the verse from being funny. One would still admire the ingenuity with which the two unrelated ideas are linked: one would still enjoy 'the subsumption of an object under a concept which in other respects is different from it'.

Eastman gives other examples, of course, where Kant's formula applies better. Among them there is a passage from Thurber and White discussing the disadvantages of a married couple separating.

If the car goes wrong (it having been chivalrously given to the wife) it is necessary to ring up the husband to fix it, causing great inconvenience to both. This could never happen if the husband and wife were living together, because then they would never be on cordial enough terms for him to let her use the car.

Here we really have been fooled. An argument in favour of marriage turns out to be directed against it. But even this can be regarded as the subsumption of an object (marital quarrels) under a concept (the advantages of cohabitation) which in other respects is different from it.

The advantage of Kant's formula is that it does explain why a purely intellectual process such as Schopenhauer describes should give rise to laughter, which is certainly an emotional disturbance. For frustrated expectation is, as Eastman points out, the dissolution of an emotional attitude.• It is in some sense a 'collapse of our pattern of experience'. It is worth noticing however that this dissolution is usually brought about, as Schopenhauer saw, by the linking of two disparate ideas. Eastman himself hints at this in his distinction between 'one-track' and 'two-track' jokes. A two-track joke pretends to be about one topic and turns out to be about another. A one-track joke sticks to one topic but fools you about what it is going to say about it. One-track jokes tend to choose topics about which we have conflicting emotions, like matrimony. They then appear to exploit one feeling and land you in the other.

The point for us is that both types bring together ideas which are normally kept in different compartments of the mind. Incidentally, this analysis of the one-track joke suggests the theory of ambivalence, which we will have to consider later.

14

RELEASE FROM RESTRAINT

I. KLINE

IN DISCUSSING non-humorous laughter we found that the laugh often expresses relief from restraint. We may laugh when a serious accident has been narrowly averted, like the school-children who saw their teacher just missed by a hammer falling from the roof. We certainly seize every opportunity to laugh when we are under a conscious strain in church or school-room or law-court. We laugh involuntarily on the public plat-form, which may be Nature's way of providing us with relief, willy-nilly. And if we laugh at play, it is when we have thrown off decorum and are romping like schoolboys.

It is not surprising, then, that relief should be seized on as the possible archetype of all laughter. The laugh, suggests Dewey, writing on 'The Theory of Emotion' in the *Philosophical Review* for November 1894, may be of the same general charac-ter as the sigh of relief: it marks the sudden end of a period of suspense, or expectation. Something of this is no doubt present in Kant's theory; and certainly in Herbert Spencer's. But both of these made incongruity, rather than relief, the primary factor. So did Schopenhauer, even though he remarked in passing that it is 'diverting to see this strict, untiring troublesome gover-ness, the reason, for once convicted of inadequacy'.

A more thorough-going relief theory is formulated by A. Penjon in an article in the *Revue Philosophique* for August 1893, suggesting that any release from restraint, any breakdown of the monotonous regularity of the outside world, may make us laugh. And this theory is developed by L. W. Kline.

All thought, says Kline, involves a certain mental tension. In controlled and rational thought this takes the form of attention, which serves two distinct functions. On the one hand, the mind takes on a certain imperviousness, a 'hide', as it were, which pro-tects it from irrelevant stimuli. Kline calls this the 'surface tension'. On the other hand, the act of attending also serves to direct the mind along certain definite channels. When the thinking process continues organized and controlled in this manner, and progresses towards an end, it is termed rational.

But sometimes the mental tension exceeds the capacity for controlled thinking. We then have a wave of emotion. 'The mental stream has had its banks torn away and its forward movement stopped, voluntary movements are replaced by hereditary. In the more intense form a reversion to primitive conditions may occur; for we then do and say things that may shame us in our sober moments.'

Emotions may be of two kinds. If they are brought on by 'the sudden triumph of wrong and evil values', the emotion is unpleasant, ranging from mild disappointment to the tragic. If, on the contrary, the disruption is caused by a sudden triumph of good values, a pleasant emotion results.

Kline continues:

the humorous process occurs in just such a disrupted consciousness at the triumph of good and pleasurable values preceded by a mental tension similar to, but not always equal to, that preceding emotions . . . . The function of the humorous stimuli consists in taking the hide off consciousness, as it were, and in breaking up, in part only, its organization, which is at once followed by the humorous feeling, the next wave in the stream of consciousness.

Humour, then, always involves a sudden disruption of the orderly processes in thought, resulting from the triumph of good and pleasurable values. But in this it does not differ from any other pleasurable emotion, such as admiration or joy. Humour is the triumph of a particular set of values, causing pleasurable feelings of a particular sort, and only occurs when the stimuli are of a certain kind.

What are these humorous stimuli? They are 'departures, exaggerations, even violations of the laws, uniformities, concepts and what not that have evolved out of man's experience'. More specifically, they are useless actions, as when Newton put his watch in a kettle, and timed it with an egg; unusual and eccentric clothes; distortions of words, including mis-spelling, mis-pronunciation, repetition, foreign accents, dialect, localisms, etc.; the quaint and unusual in language, including slang, catch-words, verbosity, the mock-heroic and so on; illiterate, ignorant, inexperienced, credulous, sceptical, superstitious, over-serious, vain or prosaic thoughts; animals or men of one class doing tasks common to another class, as when an ox pulls a buggy; unusual physical features, odd shapes, Falstaffian proportions. All these are departures from the norm, violations of our preconceived ideas of the way things should be. They will, therefore, be humorous stimuli so long as they do not disturb the recognized values of good and evil. The mind must maintain a disinterested attitude towards them—the æsthetic rather than the practical attitude. 'If we seek the practical, humour ceases, issuing in bitterness or joy, sarcasm or flattery, indignation or admiration. Humour, then, is an end in itself and has no practical interest in its object.' This, says Kline, is the first differentia of humour, distinguishing it from other emotions.

But if the humorous stimuli do not 'disturb the recognised values of good and evil,' what becomes of the triumph of good values, which we understood to be essential to humour? The answer, apparently, is that the good values are of a special type. They consist in the sense of freedom, which, Kline says, is the second differentia of humour. For humour is essentially a rending of the veil of uniformity.

It appears as the only objective fact in our experience that dares to defy the world order with impunity, that can violate ruthlessly, without pain and without apology, the manifold human contrivances, social customs and relationships, and thereby not only creates the sense of freedom but also assures us that we may temporarily escape from the uniformities and mechanism of life.

Humour, then, performs an important psychological and biological function in our mental evolution. In its more trivial aspects, it is useful in cutting the surface tension of consciousness, in affording relief from the strain of attention necessary in learning to master our environment. 'It spells the mind on an uphill pull.' But the larger function of humour is to detach us from the world of good and evil and make us see it in its proper perspective. It is true that some mechanization of mind is necessary in learning to cope with our environment. We could not live without habit. But it is also important that pliancy, initiative, and awareness should be retained. Humour, like play, 'prevents the mental life of the race from hardening into instinctive and hereditary forces'.

We have here an attractive, clear, and comprehensive theory. Notice in the first place how skilfully Kline has managed to incorporate the main features of many rival theories. The unexpectedness of humour, its element of shock; incongruity, and

especially that form of it which we have called inappropriateness; the æsthetic attitude; the kinship with play; and finally
the Bergsonian insistence on elasticity of mind—all are fitted
into place.   Obviously he has taken account of a good many of
the facts.   But does he explain all of them?

There is one obvious omission.   Kline has no time at all for
superiority.   He declares quite definitely that superiority is not
part of humour, and that the sense of power, while it may yield
pleasure, cannot yield humour.   This view leads him to slur
over those 'humorous stimuli' on which Hobbes and his followers
lay most stress.   Small misfortunes are considered only in so
far as they represent departures from uniformity.   Fatness, for
example, is just an odd shape.   Illiteracy, ignorance, inexperience
and the rest are funny only because they lead to actions out of
time and place.   The man ahead of his time, like the inventor,
is just as likely to cause laughter as the boor or the half-wit.

There is obviously some truth in this contention.   But ultimately it means that all comic misfortunes are reduced to mere
novelty and oddity, and all comic vice to eccentricity.   This is
to ignore the whole phenomenon of derisive laughter.

In one place, indeed, Kline seems to deny that vice is ever
funny.   He gives us a list of 'non-humorous stimuli': events
which never inspire humour.   These are, first, the macroscopic
things of the world—the immensity of space, the infinitude of
time, the heavenly bodies, etc.—together with their laws, order,
harmony and rhythm; secondly, those things inimical to life and
freedom, which inspire aversion and loathing, never humour—
parasites, creeping, crawling, slimy things, skin diseases, tyranny,
bullying, poltroonery, treachery, ingratitude, and 'the entire
catalogue of vanities given to Solomon'; thirdly, those things,
largely of the social order, which have become habitual, regular
in occurrence, and necessary to human comfort—all natural
forms of locomotion and movements, all common and customary
occupations, all actions and events of familiar notice.

The second of these three classes is obviously questionable.
Kline seems to have forgotten that fleas are a common music-
hall joke; and the whole list has an odd resemblance to Eastman's catalogue of unpleasant things which, in his view, are
especially and intrinsically funny.   This is a striking proof of
how little, in the field of humour, can be regarded as agreed
and undisputed fact.   But, since Kline includes vices here, it

would seem that his later list of comic 'thoughts'—credulity, scepticism, superstition, and so on—are to be regarded as eccentricities rather than immoralities.

Oddly, Kline does not seem to have seized on the explanation of comic vice which fits his theory best. This is that we laugh at cowardice, selfishness and the like because they gratify our own desire to escape from the tyranny of moral standards. Perhaps something of this is implicit in his later statements. He certainly stresses, much more than Bergson, the utility of humour in preventing the inevitable acceptance of over rigid codes of behaviour.

But this brings him up against the opposing difficulty. The 'biological function' of humour is often to preserve codes of this kind, rather than to destroy them. For Bergson, as we have seen, inelasticity seems often the eccentricity of the man who refuses to conform to conventions. Kline, when he speaks of the inventor ahead of his time, seems to recognize this.

But his theory hardly accounts for it. For why should we get a sense of freedom when we see someone transgressing our conventional code unless it is that, either consciously or unconsciously, we question the code? Why should laughter at the nonconformist lead us, as it unquestionably does, to remain smugly confident of the need to conform? Kline mentions that we laugh at the customs of foreigners, and they at ours. But his theory would lead us to believe that this results in a mutual questioning, each of his own customs. For why else should the sight of foreign customs make us feel free?

Sully seems much nearer the truth when he says that the function of such laughter is to protect the mores of our group from the intrusion of alien manners. For the fact is that laughter often is derisive. Bergson recognizes this: and it leads him to ignore the many occasions when humour does question the validity of the codes themselves. But Kline has made the opposite mistake, and ignored the conventional side of humour altogether.

But perhaps we are giving this conception of freedom a twist that Kline does not always mean it to have. After all, he has defined it as an escape from the monotony, the uniformity, of life. A glimpse of foreign customs might well give us that, whether we approve of them or not. We can laugh at an eccentric departure from the code without necessarily rejecting the code; and it would still be true that this exercise would help to keep our minds fresh and pliant, would make them more ready to make that rejection if ever the need arose.

This defence is valid as far as it goes; but it still leaves out of account the positive, conservative role that humour often plays. It is perhaps difficult to reconcile this with humour's other function of destroying codes that have become rigid or obsolete. It can probably best be done by remembering that the code is itself condemned only by reference to some wider standard of values. But if we insist on this we can hardly make freedom the main differentia of humour.

Kline's treatment of incongruity is interesting. It comes fairly close to our own concept of inappropriateness. Whatever is out of time or place, or twisted out of its normal shape, or divorced from its proper function is, according to him, food for laughter. He does not seem, however, to lay much stress on incongruity as such, or to explain why it should bulk so large in humour. He reduces it, once again, to mere novelty and oddity. It is true, of course, that incongruity has this side. But there does seem to be some special delight in tracing unusual connections that goes beyond this. But this need not delay us long because Kline's theory does explain incongruity fairly well. Relief from uniformity and monotony probably is the essence of the process.

Oddly enough, Kline makes no mention of the two types of humour that his theory best: indecency and nonsense. Indecency pretty obviously is a release from a tyrannous moral code: and nonsense is probably best explained as a revolt from 'that strict, untiring, troublesome governess, the reason'.

15

RELEASE FROM RESTRAINT

II. Freud

THE DEVELOPMENT of psycho-analysis was almost bound to give a new impetus to relief theories of humour. Dewey's notion of laughter as 'a sigh of relief' can be carried much further once we think of man's mental life as a continual struggle against oppressive inhibitions. 'Relief from what?' is the obvious question any relief theory has to answer. And whatever restraint we decide on must be something common to all men and to all phases of life, and yet not so vague as to rob the theory of most of its meaning. 'Inhibition' seems the perfect answer.

Yet Freud's own theory of humour does not give this answer quite as simply and definitely as that. In the first place, he is careful to tell us that he is not investigating the whole field of humour, but only part of it: wit. And even then his theory, when it emerges from a closely argued and somewhat tortuous discussion of the technique of wit, is overlaid with reservations, distinctions, and the usual Freudian crop of specially invented technical terms.

Impatient disciples have been tempted to remove these ornaments and present the theory in the charm of naked simplicity. One of these, Mr. Edwin B. Holt, summarizes it as follows: Humour, he says, is simply 'letting the cat out of the bag'. What is the cat? A suppressed wish. What is the bag? The psychic 'censor'. And that is all there is to it.

Now it is obvious that we can apply this formula to our classification of humour with some success. Indecency is one very large and obvious cat; malice (which includes all that the Hobbists find in humour) is another; vice is a third; nonsense (if we remember Schopenhauer's remark about Stepmother Reason) is a fourth. But it is obvious, too, that we are going to run into some difficulties. No doubt it was because Freud foresaw the difficulties that his theory is considerably more complex than Holt's paraphrase of it.

He does not unequivocally explain all humour, or even all wit, as springing from inhibitions. On the contrary, he distinguishes between 'harmless wit' and 'tendency wit'. Harmless wit is indulged in for its own sake: tendency wit grants us, in addition, the opportunity to gratify our repressed hostility to others or our repressed sexual desires. The existence of harmless wit proves that the technique of wit alone can cause pleasure; tendency wit taps a further source of pleasure as well.

What, then, is the explanation of harmless wit? Freud's detailed examination of technique provides him with the answer. Altogether, he enumerates twenty-three main types of wit, but some of these are grouped together, so that we need not consider them all in detail. To begin with, we have a distinction between word-wit and thought-wit. This cuts across his other distinction, between harmless and tendency wit. A play upon words (upon a person's name, for instance) may have insulting implications: it would then be both word-wit and tendency-wit.

Word-wit can be divided into three main groups, or witty devices, each of which is capable of a number of variations. The first device is condensation. Freud's key example of this is a remark of one of Heine's characters, Hirsch-Hyacinth, who boasts that Rothschild treated him 'quite famillionaire'. Here the condensation consists in telescoping two ideas into a single word. Similar examples of this 'mixed word formation' are 'alcoholidays' and 'anecdotage'.

But this type of condensation can also be achieved by a slight modification of a familiar phrase. Examples: 'I was driving with him *tête à bête*; 'He has a great future behind him'; 'Like Cincinnatus he returned to his place before the plough'. Here a very slight change in the wording has enabled us to smuggle in a considerable change in the sense.

The second device Freud calls 'manifold application of the same material'. Here a particular combination of words or syllables is repeated with some variation which entirely alters the sense. Thus the name Rousseau becomes *roux sot*—a red-headed fool. Or there may be a change of order, as in: 'Put not your trust in money, but put your money in trust.' Or a slight modification of the material itself, as in 'traduttore—traditore' (translator—traitor).

The third device is double meaning. This may depend on the existence of homonyms in the language, on the use of the same word in a metaphorical or a literal sense, and so on. Freud's chief example is the description of Napoleon III's confiscation of estates shortly after succeeding to the throne: 'C'est le premier vol de l'aigle', where 'vol' may mean either 'flight' or 'theft'. Another example: 'This girl reminds me of Dreyfus. The army does not believe in her innocence.'

These three types of wit, Freud concludes, are closely related. 'Application of the same material is only a special case of condensation, and play upon words is nothing but condensation without substitutive formation.' Even where condensation, in the strict sense, is not present, there is at least economy. Economy, then, appears to be the common feature of all word-wit. But, at the same time, Freud notes that all laconisms are not witty, and that the economy, regarded merely as a saving of effort, is not very impressive. It would be easier to express the thought in the longer, but more obvious way.

Now what of thought-wit? This takes many forms, and is not nearly so easy to summarize. But one important group, which is capable of many variations, is indirect expression or allusion. The meaning may be expressed through associations, as in the story of the two American business men who had their portraits hung side by side, and asked an art critic for an opinion on them. 'Where,' asked the critic, 'is the Saviour?'

Or it may be conveyed through omission, as in the epigram: 'A wife is like an umbrella; at worst one can also take a cab.'

Or the thought may be conveyed through its direct opposite: 'This woman resembles Venus de Milo. She is very old, has no teeth, and has white spots on the yellow surface of her body.' A favourite form of this is an apparent defence which really adds still greater reproach. 'It is not true that she dyes her hair black. It was black when she bought it.' Many of the catty remarks in *The School for Scandal* are of this type.

Freud lists other types of thought-wit. Three of these are important, and had better be discussed here. They are: *displacement, unification* and *nonsense.*

An example of displacement occurs in this dialogue between a horse-dealer and his customer. 'If you mount this horse at 4 a.m. you will be in Monticello by 6.30.' 'But what should I do at Monticello at 6.30 in the morning?' Here the point of a remark has been twisted so that an unimportant element has been given all the emphasis.

Unification is the establishing of an unexpected identity between ideas, in their relations to one another, or a common third. An example is the story of the emperor, travelling through his domains, who came across a peasant with a remarkable resemblance to himself. 'Was your mother ever employed at the palace?' 'No, sire, but my father was.'

Or again: 'The inhabitants of Gottingen are divided into Professors, students, Philistines and cattle.'

Freud treats nonsense rather timidly: he seems anxious to show that it is really good sense. This is surprising when one realizes that nonsense is one of the best arguments for a relief theory, and that Freud himself does suggest later on that irrational thought is itself a release from inhibition. But here he merely notes that jokes depending on nonsense often have as their point the revealing of nonsense on someone else's part. Example: 'Never to be born would be best for mortal man. But hardly one man in a thousand has this luck.' Here, says Freud, the comment exposes the nonsense of a sham aphorism. He goes on to say that this is not true of all nonsense; but none of his examples are really nonsensical in the sense that the drawing of the man on skis passing through a tree is nonsensical. Freud even rationalizes the 'shaggy dog' story. Although he does regard them as 'liberating the pleasure in nonsense', he goes on to say: 'These witticisms are not altogether without tendency. They furnish the narrator a certain pleasure in that they deceive and annoy the hearer. The latter then calms his anger by resolving to take the place of the narrator.'

Now we can return to our original question: What is the explanation of harmless wit? In one type, says Freud, the technique consists in directing the psychic focus on the sound instead of the sense of the word, and in allowing the acoustic word-disguise to take the place of the meaning. We are justified in assuming that great relief is thereby accorded to the psychic work: in the serious use of words we refrain from this convenient procedure only at the expense of a certain amount of exertion. Such word-sound associations are common among certain mental patients and in children. In wit we reach, through the sound effects of words, connections between sets of ideas normally remote. The greater the distance the greater the pleasure. This is due to psychic economy: moreover, we make use of a short cut rejected in serious thinking. A joke is good if a real connection is found between the two ideas connected by this short-cut, as in *traduttore—traditore;* poor if there is no real connection.

Now what precisely does this mean? Is 'psychic economy'

merely a short cut, a form of brevity or condensation which for some reason gives us pleasure simply because it is a short cut? Or is it the point that this sort of word-association is rejected in serious thinking'? Have we, that is to say, formed an inhibition against word-play, and does our delight in it spring from this? Freud continually hints at this view, but he never quite commits himself to it.

So far, however, he has been talking about only one kind of harmless wit. He goes on to discuss others.

A second group of technical means of wit—unification, similar sounding words, manifold application, modification of familiar idioms, allusions to quotations—all evince one common character, namely, that one always discovers something familiar where one expects to find something new instead. To discover the familiar is pleasurable and it is not difficult to recognize such pleasure as economy-pleasure and to refer it to the economy of psychic expenditure.

Reinforcing this conclusion is what Freud calls the factor of actuality. This is the familiar fact that a local or topical allusion will always help a joke. The joke about the girl who was like Dreyfus is not as funny now, Freud points out, as it was when the Dreyfus affair was a topic of absorbing interest.

Just why is the rediscovery of the familiar a form of psychic economy? Presumably because we find it easier to deal with familiar ideas than with new ones. Freud adds that rhyme, alliteration, refrain and the like also owe their appeal to this factor. But the whole argument seems unsatisfactory. Most of the forms of humour he cites could just as easily be described as the discovery of something new where we expected the familiar. The modification of familiar idioms is a case in point. It is not because we recognize the dear old hack phrase in spite of its transformation that we laugh, but because the hack phrase has taken on a startlingly new application.

We may, it is true, get a thrill of recognition at hearing a quotation neatly applied. But it will not be comic pleasure. We will not laugh unless the quotation has been misapplied: unless, that is to say, it has taken on a new and startling meaning. It is true, as Freud points out, that many jokes do combine the new and the familiar. But to explain them as the rediscovery of the familiar is to approach them from the wrong end. The point is not that we sink back into the dear old familiar rut, thereby achieving psychic economy. The point is rather that we have been suddenly jolted out of the rut.

The third type of harmless wit is false logic, absurdity, displacement, representation through the opposite, and the like. This again is due to economy of psychic expenditure.

It is quite obvious that it is easier and more convenient to turn away from a definite trend of thought than to stick to it; it is easier to mix up different things than to distinguish them; and it is particularly easier to travel over modes of reasoning unsanctioned by logic; finally in connecting words or thoughts it is especially easy to overlook the fact that such connections should result in sense.

Freud then proceeds to elaborate his tentative suggestion about an early inhibition against these modes of thinking. Children enjoy playing with words and thoughts, but they are gradually compelled, by parents and teachers, to develop 'along the lines of right thinking', and to 'separate reality from fiction'. The child tends to resist; and the resistance is far-reaching and persistent. It results in a general and universal pleasure in nonsense. This manifests itself most strikingly in the 'rags' and rowdyism of the undergraduate.

What, then, is 'psychic economy' precisely? The line of least resistance, or release from inhibition? Freud does not make the problem any easier by pointing out that thwarting an inhibition is itself, in a sense, following the line of least resistance. Or, as he puts it, psychic expenditure is required for the retention of an inhibition. The pleasure in its removal, therefore, 'corresponds to the economy of psychic expenditure'.

It is clear, however, that when Freud talks of psychic economy he does not always mean the removal of inhibitions. This becomes apparent in the distinction he makes between play, jest, and wit.

Play appears in children while they are learning how to use words and connect thoughts . . . . During this process he experiences pleasurable effects which originate from the repetition of similarities, the rediscovery of the familiar, sound-associations, etc., which may be explained as an unexpected economy of psychic expenditure . . . . Playing with words and thoughts, motivated by certain pleasures in economy, would thus be the first step of wit.

The child, however, is not allowed to continue this harmless game. He is checked by 'the growing strength of a factor which may be called criticism or reason'. Reason says in effect: 'Don't be silly!' and the desire to appease this stern critic results in the second stage of wit, the jest. There is but one way to accomplish this appeasement: the senseless combination of words or the absurd linking of thoughts must make sense after all. But the jest is still only half-way to wit.

The jest is content when its utterance does not appear utterly senseless or insipid. But if this utterance is substantial and valuable, the jest changes into wit. A thought, which would have been worthy of our interest even when expressed in the most unpretentious form, is now invested in a form which must in itself excite our sense of satisfaction.

The childish play-pleasure can thus be made to embellish thought; for a witty thought appears more profound than it really is. And finally, in tendency wit, the same play-pleasure is used as a means of breaking down inhibitions.

The point to notice here is that Freud uses 'psychic economy' of a stage before the inhibiting effect of reason is felt. Apparently there is something about the rediscovery of the familiar, for example, that is pleasurable purely in itself. This pleasure is, it is true, a form of 'psychic economy'; but apparently a different kind from that afforded by release from inhibition.

Harmless wit, then, consists simply in exploiting this childish play-pleasure. Release from inhibition occurs, if at all, only in the special form of pleasure in nonsense. This basic play-pleasure remains in all examples of wit; but in most of them it is tremendously reinforced by relief from other inhibitions—'the great struggling suppressed tendencies' which, according to Freud dominate most of our lives. And that is what is meant by tendency wit.

What are these tendencies? At first Freud limits them to two: sex and aggression. Later, as we shall see, he admits other types: but he still regards most jokes as either hostile or obscene.

Smutty jokes are in essence a form of sexual aggression. The basic form is a reference to a sexual organ, or to excrement, which is an infantile form of sexuality. In other words, smut is a kind of verbal exhibitionism. But, Freud adds, a lecture on anatomy or on the physiology of reproduction will not be obscene. The essence of the smutty joke is that it is directed towards a woman with the object of exciting her. This is its origin: and it may still be seen in its pure form in bar-rooms, where the smutty talk begins when the barmaid appears. In these circles the jokes may be fairly 'coarse': that is to say the sexual reference will be only slightly veiled.

In more refined company, smut changes in two respects. First, it is considered coarse to indulge in it in the actual presence of women. And secondly, the obscenity must be veiled in some way before it is acceptable. Wit then becomes the sugar coating round the pill. Not that the pill is really bitter to us: on the contrary, it satisfies one of our deepest cravings. But it is bitter to the 'censor' within, who imposes upon us the artificial standards in which we have been reared. Wit, then, is a bribe to the censor.

When we laugh over a delicately obscene witticism we laugh at the identical thing which causes laughter in the ill-bred man when he hears a coarse, obscene, joke; in both cases the pleasure comes from the same source. The coarse obscene joke, however, could not incite us to laughter, because it would cause us shame or would seem to us disgusting; we can laugh only when wit comes to our aid ... Strictly speaking, we do not know what we are laughing about. In all obscene jokes we succumb to striking mistakes of judgment about the 'goodness' of the joke as far as it depends upon formal conditions; the technique of these jokes is often very poor while their laughing effect is enormous.

So far, then, we have a theory rather like Eastman's. Wit depends, formally, on a particular technique ('psychic economy' in Freud, 'frustrated expectation' in Eastman). But added to this there is usually a further source of pleasure. The difference is that whereas Eastman regards this added pleasure as irrelevant, for Freud it is (except in harmless wit) the real crux of the joke. Further, Eastman regards the addition as a sop to our consciences, which treat the joke *qua* joke as mere foolishness. Freud, on the other hand, sees the witty technique as the sop, enabling us to wallow guiltily in the tendency.

This comparison makes clearer Freud's rather equivocal attitude to the inhibition against nonsense. Eastman, as we have just seen, also advances this notion. The adult regards verbal fooling as beneath his dignity: to pacify him, a serious 'point' is added to the joke. Freud's analysis is more complex. Like Eastman, he supposes a resistance against the infantile pleasure of mere word-play. But this resistance is overcome, not by adding a tendentious 'point', but by allowing the word-play to make sense. The censor, then, is as it were fooled twice. To begin with, he grudgingly permits the infantile delight in nonsense to assert itself. He does this because the nonsense has somehow become linked with a sensible thought. Then he allows himself to become so beguiled by this infantile pleasure, that for *its* sake, he allows an obscene or malicious reference to be smuggled in as well. One begins to understand why Holt and others have yielded to the temptation to simplify Freud.

But there is a further complication. Hitherto we have supposed that the technique of wit consisted merely in some form of 'economy', which for rather obscure reasons roused an 'infantile play-pleasure'. But it now appears that the technique has another function. Its form is dictated by this very need to deceive the censor. This is brought out by Freud in an elaborate comparison between 'wit-work' and 'dream-work'.

In the course of this Freud discovers that the main techniques of wit, condensation, displacement, and indirect representation, are all characteristic of the dream. Further, Freud thinks that wit, like dreams, originates in the unconscious. That is why wit so often comes to us as an 'inspiration', 'in a flash', and not by conscious seeking.

Freud admits that he may have found this resemblance between wit and the dream simply because that was what he was looking for. He thinks, however, that he can survive this charge; and that, however he may have come to formulate his analysis the facts will bear him out. What concerns us at the moment, however, is a different charge. The dream-work has one simple purpose: to elude the censor. It is the disguise which inhibited thoughts assume in order to penetrate the conscious. But this is not the purpose of the wit-work. On Freud's hypothesis, wit does not deceive the censor but beguiles it. It assumes the forms it does because they are pleasurable forms; capable of rousing some deep-seated infantile enjoyment. But to identify wit-work and dream-work leads one to suppose that wit uses displacement, indirect expression and the like as a means of deceiving the censor. In short, Freud seems once again to suggest that *all* the pleasure of wit lies in relief from inhibition.

His confusion on this point comes out in his treatment of nonsense. A primary, underived pleasure in nonsense for its own sake is a necessary premise on which his whole theory is based. But, although he admits this, he never seems quite happy about it. On the one hand, as we have seen, he tends to explain away this pleasure in nonsense as derived from an inhibition formed in our early years when we are mastering the difficult technique of rational thinking. On the other, he advances yet a third explanation by which nonsense is an implied criticism. Nonsense, or absurdity, in dreams, is not accidental; it indicates 'embittered criticism and scornful contradiction within the dream-thoughts'. This, Freud claims, is often true in wit also.

It is of course possible to reconcile these three explanations. Nonsense jokes are of many kinds (particularly in Freud's very wide sense of the word) and may be susceptible of different explanations. It is also possible to suppose that, by a rather striking coincidence, the techniques which afford the primary pleasure which is the esssence of wit are also those which serve best to deceive the censor. But it is also possible that Freud himself is not quite clear on these points. Certainly his theory, as he presents it, becomes a tangled skein in which it is difficult to separate different strands.

To show how tangled the skein really is, consider the following summary of Freud's position:—

(a) The primary pleasure of wit is due to its technique, and may be traced to psychic economy.

But relief from inhibition is also psychic economy.

(b) Pleasure in psychic economy may be traced to the infant playing with words and ideas. This infantile play-pleasure precedes wit and is its source.

But playing with words and thoughts is early repressed by the reason, and a strong inhibition is formed against it.

(c) Our pleasure in the technique of wit is so great that, in order to gratify it, we overcome our repressions against obscenity, hostility, etc., and so allow these repressed tendencies to be gratified at the same time.

But the techniques of wit are the same as the techniques of the dream, which originate as a means of deluding the censor.

Is it any wonder that one often doubts whether relief from inhibition is secondary or primary in Freud's theory?

Obscenity, as we have said, is only one form of tendency-wit. The other main type, hostile wit, is precisely parallel to obscenity. From our early childhood, our hostile impulses towards our fellow-beings are repressed, just as our sexual impulses are.

And just as the coarse jests of the common man become refined in more cultured circles, so the frank abuse of the fish-wife is only acceptable in polite society in the form of polished witticisms. Here again wit becomes a form of eluding the censor.

But hostility against individuals may be broadened into hostility against institutions. In this form wit becomes rebellion against authority. This obviously goes beyond hostility, and allows us to gratify an entirely different inhibition—our repressed dissatisfaction with the moral code. The aphorism about marriage ('at worst one can always take a cab') is cited by Freud as an example. This is not merely an obscenity: it also gives vent to our dissatisfaction with the whole institution of marriage. Another example is the story of the man advised by his doctor to give up drinking, which was making him deaf. After a time he took up drinking again, explaining that he had heard of nothing as good as his whisky.

Although Freud began by stating categorically that all tendency wit was either obscene or hostile, he does at this point admit that this is a third type, and not just a variety of hostile wit. He calls it cynical wit, and adds that when directed against the institution of religion, it may be called blasphemous wit.

It will be seen that Freud has been able to transform the whole argument for superiority theories into a relief theory simply by pointing out that our natural aggressiveness is repressed in early youth. This is ingenious, and obviously contains much truth. But even so, rebellion against authority obviously fits his theory much better than hostility, which is often directed against our social inferiors. Accordingly, he suggests that, in jokes of this latter kind, the real butt often turns out to be 'the system'. As an example, he gives the Jewish stories about the beggars, or 'schnorrers', whom wealthy Jews are required by their religion to support. A typical story tells of the 'schnorrer' who was a regular Sunday-dinner guest at a certain house. One day he brought a stranger with him. 'Who is that?' 'Oh, he became my son-in-law last week, and I have agreed to supply his board for the first year.'

The point here, says Freud, lies in the absurdity of the 'schnorrer' treating his patron's money as his own. But he is in fact entitled to do this by Jewish law. Hence the joke is really a veiled attack on a sacred law which even the pious find oppressive.

This story also illustrates Freud's favourite point about absurdity, or nonsense. The absurdity on which the joke depends serves to reveal a real absurdity in the Jewish code. It is therefore, as in the dream, a form of 'embittered criticism.'

Freud adds a fourth type of tendency-wit: sceptical wit. He elucidates this by an example:

Two Jews were at a railway station.
'Where are you going?'
'To Cracow.'
'You liar! You wish me to believe that you are going to Lemberg, whereas really you are going to Cracow all the time!'

This joke, says Freud, poses a real problem. Does it constitute truth if one gives the exact facts without taking into account the interpretation the hearer will put upon them?

One may doubt if this type of story is really common enough to constitute a distinct class of its own. But it is at least clear that Freud is quite willing to recognize other repressed tendencies, besides hostility and obscenity. He has in fact anticipated Eastman's extension of this theory, already referred to.

Freud does not claim to be advancing a general theory of laughter, or even of humour: in the main he confines his attention to wit. He does, however, in a final chapter, say something about the relation of wit and the comic. And this leads him to elaborate his notion of psychic economy, which has hitherto remained obscure.

In wit, Freud says, three persons are required: the wit, the butt, and the audience. In obscene wit the second person is the woman (for example, the barmaid). In actual fact her presence is usually dispensed with, but she is, according to Freud, always theoretically present.

It is the third person who laughs. Why? Because, Freud says, the third person has produced in him, without effort on his part, an idea whose formation was resisted by great inner hindrances. To bring it about spontaneously like the first person he would have had to put forth a good deal of psychic expenditure. He has been saved this expenditure: his pleasure results in economy.

At this point Freud introduces Herbert Spencer's theory, by which laughter is explained as a sudden discharge of superfluous energy. Freud accepts this with only slight modification.

Inhibition, he suggests, uses a good deal of energy: this has suddenly become superfluous and is therefore ready to be discharged.

The comic, however, requires only two persons. Where wit is made, the comic is found: that is to say, we see something in the behaviour of someone else which suddenly strikes us as comic.

For example, we laugh when we see someone performing 'immoderate or inappropriate' actions: a child following with his tongue the movement of his pen when he is trying to master the art of writing; a bowler, after he has released the ball, making motions as if he were still able to control it.

Why are these funny? Because, says Freud, we compare the motions actually made with those which seem to us really necessary. How do we make this comparison? By putting ourselves in the place of the other person. 'I obtain an idea of an actual simple motion by performing it or imitating it. When I perceive a motion in someone else I carry it out imitatively.' We are, then, really comparing two different motions of our own: the one which experience has taught us to associate with the act in question, and the one which we actually observe being performed. The difference between the two reduces itself to a difference in expenditure of energy.

But, just as in reading we no longer spell out words, so through long habit we have learned to make these motions mentally, through memory traces. Nevertheless, some sort of innervation still occurs, and expenditure is still greater or less.

Nor is this process confined to our observation of movement. The same mechanism, Freud declares, explains our grasping of ideas. If we speak of 'a high mountain' or 'a dwarf', we may make appropriate gestures with our hands. Even if we control our hands, we are likely to make similar changes in our voice. At the very least, we will probably distend or contract our eyes. Always our idea of a large or small object is associated with greater or small innervation expenditures. And this is true, not only of physical size in objects, but also of the mentally or morally great.

This explains why degradation is comic. We have summoned all the energy necessary to deal with a 'big' notion: its sudden transformation into a little one leaves us with a reserve of energy which spills over into laughter. Freud then proceeds to apply this formula to unmasking, caricature, frustrated expectation, and other categories of the ludicrous. His conclusion is that comedy, like wit, depends on an economy of expenditure; though not the peculiar economy that comes from getting rid of an inhibition.

But wit and comedy do not exhaust the ludicrous: there is also humour. Humour, says Freud, exhibits a different type of economy: economy of emotion. For example, he quotes Mark Twain's story of the navvy who was hurled into the air by a premature explosion of dynamite. He came to earth again several miles away, and when he got back to the job he found he had been docked half a day's pay for what a later generation calls 'absenteeism'. Here, says Freud, our natural sympathy at a story of disaster is suddenly cut off by the trivial conclusion. Similarly with the convict on the way to the gallows who asked for a kerchief to prevent him from getting a cold in the neck.

Freud summarizes his theory by saying that wit originates from economy of expenditure in inhibition; comedy from an economy of expenditure in thought; humour from an economy of expenditure in feeling.

Freud's account of humour is obviously only a variant of his general formula for comedy; but nevertheless he is really giving us not one theory but three. For although he here identifies wit with release from inhibition, we must remember the other strand in his theory of wit—the infantile play-pleasure—which is essential to the whole theory. Freud attempts to link all three theories together with the single word 'economy'; but the connection is only verbal. He also suggests tentatively that all three are somehow connected with unconscious, and probably infantile, processes; but this does not seem to make things much clearer.

Of the three theories, only relief from inhibition has attracted much attention. This is far and away Freud's most fruitful contribution to the theory of humour, and we can understand why Holt and others simplified Freud so as to leave out all his other speculations. Freud himself does not seem to have realized how far this formula by itself could have taken him, had he been less cautious. He cites Falstaff, for example, as an essentially 'humoristic' character, who rouses in us 'economized contempt and indignation'. That is to say, these emotions, which are the natural response to behaviour like Falstaff's, are cut off by his charm and his wit. Accordingly we have economy of feeling: i.e., humour. Apparently this is Freud's explanation of comic vice in general. But surely our attitude to Falstaff is better explained as release from inhibition. Certainly our indignation and contempt are disarmed: that is to say, in Freud's own terms, the 'censor' is disarmed. And this enables us to indulge vicariously the propensities towards gluttony, cowardice, self-indulgence and the like, which society has forced us to suppress. This is so plausible an explanation, and so completely in Freud's line, that it seems amazing that he should have rejected it.

Before considering further the possibilities of this part of Freud's theory, however, it may be as well to dispose of the other two.

The infantile play-pleasure need not detain us long. It is always rather nebulous, and Freud himself never seems quite sure that it may not, after all, turn out to be release from inhibition. He arrived at it, you will remember, from an analysis of the technique of wit. This suggested two things: that there was a natural, pleasure-giving propensity to play with words and ideas, and that this pleasure was somehow caused by economy. This economy was at various times identified with (a) that brevity which is the soul of wit, and (b) the line of least resistance.

But Freud himself had to admit that 'the economy is not very impressive'. Eastman, commenting on one of Freud's examples, the gibe at the politician who 'like Cincinnatus, has now returned to his place before the plough', says quite truly that this is a very uneconomical way of calling a man an ass. We can of course say that this direct form of speech is forbidden by the censor: but the whole point of Freud's theory is that the censor is disarmed by some special form of economy which is pleasurable in itself: so pleasurable, indeed, that for its sake the malice in the remark is allowed to go unchecked. Certainly the release of this malice taps a further source of pleasure; but we have still to explain the original pleasure which disarmed the censor in the first place.

It seems obvious that what we have here is not economy of expression, but the sudden fusing of two disparate ideas. A compliment, with a whole retinue of pompous classical associations, has suddenly been transformed into a particularly

plebeian insult. The neatness with which the transformation
has been made is, it is true, important: in that sense economy,
or brevity, does play its part. But it is distinctly a secondary
part. The essence of the process is the sudden mingling of ideas
which are normally kept in different compartments of our minds.

In enjoying this joke, we are certainly not following the path
of least resistance. It is easier to follow well-worn mental paths
than to link them by unexpected by-ways. The hack phrase is
the line of least resistance: the comic transformation of it demands alertness and ingenuity. Playing with words and ideas
may be delightful; but it is hard to see why Freud should think
it is easy. Kline's explanation, that the pleasure arises from its
keeping us mentally fresh and awake to new ideas, is surely
much nearer the mark.

If we examine Freud's analysis of witty technique, we will
find that most wit depends far more on this mingling of ideas
than on either form of economy. Freud refers to this mingling,
under the name of 'unification', as one form of technique; but it
can be argued that condensation, manifold application, displacement and the rest are merely alternative devices by which
unification is brought about.

It is significant, I think, that Freud apparently realized that
here was one persistent element in humour that could not be
reduced to release from inhibition. He tried persistently to confuse the two: when that failed, he tried, by juggling with the
word 'economy', to prove that at least the two had the same
basis. He did show, with complete success, that this mingling
of ideas may often be pressed into the service of relief from
inhibition. But he was never entirely able to rule out this
mingling as an independent source of humorous pleasure.

Much the same may be said of his other theory, the analysis
of the comic. It is significant negatively, as showing his conviction that relief from inhibition could not explain all humour.
As it stands, it is full of difficulties. To begin with, there is the
'immoderate action' which we instinctively compare (by minute,
unconscious movements of our muscles) with our own
movements in similar circumstances. According to Freud, the
difference in innervation expenditures leaves us with a surplus
of energy which, as Spencer postulates, spills over into laughter.
One would have expected the opposite to be true. Grant that
when we see a boy writing, we have immediately present to our
minds some rudimentary movements of the hand. We then

imitate, in the same rudimentary way, the actual movements we see being carried out, and find—what? Surely that we have, not a surplus of energy, but less energy than is needed to imitate the laborious schoolboy. Freud seems to assume that we begin by imitating the process in front of us, and only then compare it with our general concept of writing. Yet he proceeds to apply his formula to the familiar facts of anti-climax, where we begin with a general notion of an exalted subject, and find that the actual exhibit in front of us is much less exalted.

Perhaps there is no real inconsistency here. But inconsistency is not long delayed, for Freud goes on to explain that a person will also be comic if he puts forth less energy than is thought proper to his activity. It is hard to see how both situations can fit the hypothesis of surplus energy.

It is true that Freud qualifies this by saying that it is only in the sphere of mental effort that too little expenditure is funny. This is the explanation of examination blunders, and comic stupidity generally. Our evolution, he explains, moves in the direction of limiting our physical actions, and increasing our mental work. By heightening mental expenditure we diminish physical expenditure. We 'use our head and save our legs'.

But, in the first place, this does not mean that inadequate mental effort is the same thing as excessive physical effort, which is what Freud's theory demands. To say that one may sometimes cause the other is obviously not enough. It may be, of course, that for evolutionary reasons we despise both excessive physical effort and inadequate mental effort; but, if Freud means this, he is abandoning Herbert Spencer for Hobbes: economy for superiority. And, secondly, insufficiency of physical effort is, as a matter of fact, funny. It is comic, no doubt, to lift a feather with a great display of effort: it would be equally comic to lift a ton weight nonchalantly with one finger. Professional comedians have been known to get a laugh out of both processes.

The truth is that Freud's attempt to translate incongruity into quantitative terms is not successful. Right at the beginning he talks of 'immoderate and inappropriate' actions. Immoderate is a quantitative term; but inappropriate is not. Freud passes from one to the other without apparently realizing that his theory ceases to apply once he is dealing with propriety rather than size. He does try to bridge the gap by his theory of 'ideational mimicry', whereby all ideas are expressed in terms of physiological expenditure. But inappropriateness goes beyond the mingling of 'big' and 'little' ideas.

Take, for instance, the wartime story of the young man who found himself sharing a first-class carriage with a brass hat. The brass hat made loud comments about able-bodied young men who ought to be in uniform, etc. The young man showed no sign until he was just about to leave the carriage. Then he turned to the brass hat and said courteously: 'I could not help overhearing your remarks. Allow me to explain, sir, first, that I am in a reserved occupation; secondly, that the body which employs me is the Foreign Office; and, finally, that if it hadn't been for the Foreign Office you wouldn't have had your bloody war!'

Now, it is possible to say that here we thought the Foreign Office was to be elevated, whereas in fact it is 'belittled'. But is this more than verbal juggling? In fact, there is nothing 'trivial' about the thought finally expressed. It is, on the contrary, a tremendous charge. It should require as much 'innervation expenditure' as any fulsome compliment. The point is, not that we were expecting something big and got something little, but that the whole direction of our thought has been suddenly changed. We are given, not something little, but something that does not fit in.

Herbert Spencer's argument is most appropriate to Kant's 'frustrated expectation' theory. Here we are expecting something (which involves, no doubt, certain physiological adjustments) and get literally nothing. On this hypothesis it is reasonable to suppose that we are left with a surplus of undischarged energy. But in actual fact, though it may be true that an expectation is disappointed, we are not left with nothing. We are nearly always given something, but it is something different. As we have seen, Eastman realizes this and gets into difficulties trying to explain it without abandoning Kant. Herbert Spencer realizes it too, and developed the theory of 'descending incongruity'. He said that what we got was always smaller than what we expected. But this too is not true. The truth is simply that we get something different.

However, all this belongs to a criticism of Herbert Spencer rather than of Freud, who is merely following him here. The interesting point is that once again Freud has difficulty in explaining away the inappropriate. He is brought up short by a stubborn residue of humour which is plainly not relief from inhibition. He is using Spencer's theory in order to pack this residue, along with relief from inhibition, into the convenient portmanteau 'economy'.

We are left then with Freud's central theory. As we have seen, it is impressive: more impressive, indeed, than he himself realized. For consider what it takes in. Misfortunes, insults, stupidity—all the facts that support Hobbes and his followers—fit in here without strain once one grasps the undoubted fact that most of us have a strong, but inhibited, propensity to malice. Indeed, it not only explains insults: it explains why veiled insults are funny, where frank ones are not. We need not believe all the ramifications of Freud's theory about the censor. But most of us would, I think, accept it in its simplest form. The difference between the drawing-room and the smoking-room joke is, after all, often a matter of form rather than content. The ideas may be the same: it is only the words which must become more decorous. Most writers on humour agree that a successful joke must avoid rousing emotions which may interfere with humour. This is not really different from Freud's thesis that humour must cloak its malice so as to disarm the censor.

Indecency, of course, fits the theory like a glove: so does nonsense, although Freud himself never seems quite easy about this. These are, indeed, the classes of humour which specifically support relief theories, just as misfortune specifically supports superiority theories. The point is not so much that the theory can account for them, as that other theories cannot.

Comic vice, at least of the Falstaff type, where we laugh with the villain, and not at him, can easily be explained as release from inhibition: the other type, of course, enables us to give vent, not to our suppressed vice, but to our suppressed malice. And there is no difficulty in accounting for the unmasking of pretences.

We are left, then, with incongruity, or inappropriateness. There is a very large area of humour which consists primarily in the linking together of disparate ideas. As we have seen, Freud himself apparently realized that relief from inhibition could not explain jokes of this type. The complexity of his theory, as against its simplification by some of his followers, is largely due to this. Freud's theory is illuminating, both in its success and in its failure.

16

RELEASE FROM RESTRAINT

III. GREGORY

A MORE thorough-going attempt to explain laughter as relief is contained in J. C. Gregory's *The Nature of Laughter*.
Gregory realizes that laughter may take many forms; but he
thinks that relief occurs in them all, as a basic and characteristic
element. Thus the laugh of triumph is primarily an expression
of relief at the successful conclusion of a struggle. The merely
scornful laugh is primarily an expression of relief at the im-
potence of an enemy. In each of these the emotion of relief is
suffused with the emotion of triumph or of scorn, so that it is
difficult to disentangle them. But it is relief that supplies the
common element, and it is this that causes them both to issue
in laughter.

Precisely the same is true of sympathetic types of laughter.
If friends laugh at greeting, it is because all social life implies
a certain tension. 'The more formal greetings between strangers
intimate uncertainty about one another and contrast with the
greater familiarity between friends. The laughter of greeting
is part of this familiarity which like all familiarity decreases
constraint.'

Relief can be found in other types of 'delighted laughter'. We
noticed in Part I that a general sense of well-being causes a
predisposition to laughter rather than laughter itself. We may
laugh at the feeblest jokes when we are feeling pleased; but we
still require something at least resembling a joke. Gregory
recognizes this; and suggests that this type of pleasurable mood
is really a sense of relaxation, 'a diffused mental relief that is a
source of many laughters without being one of them'. He also
anticipates our point that play does not cause laughter when it
is tense and purposeful, as in football or chess. In general, he
would argue, it is the relaxed pleasure, the mere irresponsible
romp, that provokes laughter.

It is because relief can enter into so many human activities
that we have become confused about the essential nature of
laughter. In a belligerent society, where men seldom feel secure,
relief, and hence laughter, occurs most naturally as an expres-

sion of triumph over a fallen foe. In a more secure society, other more friendly forms of laughter are likely to develop. 'A modern writer like Eastman is amusing in his perplexity over Hobbes and his followers. He cannot understand unsympathetic or anti-sympathetic theories. There need be no perplexity if Hobbes lived in a less sympathetic age than the present.'

Gregory, then, agrees with Leacock that laughter has been gradually humanized, without drawing the conclusion that hostility is its essential basis. Laughter arises out of hostility only when a hostile threat has been successfully overcome. This in itself gives sympathy a chance to creep in. 'Relief, by cutting short the hostile act and breaking in upon the hostile mood is a step towards sympathy.' But, Gregory continues, paradoxically, animus lingers in the laugh for the same reason that it leaves it. The relief of laughter, in the very act of relaxing from aggression, hints at the foolishness or worthlessness of the person laughed at. This explains the sting of laughter, which Ludovici and other followers of Hobbes make so much of.

This, in outline, is the way Gregory explains what he regards as two main varieties of laughter: the 'ungracious' and the 'delighted'. He distinguishes another main type, 'amused laughter', and to these he adds a fourth, 'the laugh of sheer relief', which, he claims, is the basic type to which the others can be reduced. As we might expect from our consideration of Freud, it is the third type, amusement, the distinctively humorous laugh, which he finds most difficult. But before discussing his treatment of this, let us see how successful he has been with the first two types.

Is all laughter at misfortune of the same essential nature as the laugh of triumph? No doubt we feel relief when we see an enemy overcome. But why should we be relieved at the downfall of a perfect stranger who slips on a banana-skin? Pretentiousness and pomposity may strike us as a menace to our own self-esteem, so that we welcome their exposure; but why should we wish to triumph over a harmless, unassuming, sympathetic figure like Charlie Chaplin?

This is a difficulty for Gregory; but not more so than for Hobbes. All superiority theories do after all presuppose some basic hostility between men. If we were in thorough sympathy with our fellows, their misfortunes would not make us feel superior. They would, on the contrary, increase our own feeling of insecurity. Superiority theories are only plausible if we suppose that most of our insecurity is caused by other men. This is a sad comment on the human situation, but it may well be true. The point here is that if we accept it, then relief is involved in derisive laughter quite as much as superiority. And, since relief enters into other types of humour where superiority does not (or at least not obviously) Gregory can claim with some justice that relief is more likely to be the basic element.

There is, of course, a further argument open to Gregory, the argument from repression. As we saw when discussing Freud, this does provide a simple and convincing link between hostility and relief. Hostility may not play so universal a part in human affairs as Hobbes supposed; but it certainly does occur, and it certainly is suppressed in most civilized society. Gregory does adopt this argument; but he does not make quite as much of it as one might expect. 'Freud's theory,' he says, 'centres, and, it may be added, centres too exclusively, on the providing of laughter with its situation of relief by the release of a repression.' The release of repression is one type of laughable relief, but not, Gregory would say, the only one. Even laughter at profanity, Gregory insists, is not entirely due to the convention against its use. We laugh at an oath, on the stage or off it, because 'relief, by mental explosion, is the essence of the "damn". Laughter is thus provided with its fundamental situation.' The spectator shares this through sympathy, and it is he who laughs, because his vicarious relief is free from the annoyance that may curb laughter in the swearer. The public flouting of the ban against swearing heightens the relief by supplying an element of release from repression, but is not the sole, or even the primary, cause of laughter. 'There seems to be an abundance of relief in the oath: it scatters a gathered anger, defies a public convention, and may also suggest to the spectator an attack which fails to mature by converting a blow into an expletive.'

Here Gregory, in his anxiety not to narrow his theory by identifying relief with release from inhibition, is surely going too far. Our society has two main types of verbal taboo: oaths and words describing sex or excrement. Of these, only the oaths express 'relief by mental explosion'. Yet the oath, in spite of its 'abundance of relief', is only very mildly funny. The others, which (presumably) cause only the subsidiary laughter of relief from inhibition, play a much bigger part in humour.

This, however, is a minor point. The main one for us here is that Gregory, like Freud, realizes that release from inhibition will not explain all laughter. We may grant, however, that by combining Freud's explanation with Hobbes' he does manage to account at least as well as most theories for the hostile element in laughter, and hence for the first of his three varieties, 'ungracious laughter'.

Can we say the same of 'delighted laughter'? We have seen that there is some force in the contention that we laugh at the relaxed pleasures rather than the tense ones. But Gregory also makes the point there that his theory can account for the pleasurable tinge generally admitted to be an essential part of laughter. All pleasure is not laughable, but most laughter is pleasurable. This is 'simply because the sense of relief is pleasurable'.

One obvious corollary is that Gregory must distinguish sharply between relief and disappointment. Relief for him cannot be simply 'frustrated expectation'. It cannot be enough that our mental pattern is somehow disrupted; what is broken must have contained something irksome.

It is not clear that Gregory always recognizes this. He does indeed tell us that 'news of defeat when victory is expected is not laughable'. But, provided that there is no very violent disappointment of this kind, he seems to think he can take over the whole theory of 'frustrated expectation' and identify it with 'relief'.

He sees, for example, no disparity between his theory and Herbert Spencer's.

Herbert Spencer expressed this fundamental necessity for relief in the ludicrous break in expectancy by describing the occasion of laughter as a 'descending incongruity'. A sneeze in the middle of Beethoven's symphony releases the audience 'from an irksome attitude of mind'. A flow of serious expectancy, not necessarily 'irksome', follows the demand of the music; then it is suddenly unverified, the sneeze satisfies attention for a moment, relief blends with a perception of the incongruous sides of the break, and a laugh, expressing relief and charged with a sense of the ludicrous, spreads through the audience.

This version of Spencer's argument is not quite fair. The passage in question is part of an answer to Bain. In it Spencer is denying the claim that laughter is always due to degradation

of those serious interests to which we give unwilling attention.
Spencer also says:

But no explanation is thus afforded of the mirth which ensues
when the short silence between the andante and allegro in one
of Beethoven's symphonies is broken by a loud sneeze. In this,
and hosts of like cases, the mental tension is not coerced but
spontaneous, not disagreeable but agreeable; and the coming
impressions to which the attention is directed promise a gratifi-
cation which few if any desire to escape. Hence, when the un-
lucky sneeze occurs, it cannot be that the laughter of the
audience is due simply to the release from an irksome attitude
of mind; some other cause must be sought.

The question is whether this argument, against Bain, does not
also tell against Gregory. In order to call Spencer as a witness
in his defence, Gregory has to admit specifically that the mental
pattern which the laughable situation disrupts is not necessarily
irksome. But, if that is so, can we call the disruption 'relief'?

Gregory's answer is that any activity, even a pleasurable one,
calls for a certain mental tension. 'There are pleasures of tension and pleasures of relief.' But the pleasures of tension are
apparently not unmixed with pain. Any sudden shattering of
tension, even of pleasurable tension, is, one gathers, itself
pleasurable. It can therefore be justly called 'relief.' And,
since any activity involves attention, and all attention involves
tension, it follows that any break in any activity enables
Gregory to introduce his formula. The only exceptions are those
cases where some other emotion, such as frustration or rage,
intervenes to inhibit laughter.

We may ask whether the whole concept of relief has not become rather tenuous here. If relief is merely the slight easing
of strain which accompanies any break in attention, is it enough
to justify the very strong association between laughter and
pleasure? Or does Gregory's theory depend on a verbal ambiguity? Sometimes he requires us to interpret relief in the fullest
emotional sense of the word, as implying the lifting of an almost
intolerable burden. At other times he uses it in the relatively
colourless sense which implies little more than a break in con-
tinuity, as when the fashion books speak of a black coat relieved with white.

We have anticipated Gregory's treatment of his third type of
laughter, 'amused laughter'. By this he means humorous

laughter, which, he says at once, implies incongruity. 'Relief is a break, and the two sides of the break constitute an incongruity.' This seems to mean that incongruity occurs when we focus attention on the contrast between what we expected and what actually occurs.

This enables Gregory to take over bodily Kant's formula of frustrated, or, as he prefers to call it, 'deceived' expectation. No doubt Gregory makes the change because frustration sorts rather oddly with relief. But so, for that matter, does deception.

Consider, for example, Gregory's account of exaggeration.

An angler tells a listener that he has caught a very large fish. The listener is expectant. 'It was so big that'—the listener is on tip-toes—'when I pulled it out the level of the water in the lake sank two feet'—expectation is disillusioned and the listener laughs. Exaggeration deceives expectancy by enticing it up higher than it should go. When the fraud is discovered, promise and performance incongruously contrast, attention relaxes, and amused laughter results. The fraud must be soft enough for amusement to be a sufficient recompense—the exagerative deceit must end in relief.

This analysis is not essentially different from Kant's, or Herbert Spencer's, or Eastman's. At first sight, it seems a little odd to say that expectancy has been enticed higher than it should go. It is the story that is tall, while expectancy is obviously not high enough. But Gregory's point is clear enough. The listener has expected something credible. He has built up a pattern of serious attention on that assumption, and it is the sudden collapse of the pattern that causes laughter.

We have already discussed this theory when considering Kant and Eastman. Gregory differs from them only in insisting that this mental disruption must be regarded as essentially relief. We have already raised the question whether the element of relief here is really strong enough to bear the weight he puts upon it. But there is another objection, which is probably more serious.

Gregory's analysis deprives humour of any positive content. Laughter, he says, is essentially a desistance from effort, a pleasant interruption of the serious business of life. But we have seen that the shattering of mental concepts involved in incongruity may lead to a clearer view of the real relations between things. Gregory himself recognizes this up to a point. Although he warns us that laughter, since it is essentially a pleasant relief from earnest, may be overdone and lead to permanent idleness of mind, he also tells us that a sense of humour is 'almost indispensable to sound judgment'.

Pomposity and dogmatism wane when men perceive the contrast between their own little pretensions and the greatness of the universe. A quiet humility descends when the fuss made by any individual is humorously contrasted with the cosmic placidity that ignores him. We cannot fit the universe, or any part of it, neatly together, as a clock-maker fits our watches; we cannot assign man to his precise niche nor say exactly what he is nor what he should be; and humorous perception of the incongruities in our own muddled versions of things prevents us from suffering too acutely from our own failures and presuming too much upon our own insight. Relief by laughter from the seriousness of life is a good thing . . . .

In this passage Gregory seems to be hinting at what we have called the god's-eye view. There is also the suggestion that humour may break down a rigid compartmentalism and correct the faults inherent in the generalizations by means of which human beings try to understand the universe. But if this is true, can we still think of humour as merely a break from the strain of attending to these generalizations? Gregory's argument seems to be that we must behave as if our aims were important, and that the god's-eye view is just a momentary relief from this striving, useful as a holiday, but fatal if it becomes a permanent habit of mind. There is certainly something to be said for this view. We are always part of the struggle even when we try to rise above it. But surely there is some permanent value in the attitude of mind which can rise above it? To speak of it as a momentary relief hardly allows for this, and certainly does not explain why it should be 'almost indispensable to sound judgment'.

We may, however, be reading rather more into this passage than Gregory intended. Although he regards humour as essentially incongruity, and incongruity as the collapse of a mental pattern, he does not quite make the transition to universe-changing or attitude-mixing. For him an incongruity is simply something unexpected. This becomes apparent in his treatment of wit. Harking back to the earlier meaning of the word, he denies that wit is necessarily amusing, and defines it simply as 'a quick, vivid illumination of a truth'. If laughter belongs to it in its own right, it is the laughter which 'accompanies the relief of achievement'. But wit is also specially suited to the development of other kinds of laughter. 'Its efficiency, which is part of its nature, invites its use as a sword', provoking the laughter of triumph. Again, wit often consists in finding un-expected likenesses. But 'when wit reveals an unsuspected similarity between two things it will also display an incongruity between them'.

It is clear that Gregory regards incongruity as simply the coming together of 'an ill-assorted pair'. He does not regard this as merely one step in the process of finding new connections between things, with a consequent shattering of mental com-partments. Otherwise, he might have been less ready to sup-pose that the ludicrous is only a trivial by-product of wit. On our view, 'a quick and vivid illumination' is part of the essential nature of humour itself. Only by so regarding it can we under-stand the full force of the mental disruption, the shattering of the pattern that is necessary to his own theory. Gregory, how-ever, reduces this to little more than unexpectedness. He says flatly that 'the predilection of the witticism for remote identities . . . . should have prevented the identification of wit with the comic.' But 'remote identities', as we have seen, are necessary to the process of universe-changing which we have suggested is the real essence of the comic. It is because he does not realize this that Gregory, like Eastman, tends to reduce humour to a purely formal element. The rich, satisfying content becomes something extraneous which may be added, but is not the real cause of laughter. As we have seen when discussing Eastman, this amounts to emptying out the baby with the bath-water.

What, then, is our final verdict on Gregory's theory? He adopts many of the explanations that have been advanced by his predecessors. He agrees with Hobbes that some laughter is due to superiority, with Freud that some laughter is due to release from repression, with Kant that some laughter is due to frus-trated expectation. But he claims that each of these formulas can be better described as relief, whereas there is also the sheer laugh of relief which cannot be reduced to any of them.

His case is quite impressive. We have suggested that it de-pends in part on juggling with the word 'relief'. The whole concept of relief becomes a little attenuated when it is identified in one place with the removal of a threat, in another with the satisfaction of achievement, and in a third with a break in attention. At the same time, it seems likely enough that there is an element of relief in all laughter. The real question is whether it is the important and essential element. Gregory's analyses are usually reasonable enough as far as they go, but they do not always seem quite adequate. Our laughter at misfortune has a positive content that cannot be quite explained as the removal of a rather hypothetical threat to our own security. Laughter at greeting a friend contains a positive access of pleasure that is something more than the absence of the uneasiness that sometimes attends our contact with strangers. Our laughter at incongruity is something more than the break in attention which results from some interruption in the smooth flow of expected happenings.

17

AMBIVALENCE

I. Greig

WE HAVE SAID that there are three main theories of humour: superiority, incongruity, and release from restraint. Perhaps one should add the play theory; except that this is not so much a theory as a tentative speculation. Most writers would agree with Sully that humour has much in common with play; but it is difficult to see where this leads us. Even if one grants that humour is a form of play, it is still necessary to discover what, specifically, constitutes humour.

There is, however, a fourth theory which has had one or two advocates. This is the theory of ambivalence, or conflicting emotions. According to this theory, we laugh whenever, on contemplating an object or a situation, we find opposite emotions struggling within us for mastery.

A comparatively recent exponent of ambivalence is J. Y. T. Greig. Rather oddly, Greig regards his theory as little more than an off-shoot of Freud's; and he is, as will appear, a good Freudian on most other matters. Actually, however, he has done more than merely modify Freud here and there: he has changed the whole basis of his theory.

Following the lead of both Freud and Sully, Greig looks to infant behaviour to solve the riddle of laughter for us; and he comes out with a full-fledged theory of the origin of the laugh itself. Smiling, he suggests, begins as a sort of rudimentary sucking—'a feeble and vacillating continuation of the behaviour of feeding'. The first smile of infants generally occurs after a full meal. It becomes associated with the secondary result of infant feeding, the stimulation of the instinct of love, through the nursing embrace of the mother.

The smile, then, is the outward sign of love. But when does the smile develop into a laugh? When, says Greig, the love response is interrupted by other emotions, like fear. This is a modification of Spencer's theory. 'An indeterminate amount of the psycho-physical energy of the infant is working itself out in the behaviour of love. The behaviour is suddenly opposed or

blocked.' In bracing himself against the obstruction, the infant
takes a deep breath. If he cannot overcome it, his gathering
psycho-physical energy will express itself in crying. But if he
overcomes it suddenly, or if the obstruction vanishes, the surplus energy will escape in laughter. The essence of laughter,
physically, is that one takes a long breath, and then vents it in
short, sharp, explosions of sound. And the essence of laughter,
psychologically, is that 'love behaviour' is checked by some
interruption which is, however, speedily overcome.

One may note in passing that there seems no reason, on
Greig's showing, why it should be love behaviour that is thus
interrupted. He has connected love with the smile; but he has
not connected the smile with the laugh. All that his theory of
laughter demands is that *some* behaviour should be sharply
checked. It is true, of course, that in popular thought the smile
and the laugh are inseparably connected; but in popular thought
the laugh is regarded as an intensified smile; and Greig specifically denies this. It would seem, then, that Greig can hardly
rely on the smile to connect laughter with love. However, he
himself assumes that he has made the connection, and goes on
to consider examples.

He details six main causes of child laughter: tickling, peep-bo,
romping, the chase, teasing, and rebelliousness.

Tickling is considered at some length. Some of his comments
have been mentioned earlier. Greig finally favours the theory
that the ticklish parts of the body are the 'erotogenic zones'.
The first erotogenic zone, says Greig, is the mouth, lips, chin
and cheeks, and at first a touch on this zone will cause the
infant to suck. Later a touch on this zone will elicit sucking if
the child is hungry, smiling if he is not. Later still, other parts
of the body become erotogenic. As soon as the child is old
enough to recognize in the person who touches something that
may hurt as well as soothe, the touch will still elicit love behaviour, but obstructed by fear, and, if the stimulus recurs more
rapidly than the normal rhythm of nervous conduction, by pain.
So long as the obstructions are overcome from moment to
moment, the child will continue to laugh. In the end, the habit
will be established, and the man may laugh even when the pain
predominates.

Greig's theory of tickling obviously hinges on the assumption
that the ticklish spots are the erotogenic zones, and this is highly

doubtful. Greig does not explain how the soles of the feet fit this definition: a particularly glaring omission since he severely chides Robinson for neglecting the soles of the feet in framing *his* theory. In any case, the most ticklish parts of the body are probably the arm-pits and the ribs. These do figure, no doubt, in amorous play, and are to that extent erotogenic zones, but then, on that criterion, so is almost every other part of the body. This is the biggest objection to Greig's account of tickling. We have already considered other points that may be made against it.

In peep-bo, says Greig, the object of affection vanishes and reappears. This corresponds to numerous situations in infant life. Objects are continually being whisked out of the range of vision. The situation exactly fits Greig's formula.

Romping about, which in infants takes the form of being tossed about, riding cock-horse, etc., causes laughter because the fear of falling intervenes in the love behaviour. Further, direct stimulation of the erotogenic zones may also take place, as when the child is jiggled on his mother's foot. Greig allows some weight to the joy of exercising new bodily powers, but regards this as secondary.

Greig would probably have some difficulty in extending this account of romping to include the child as well as the infant. Most people who have watched children will, I think, disagree with him when he minimizes the importance of the exercise of bodily powers. The fear of falling may, of course, play a part in romping: the child gets many unexpected knocks and bumps, and this may cause a sort of fearful joy. But sheer delight in bodily prowess often seems to be the main cause of laughter.

In the chase, says Greig, 'it is only when (the child) oscillates between the wish to get away and the wish to be captured that he may laugh . . . . As the danger of being caught becomes more imminent, the unconscious memory of past caresses becomes more urgent, and the struggle between the wish to be caught and caressed, and the wish to run away toward freedom, becomes more intense.'

This seems unnecessarily ingenious. Greig might have made his point without supposing the highly dubious 'unconscious memory of past caresses'. Why not simply say that the child oscillates between the fear of capture and the joy of eluding capture by his own efforts? This would be plausible, and allows

for some ambivalence. Greig, however, is apparently insistent
that it must be 'love behaviour', and not joy in general, that is
interrupted.

Teasing is something of a poser for Greig, since at first sight
it seems to support Hobbes. But Greig insists that aggressiveness originally plays no part at all in the action of a child who,
let us say, pulls his sister's hair. The first time the child does
this he is simply exercising his grasping impulse. Unwittingly
he causes an unexpected reaction (a scream) which interferes
with the love situation. Later, says Greig, aggressiveness may
develop, but even this is a form of twisted love.

In much the same way, Greig suggests that rebelliousness in
itself will not cause laughter. Laughter occurs only when the
rebellion is tempered by love.

In all this, the ordinary reader cannot help feeling that, while
Greig is extraordinarily ingenious, he is somehow just not convincing. This feeling is likely to be intensified as Greig goes on
to apply his formula to the occasions of adult laughter.

Just as Freud puts most emphasis on the repressed impulses
towards sex and malice, so Greig pays most attention to indecency and mishaps. Indecency, of course, gives him no
trouble. Our attitude to sex, he points out, is ambivalent from
the beginning. He cites Havelock Ellis to prove that modesty
occurs very early in man's development. In primitive man, it
is a natural outcome of the male's fear of interruption by a rival,
and of the female's fear of sexual aggression at the wrong
moment. Hence any reference to sex is likely to cause a conflict
between sexual desire and modesty. Laughter occurs when the
modesty is overcome. This enables Greig to incorporate Freud's
point about the devices of wit being essentially a means of disarming modesty. Freud, as we have noticed, is never very clear
on this point: on the one hand, the censor is disarmed because
the witty technique is pleasurable in itself: on the other, the
'wit-work' is simply a disguise, like the dream-work. Greig's
theory requires him to adopt the second explanation and ignore
the first.

Every age, says Greig, draws the line between sex and
modesty at some point, higher or lower in different ages. Every
age also desires to go beyond that line on occasions, provided it
can be done with some appearance of decency. Hence the
smutty joke.

Apart from the directly sexual joke, however, women have been a common source of jokes from Aristophanes to Shaw. This is because our attitude to women is ambivalent. It is predominantly affectionate, but hostility is continually intruding. When hate is whole-hearted, Greig says, humour vanishes. Thus Othello calls Desdemona 'whore' without laughter. But a man might call a woman 'a little whore', and laugh. Here the adjective indicates that the hatred is modified and restrained by love. Greig is prepared to accept either love modified by hate or hate modified by love as the formula: the essential point is that our behaviour is ruffled by an interruption, which is successfully overcome.

Our attitude to mothers-in-law, says Greig, is more than usually ambivalent. This is because the son-in-law is unconsciously attracted to the mother-in-law, to whom he transfers his incestuous desire for his mother. This mingles with the dislike inherent in the relationship to give us a typically humorous situation; and the mother-in-law becomes a stock joke.

Here again Greig might have been more convincing if he had not been so anxious to adhere to the true Freudian gospel. We need not suppose an Œdipus complex to find ambivalence in the attitude to one's mother-in-law. On the one hand, convention (and his wife) require the husband to treat her with special affection: on the other hand, she is, objectively considered, a middle-aged female stranger who has suddenly assumed the right to interfere in his private affairs.

This explanation, it is true, fits Freud's theory of humour rather than Greig's. It suggests a natural dislike inhibited by the demands of convention. Greig apparently demands a real affection checked by dislike. But, since he is prepared to allow hate modified by love, he might have satisfied the needs of his theory without departing from the common-sense view.

Incidentally, it is odd that the comic mother-in-law of the music halls should always be the wife's mother. The relation between the wife and the husband's mother is likely to be even more difficult. The mother commonly feels, more or less consciously, that she has been supplanted in the affections of her son. Moreover, her special task of ministering to his domestic comfort has been taken over by a novice at the art. Consequently, she is likely to proffer advice: which is just as likely to be resented as criticism. And yet once again we have a conventional requirement of more or less ostentatious affection. The situation is much more equivocal than any that is likely to develop between the husband and the wife's mother. Yet it has been ignored by the music-halls, except in the stock joke about 'the cakes that mother used to make'. Greig might perhaps see this as evidence that his Œdipus complex theory is right after all. But probably it only goes to show that our conventions consider the man's point of view rather than the woman's.

Why is the cuckold funny? Greig suggests that laughter at the cuckold is primarily laughter *with* the wife. The husband is simply the obstacle to her love with her paramour, and we rejoice in seeing the obstacle overcome. As an example, Greig cites the mediaeval story of the woman who was surprised by her husband, while her gallant hid under the bed.

'What would you have done if you had found a man in bed with me?'

'Cut his head off with this sword.'

'I'd have prevented that; I'd have thrown this cloak around your head, as if in jest, thus, and he'd have escaped.'

She suits the action to the word, while the gallant does in fact escape; and she shouts to her laughing husband, all entangled in the cloak, 'Run after him! He's gone!'

Now it is true that we admire the neatness and ingenuity of this device. But does the humour rest on Greig's formula? The point is surely that the wife should get out of the situation by, in a sense, revealing it. The last sentence, in particular, brings this out. On the other hand, it is probably true that most of us have a sneaking sympathy with all illicit love; and this certainly adds to the appeal of the story. But Freud's theory fits the psychological facts much better than Greig's. He would presumably say that we laugh primarily and ostensibly at the technical device of representation through the opposite, and that incidentally this enables us to gratify an inhibition. It is not that the arrival of the husband acts as a check on our vicarious love behaviour: as a matter of fact that has been irrevocably checked anyway, and the escape of the gallant does not remove the obstacle. It is the demands of conventional morality which check our sympathy for the illicit love affair. We give reign to this sympathy by laughing at the paradoxical situation in which the husband finds himself. The point to be noticed is that this paradoxical situation is funny in its own right, as well as being a means of disarming the censor.

I think Freud is substantially right here: and that there are at least two elements in this joke, and probably a third. They are: the paradox by which revealing the situation saves it; the pleasure of a forbidden subject—illicit love; and pleasure in seeing one person outwit another.

Smutty jokes may, of course, be excremental rather than sexual. Greig adopts the Freudian view that pleasure in excrement is infantile sexuality. Disgust takes the place of modesty, and our attitude to excrement, like our attitude to sex, is essentially ambivalent.

Physical deformity, bodily mishaps, and misfortunes generally give Greig more trouble than indecency. This is because he is not content, with Freud, to accept hostility as a repressed impulse on a par with sex. At times, Greig falls back on this explanation, restated as 'hate modified by love', but he is obviously happier when he can find a sexual explanation.

Physical violence, for instance, is funny only when our attitude to it is ambivalent. 'If I horsewhip another man, I go through it without laughter, for hatred is in undisputed possession.' Similarly, a close friend of the victim, watching, will be all sympathy, and will not laugh. Only the impartial spectator will laugh, because he sympathizes with both sides. That is why we laugh at Punch and Judy: the audience sympathizes with Punch, but also to a lesser degree with the characters he belabours, especially Judy. Further, since flagellation is a sexual perversion, the love behaviour is reinforced unconsciously. Punch himself inspires an ambivalent attitude, because he is essentially a doll, to which the child responds with love. But he is an unusual doll. The sight of his deformities causes a check in the love behaviour, which is however soon overcome. Furthermore, the particular deformities of Punch (the hump or horn, the pointed nose, the pointed hat) are unconscious phallic symbols, thus stimulating the love behaviour.

It is not difficult to find flaws in this ingenious argument. In the first place, the child who laughs at Punch will also laugh at a deformed man who is not a doll, and whose deformities do not suggest phallic symbols, except in so far as everything is a phallic symbol to a Freudian.

Secondly, it is by no means certain that when we laugh at

physical violence we sympathize with both sides. The villain who gets his just deserts will often be greeted with derisive laughter, especially by children. This is once again more easily explicable on Freud's terms than on Greig's. It does suggest that what we are looking for is a reputable means of venting our unconscious malice.

But the more typical butt of slap-stick fits neither theory. We laugh at Chaplin even though we sympathize with him a good deal, and not at all with his persecutors.

Greig goes on to discuss street mishaps, such as collisions, falls, losing one's hat. Collisions, he says, are only a special case of physical violence. But are they? Greig's account of physical violence requires it to be intentional, so that our love (sympathy) for the victim may be checked by the hate which we share with the persecutor. But in street collisions we should merely sympathize with both parties. Hate does not enter into our feelings at all.

Falls have sexual associations. Greig quotes Juliet's nurse (or rather, her husband): 'Dost thou fall upon thy face? Thou wilt fall backward when thou hast more wit.' There is also the phrase: 'fallen women'. But the fall is principally to be regarded as a check to our natural love behaviour (sympathy) which will affect our attitude even towards strangers. 'It is a better joke if the old gentleman who slips on a banana skin has been in view for some time, than if he suddenly turns a corner and falls plump at our feet.' In other words, we must have time to adjust ourselves to him; and this implies some sort of attitude, usually vaguely sympathetic.

He does not, however, explain why this 'love behaviour' should be checked by a fall. Our natural sympathy for a fellow man should simply be reinforced by our sympathy for the victim of an accident. Perhaps he assumes, with Freud, that there will always be some malicious rejoicing at others' misfortune. But he does not say so.

Hats, says Greig, are sexual symbols. It is funnier for a woman's hat to blow off than for a man's. This is because uncovering the head is unconsciously interpreted as a sort of obscene exposure of the person.

This explanation is not merely fantastic in itself, but it does not even square with the theory that hats are phallic symbols. Greig cites, as an example, a mediaeval tale about a woman

whose head had been shaved because of sickness. She inadvertently went out into the street without a hat. Rebuked by
a neighbour, she tried to cover her head by whipping up her
clothes over it. The spectators laughed 'at her folysshenes,
whiche to hyde a lyttel faute shewed a greatter'.

This story tells against Greig, not for him. The exposure of
the head is only blameworthy because of the special circum-
stance that the head had been shaved. Greig may, of course,
argue that this only accentuates the 'indecent exposure', but in
any case the real point of the story has been admirably sum-
marized in the last sentence. It lies in the paradox by which
an attempt to redeem the situation makes it worse.

Greig cites another story to illustrate the humour of gaucherie.
This time it is a scene from a French comedy: A lover visits his
lady and' her mother. She drops her cotton. Both lovers
stoop to pick it up, and bump their heads together. In despair
at his clumsiness the gallant beats a retreat, but knocks over a
prized piece of porcelain; then slips on the floor, newly waxed
for the wedding; clutches at a mirror, bringing it to the floor;
and finally breaks a guitar.

Greig finds sexual stimuli everywhere. First, the hero is a
lover, and 'all the world,' he says, 'loves *with* a lover.' Secondly,
the head-bumping rouses the obvious association of lovers
touching, i.e., love-behaviour, which is interrupted by the substitution of a painful bump for a pleasant touch. Thirdly, the
porcelain rouses an ambivalent attitude. On the one hand it
is an *objet d'art*, impossible to replace, to be regarded with
veneration; on the other, it is a woman's knick-knack, to be regarded with contempt. Fourthly, the mirror suggests Narcis-
sism; and, finally, a guitar suggests love serenades.

All this is pretty obviously wrong-headed. The real point of
the hero's being a lover is, obviously, that the object of the visit
is to ingratiate himself. He accomplishes the direct opposite,
and every attempt to retrieve the situation only brings further
disaster. Over and above this, there is, of course, a sheer joy
in knockabout. This requires some explanation, but Greig's is
hardly convincing.

Summing up his treatment of physical mishaps, Greig says,
re-stating Bergson: 'Any action is potentially comic that calls
our attention to the physical in a person: (i) when this serves

to check . . . love behaviour . . .; (ii) when this brings to focus
hate behaviour that is still discoverably ambivalent and/or
(iii) when the physical is consciously or unconsciously interpreted in terms of sex.'

It is to be noted that the relation of (iii) to the general formula, as set out in (i) and (ii) is never quite cleared up by
Greig. Again and again he seems to think he has made his
point provided he can find any sexual association, however
remote, as when he reminds us that guitars suggest love
serenades. The point may be that, since our attitude to sex is
always ambivalent, any sexual reference is automatically funny.
But then we would have to suppose that hats, for instance, are
funny in themselves, even when they do not blow off our heads.
At other times he is content to say vaguely that the sexual
association 'reinforces the love behaviour'.

Greig is rather more successful in accounting for comic vice.
The ambivalence here, he says, is due to our sympathy for the
rascal, caused by our own incipient immorality, on the one
hand, and our moral disapproval on the other. The sympathy
must triumph, and to this end humorous writers use various
devices to disarm our disapproval.

This is, of course, Freud's inhibition theory, and, as we have
already noted, does explain one type of comic vice very well.
The other type, when we laugh at the villain and not with him,
can also be explained well enough by Freud. It is not clear
how Greig would explain it.

But Greig is not content with this. Particular vices, he explains, may reinforce unconscious sexual associations. Drunkenness, for instance, is funny to a child because the drunk man
often falls, or collides with someone. But the child's attention
is diverted from these comic accidents by his parents, who
suppress his interest in drunkenness. Hence it becomes associated in his mind with sex, which is similarly suppressed. As
proof of this association we have the phrase: 'woman and wine'.
'Drunkenness,' Greig concludes, 'is always a substituted, unconscious stimulus of sexual behaviour in the spectator.'

Disguises, says Greig, always create an ambivalent situation.
The disguise is a variant of peep-bo. The child confronted by
a member of his family in disguise, whether intentional or
merely caused by unfamiliar clothes, will be a prey to conflicting emotions. With the removal of the disguise, these vanish,

and laughter follows. The child must half penetrate the disguise, and be uncertain which attitude to adopt.

This childish attitude, Greig continues, persists into adult life, making disguise a favourite device in stage comedy. Moreover, in Shakespeare's comedies Julia, Viola and Rosalind all don doublet and hose for various reasons, but for one essential purpose—to introduce a check to the smoothness of their love affairs.

It is quite obvious, however, that the situation on the stage does not correspond to the childish experience described here. On the stage the actor is completely deceived, and the spectator (who laughs) completely undeceived. The point is that apparently appropriate behaviour is really inappropriate. There is no ambivalence.

Greig apparently realizes this, but he does not think it affects his explanation. As the result of childish memories, he explains, merely seeing through a disguise becomes automatically funny. In other words, we are not laughing at the situation before us at all, but at the unconscious memory of a totally different one! And this is not the only time that Greig uses this explanation.

Verbal play is obviously difficult to fit into Greig's formula. Actually he tends to slide over it. Since he regards his whole theory as little more than a gloss on Freud, he thinks he can rest content with Freud's analysis of wit, or at least of tendency wit. Freud specifies two inhibitions, sex and hostility. In other words, love and hate. Therefore, Greig says, Freud's formula corresponds to his own.

But Freud realizes that verbal play is funny in its own right. As we have seen, his theory depends upon this. Greig thinks he can overcome this difficulty simply by denying the existence of harmless wit. On closer examination, he suggests, every piece of word-play will be found to contain some point.

But this leaves unexplained the purpose of the witty technique which Freud has so painstakingly analysed. Greig does not attempt to meet this difficulty. He might of course fall back on Freud's alternative theory that the purpose of the wit-work is simply to deceive the censor. But as a matter of fact Greig is inclined to reject the concept of the censor altogether. His theory does not depend, as Freud's does, on the existence of deep-seated inhibitions. Love behaviour, for instance, may be checked by modesty, but it may also be checked by some other emotion. All that Greig demands is a conflict of emotions: he is not concerned, as Freud is, with the relief of *continually* thwarted desires.

In rejecting this part of Freud's theory, Greig has, I think, lost much that makes it valuable. When we think of laughter as a release from inhibition, we do understand much that may otherwise puzzle us. The delight in nonsense, for example, (which Greig incidentally ignores altogether) is best explained as a reaction against 'stepmother Reason'. Dewey noted that the laugh has much in common with the sigh of relief: Sully said that any theory of laughter must allow for the element of childish delight in the gloriously new and extravagant, and for the sense of relief from restraint. These two, he added, are closely connected. The notion of inhibition does give a plausible and far-reaching explanation of all this. Greig's formula is obviously much weaker and much less comprehensive.

Further, Greig is without the saving caution which made Freud insist on a place in his theory for verbal play as such. He tried hard to bring the whole of wit within the formula of release from inhibition, but apparently he sensed that there was always something left over which refused to conform to his most ardent theorizing. That is why the curious double strand continually recurs in his treatment. Freud's instinct here was sound. He is a much more moderate Freudian than Greig. The more far-fetched speculations about phallic symbols and the like occur only in the disciple, and never in the master.

In fact, it is hard to find any advantages at all in Greig's theory as compared with Freud's. Like Freud, he can explain jokes which turn on sex or malice: but his explanation of both, and especially the second, is much less convincing than Freud's. Unlike Freud, he does not make any serious attempt to come to grips with the large part of humour which is better explained by the incongruity theories.

On the other hand, the occasions of humour are so frequent and so varied that it is hard to believe that they always touch on some deep-seated inhibition. No doubt this is why Greig felt the need of some more elastic formula. But 'love checked by hate' is still too narrow a conception to enlarge Freud's field very much. Greig might have been more successful if he had carried the notion of ambivalence further.

18

AMBIVALENCE

II. Menon

ALTHOUGH, unlike Greig, he does not use the word, a much more thorough-going theory of ambivalence is offered by Mr. V. K. Krishna Menon.

Menon insists that laughter is essentially subjective. The laughable is not a quality in things: if it were, we should all laugh at the same things, just as we all recognize that sugar is sweet. The truth is that laughter is a product of our own emotional reactions to things. What makes one man laugh makes another angry. People laugh in circumstances or situations, not at them.

Menon agrees with Spencer that physiologically laughter is an outburst of surplus energy. But it is energy of a particular kind. Better food and good digestion may increase our nervous energy, but do not normally find vent in laughter. The energy liberated in laughter is felt to be different. It is emotional energy. And emotion is the affective side of instinct. We feel it when an instinct has been stimulated.

Normally, when an instinct is stirred, it finds its outlet in the conative activity appropriate to the instinct. Laughter occurs when this activity is, for some reason, checked. The stirring of the instinct means that the organism has been, physically and psychically, mobilized for action. Laughter is, on the contrary, a demobilization of forces. Normally this occurs gradually in the course of the activity toward which the instinct is striving. But, when this activity is prevented, the release of energy is sudden and explosive.

One illustration is the laugh of victory after a fight. The victor still has some energy unused, and this energy breaks up into shouting and laughter. If he is nearly exhausted, he will feel satisfied, but will not laugh.

But laughter of this kind, though he believes it to be 'pure' laughter, the primary kind of laughter, is, Menon recognizes, rare. He does cite one or two other instances. One is the smile of a mother on seeing her child at play. Her maternal instinct is roused by the sight of the child: that is, presumably, she feels some urge to action. Menon does not tell us what action: but one may suppose that she wishes to fondle and caress the child, or in some way to busy herself in caring and fending for it. Seeing the child happily occupied in play, however, she is content to leave it alone for the moment. Slightly more energy has been liberated than the occasion demands, and the surplus, Menon tells us, is freely let off in smiles. Another, similar, example is the laughter of lovers when talking together.

But such pure laughter is rare. Man is a complex animal, and usually it is not a simple instinct that is brought into play, but a sentiment. A sentiment is defined in McDougall's terms as 'an organised system of emotional dispositions centred about the idea of some object'. Sentiments are built up as the result of experience: and, because a man may have many and varied experiences, it is possible for an object to become the central point of different sentiments.

When this happens, the object may give rise to contrary impulses. And this is the ideal situation for laughter. We have said that laughter occurs when an instinct is checked: but in fact the checking must be of a particular kind. If we are merely thwarted by an external obstacle, we will not laugh: we will feel resentful and will probably use our energy in struggling against the obstacle. The checking, then, must come from within ourselves. This will happen if we suddenly realize that the object which stimulated the instinct is not, after all, what we imagined it to be.

Laughter can result only from the action of two processes within ourselves: the impulse to activity or cognition and the check to that activity or re-cognition, the re-cognition operating in the reverse direction. There is, then, a conflict of two opposite impulses: the impulse to proceed and the impulse to draw back. A positive and negative current meet, so to say, and flash forth into sparks of laughter. As a result of the collision there is, as it were, a bursting-out of the energy and hearty spontaneous laughter arises, giving us as much satisfaction as if we had won our goal.

Menon does not explain why we should feel this great satisfaction. No doubt the release of thwarted energy may be regarded as a relief: but this seems hardly enough to explain the pleasure of laughter. On Menon's hypothesis, one would still expect some irritation or disappointment to remain.

This, however, is an incidental criticism. It is more serious that Menon does not give us enough examples to enable us to picture very clearly the situation he is describing. But let us vary his earlier examples a little. After all, mother love, though no doubt a primary instinct, can also be the basis of a sentiment. Let us suppose, then, that a mother finds her love checked by the recognition of hateful traits in her child, which exactly neutralizes her natural 'tender emotion'. Or suppose the lover finds himself forced to cry, like Catullus, 'Odi et amo.' Will either of them laugh?

Menon would probably explain that the opposition here is not complete: the original conative impulse is stronger than the new, neutralizing one. It therefore persists, though checked, and the result is pain and dissatisfaction.

Probably a better illustration would be something like this: The lover sees his lady approaching in the distance, and is suffused with a wave of 'tender emotion'. She comes nearer—and turns out to be someone else.

Here he possibly would laugh: and the situation exactly fulfils Menon's requirements about re-cognition. Moreover, it corresponds, in general outline, to a stock device of stage comedy—disguise. But can we say that the impulse has been checked by an opposite impulse? That would apply much better to Catullus. The point is simply that the emotion is found to be inappropriate.

Menon, of course, is speaking in terms of McDougall's psychology: and consequently considers that all activity is directed by conative impulses. McDougall is indeed to Menon what Freud is to Greig, and while Menon's instincts and integrations and so forth are never as far-fetched as Greig's phallic symbols, one sometimes feels that he is manipulating the facts to fit these preconceptions.

It is because laughter depends on the sentiments that Menon insists that it is subjective. Sentiments will obviously vary from person to person. A common background of experience will of course make for similar sentiments, and so for a certain amount of common laughter. That is what makes national humour, or professional humour, possible. But essentially humour is in ourselves, not in externals. It is best defined as a mental state: 'a conflict of perceptions or impulses'; and laughter as 'the natural expression and resolution of a mental conflict of a specific kind'. There is incongruity present, but the incongruity is not in the object: it is in ourselves. 'It is an incongruity between our present perception of the object and our previous knowledge of it.'

The most distinctive thing about humour is that it involves a change of standpoints or attitudes. The humorous mind must be capable of viewing an object first in one light and then in another: it must, then, be rich in varied experience. 'The man of greatest humour is he who has the most curious, observant and reflecting mind, who has a mind richly stored with experiences, whose mind is capable of this Puck-like alertness of movement, springing from point to point.'

This movement of the mind Menon calls 'hopping': and he points out that the change must be sudden, and must swing from one viewpoint to its direct opposite. A systematic, logical examination of the object, involving a continuous change of ground, is not enough: there must be a direct and violent opposition. This is the place of contrast in humour: but contrast by itself, like incongruity in itself, is not enough. It must be this particular type of incongruity.

Further, the opposition must be complete. If you shift your viewpoint to another, only slightly opposed to the first, the laughter is not whole-hearted. 'There is laughter, but there is also some kind of dissatisfaction according to the degree of unfulfilled instinctive activity.'

It is for this reason that vanity is the enemy of laughter. Our self-regarding sentiment is very strong: and few of us are prepared to develop those viewpoints which would oppose it. The self-assertive instinct 'can get opposition only from the region of the self-abasement instinct . . . If this latter is not sufficiently developed such impulses are rare . . . On the other hand, it is to be noticed that any very excessive development of the self-abasement instinct is also not a proper condition for laughter, for then the scope for opposition of impulses from the other region is necessarily limited. It is a well-known fact that religious saints, with their characteristic humility, often reveal but a poor sense of humour.'

Now, this theory of Menon's obviously does explain a good deal in humour which other theories tend to ignore. In our early analysis we placed a good deal of emphasis on 'attitude-mixing', and my own tendency (which may or may not be justi-fied by an objective survey of the facts) is to make this the basis of a theory of humour. Menon is describing the same phenomenon: and one reads on with great interest to see how he will apply it.

Unfortunately he does not apply it. Perhaps because he re-gards humour as subjective, he gives us very few examples, and no exhaustive account of the different types of humour. Instead he gives us a rather inconclusive analysis of Falstaff and one or two other characters in literature, and then goes off into a dis-cussion of tragedy and of æsthetics in general.

If we wish to see how this theory applies to our different classes of humour, then, we shall have to apply it ourselves with little or no help from Menon.

He does, as we have seen, refer to incongruity; and this is obviously his strongest point. Incongruity probably does mean that we are forced to view an object from two opposing stand-points: and that two opposite attitudes, or sentiments, do come into collision. Even here, however, we may doubt whether there is really a conative impulse which is neutralized by an opposing one.

As an example, consider the George Price drawing of a man lugging a grandfather clock to the watch-maker to be repaired. With an expression of extreme exasperation, he is saying: 'It goes "Hickory, Dickory, Dock," and then a damn mouse runs up it!' Opinions may differ about the cause of our laughter here. There is certainly an element of sheer, wild absurdity: but it is probably true to say that we have here the collision of two 'universes of discourse': the world of the nursery rhyme and the world of practical, everyday affairs. A precisely similar collision occurs in another drawing, by Charles Addams. Hansel and Gretel are gazing entranced at the lollipop house of the fairy tale. The picture might have been an illustration in a volume of the brothers Grimm except for one detail: the house has a sort of plaque on it inscribed with the details required by U.S. law to be printed on all packets of candy: 'Contains glu-cose, skim milk, oil of peppermint . . . .'

Now here we are undoubtedly forced to look at an object from two opposing view-points: and each view-point has its own proper background of sentiment. The house is, from one point of view, part of a fairy-tale, and so idyllic, whimsical, nostalgic, tender; from the other, it is an article of commerce, over which the makers will probably swindle us unless we are protected by law: our attitude is therefore prosaic, hard-headed, calculating, tough.

Menon could ask for no better illustration of his theory. But what are the conative impulses involved here? To what course of action would our instinct drive us if it had not been checked? Both attitudes are essentially contemplative. No doubt it can be claimed that our impulse is to indulge ourselves in the airy-fairy whimsical attitude: and that this is suddenly sharply checked, with a consequent release of emotional energy. But it must be admitted that this is only a hypothesis. We may grant that an emotion like fear may result in a definite predisposition to action: the action of running away; and that certain preparatory movements of the muscles will take place, and a certain amount of nervous energy be generated. But it is hard to see that the more complex emotional attitude involved in thinking about a fairy tale will have any effect on our muscles, or will involve any appreciable amount of energy. Of course, it may be said that all activities involve energy: but, in that case, the dissolution of the attitude would not involve a sudden release of energy in laughter. It may indeed be argued that the effort of grasping the implications of the changed attitude would involve just as much energy, if not more. That is no doubt why Menon insists that there is a special type of emotional energy. Any sudden dissolution of an emotion therefore makes an overflow of energy available. This theory cannot of course be disproved: and it has some plausibility. But it is as well to realize that its connection with conative impulses demanding definite physical action is somewhat remote: and that most of the attitudes dissolved in laughter do not seem to call for any particular physical action that can be specified.

This is not however a very damaging criticism: and Menon's theory stands up very well when applied to incongruity. The difficulty is to apply it to other types of humour; and particularly to derisive laughter.

Menon makes an ingenious but quite unconvincing attempt to explain malice in humour. He reminds us that laughter is often incomplete: because we are not always able to shift our minds to a completely opposite viewpoint. Usually the opposition is only partial.

Any instinctive activity checked rouses anger. When it is checked in the manner required for laughter it finds vent in laughter. But where there is only partial laughter, there is some dissatisfaction and anger consequent on the non-fulfilment of the activity. A part of the emotional energy dissolves itself into laughter; but a part remains. We saw how in ordinary life the chances for partial laughter are greater than those for complete laughter. Even in a well-filled mind, there is sometimes bound to be insufficient opposition. If this is so, anger and pain are bound to be in actual occurrence a frequent concomitant of laughter, and we can understand how Bain came to regard laughter as springing from malignity. He speaks of 'the inexhaustible pleasures of malignity,' as he calls it, and associates it with vituperation and ridicule. And of humour he remarks 'there is a kind of laughter that enters into the innocent pleasures of mankind; it still grows of the delight in malignity, which, however, is softened and redeemed in a variety of ways.' If by malignity we take Bain to mean anger and pain, he is right to a great extent; we cannot, however, admit that laughter springs from malignity or that malignity is always present in laughter, but that malignity is often found accompanying laughter may be admitted.

It is fairly obvious that the dissatisfaction which comes from a frustrated impulse is not the same as malignity, and certainly the whole of the derision theory cannot be disposed of so lightly. Menon quotes no examples to show that they are the same: but let us try to repair his omission.

When a lover rails bitterly at his former mistress, it is true enough that his original impulse has not been entirely neutralized. It still persists: and, because it is checked, the result is, as Menon says, 'pain and anger', and it is this pain and anger which causes the bitterness. But such railing, though it may be savagely satirical, is not usually funny. On the other hand, consider any of the more amusing shafts of satire, like Pope's

> The rest to some faint meaning make pretence,
> But Shadwell never deviates into sense

or Carey's acid comment on Ambrose Philips' nursery lyrics addressed to the infant Carteret:

Namby Pamby Pilli-pis
Rhimy-pimed on missy-mis
Tartaretta Tartaree
From the navel to the knee;
That her father's gracy-grace
Might give him a placy-place.

To neither of these is the application of Menon's formula
very obvious: but to both it can be made to apply without
much strain. Pope's couplet (which needs of course to be considered in its context) does depend on the adoption of a viewpoint exactly opposite to the usual one. Dullness is the supreme
virtue, and sense a deviation. But we do not completely accept
this view: indeed, we do not really accept it at all. When we
find that this novel set of values enables a poet to be praised,
we laugh with malicious pleasure: malicious, because we are
fully conscious that praise on these terms is really blame. This
is so because the original viewpoint persists. But does this
mean that our malice is really anger and pain at bad poetry,
which frustrates our real impulse, which is towards truth and
beauty? I think this is the best case that can be made for
Menon's contention, but it is still inadequate. Of course, whenever we enjoy scoring off anyone, something about them will
probably have annoyed us, and to that extent frustrated our
impulses. But this can hardly explain the peculiar malicious
pleasure which satire does give us. It is really much more
plausible to suppose, with Hobbes, that our own vanity has been
gratified by an implied comparison; or, with Freud, that we
enjoy a momentary relief from the burden of feeling, or at least
professing, unflagging goodwill towards our neighbours.

As for Carey, here again we have an odd mingling of view-
points, or sentiments. On the one hand, the sugary silliness of
Philips' manner and metre; on the other, the hard-headed cal-
culation which is alleged to inspire him. So far, so good, and
probably in accordance with Menon. But what precisely are
the conflicting impulses? Is the malice here really only anger
and pain because the interested motive is after all transparent,
the hypocrisy not entirely successful?

Furthermore, how would Menon explain the low comedian
who falls off a ladder?

To these questions we get no answers. Menon has indeed a
chapter which begins, encouragingly: 'It remains for us to con-

sider some of those forms of humour so-called — vituperation, ridicule, satire, sarcasm and wit.' But he is content to remind us that the modern reader can get satisfaction out of the *Letters of Junius,* without sharing the author's antipathies. Like Eastman, he apparently regards the humour as residing entirely in the technique. The pleasure of malice is something additional and extraneous, and the humour can persist without it.

We have already seen that there is some force in this argument, but that it is not entirely convincing. Against Menon's version of it, it might be retorted, first, that the human animal is so constituted that he takes pleasure in seeing anybody done in the eye, even a complete stranger. Perhaps that is what the Junius example really proves. Secondly, that when satire has endured, it has usually been because its application was universal. We skip those parts of Aristophanes that can only be understood by reference to learned notes: we enjoy the gibes at women, pedants and warmongers, none of whom are yet extinct.

Although he adopts McDougall's general psychology, Menon disagrees with his theory of laughter, that it is an antidote to sympathy. Laughter, says Menon, *may* serve as an antidote to sympathy, because it is an antidote to all pain, for all pain is due to unchecked instinctive activity.

The wiser a man, the greater are his consolations in pain. But more than consolation, it is pure relief and satisfaction if there is laughter. But it is not generally possible for a man to get round to the other point of view in every case. Man's capacity for knowledge and experience seems to be limited, and to that extent the obstacle to our fulfilment of the instinctive activity stands immovable and we suffer . . . . that sometimes in actual life we are not able to get rid of our pain through laughter is no evidence that laughter is only a device against minor mishaps.

There seems a confusion here. On the one hand Menon argues that all pain is due to unchecked instinctive activity, and on the other that it is due to the checking of instinctive activity. What he means, apparently, is that when an instinct is frustrated by an external obstacle, we can console ourselves by adopting the point of view which checks the instinct itself. But, even then, laughter is hardly an antidote to pain. It is a by-product of the antidote — the means of using up the surplus energy left over from the original instinct. But the point for us here is that Menon entirely ignores the facts which make

McDougall's view plausible: that small misfortunes are often the objects of laughter.

Menon probably means that all misfortunes are really the thwarting of some instinct. Through sympathy, this applies to the misfortunes of others as well as to our own. Hence we are led, in both cases, to find the opposing viewpoint which will check the instinct involved. This sounds all right on paper, but it is not easy to see how it applies to the throwing of custard pies or to slipping on banana-skins. Moreover, if this is Menon's meaning, he has reversed both McDougall and the facts by making our own misfortunes the primary cause of laughter, the misfortunes of others secondary. On McDougall's view, we need most of our sorrow for our own mishaps, and so resist the demands of sympathy except in real disaster. Otherwise, in a cruel world, living would be intolerable. But if laughter is the antidote to pain itself, and not merely to sympathetic pain, it is a little odd that we should apply it so readily to the misfortunes of others, and so reluctantly to our own. The reason may be, as Menon suggests, simply that we are not very wise in these matters. But it is more plausible to suppose, with McDougall, that self-pity is a luxury and pity for others rather a nuisance.

It will be necessary for us to consider how far 'mental hopping', or attitude-mixing, can explain our other main classes of humour, but perhaps we had better not father our analysis on to Menon. After all, we have already put quite a lot into his mouth: and, since he gives us no guidance, it is a little futile to speculate how he would explain nonsense, or indecency, or comic vice, or the god's-eye view. Probably none of them would give him as much trouble as derision.

Menon's great merit is that he does seize on one fact about humour that has been somewhat neglected: that it involves a conflict of attitudes. His attempt to explain this in terms of McDougall's psychology is not altogether convincing: and his great defect is that he does not tell us how his theory applies to the many different types of humour.

Part III
SYNTHESIS

19

THE INAPPROPRIATE

W E HAVE completed our survey: without, it may seem, much to show for it. We have found strength and weakness in every theory. We can make out a case for all of them: we are satisfied with none of them. Must we leave the whole matter at that? With a wiseacre's nod and the irritating verdict: 'There is much to be said on both sides'?

It would, as a matter of fact, be the wisest thing to do. But the impulse to tidy up the loose ends becomes irresistible. Let us see, then, if we can fit all our odd data about humour into one single, coherent theory of our own.

Throughout this study we have tried to be objective: but we have nevertheless shown some fondness for one particular mode of explanation. We have returned continually to the linking of disparates, to the collision of different mental spheres, to the obtrusion into one context of what belongs in another. We have found this to be an element in many kinds of humour: perhaps because it was there, perhaps because we were, consciously or otherwise, looking for it. But let us see if we can build a theory of humour round this concept. If we want a convenient single word for it, we may call it inappropriateness.

But the inappropriate, though the central part of our theory, is not its starting point. One of the difficulties we have found in our subject is that its scope is not clearly defined. On the fringes of humour there is much else that cannot quite be excluded, and yet does not quite belong there. The quaint, the grotesque, the whimsical—are these forms of humour or approximations to humour?

If they are approximations, it may be because they contain an element which, without being the whole of humour, is always present in it and is an essential part of it. I think this is the element of freshness: what Sully calls novelty and oddity. Humour is plainly not just oddity: and things may be fresh and novel without being funny. But novelty and oddity is always in humour, or at any rate almost always. Popular speech distinguishes between 'funny peculiar' and 'funny ha-ha': which suggests that the two are distinct, but somehow connected.

I would suggest, then, that one stage in the development of humour (proto-humour, if you like) is our sense of delight in what is new and fresh. Children show this most clearly. Any healthy child is intensely interested in the world which is unfolded before him by the mere act of living in it. That is why he asks so many questions. But that is not all. Every time he meets some new part of this world — a new animal, a new word even — or has some fresh bodily sensation — riding on a pony, sliding down a hill — he is quite likely to shout with excited laughter.

But, even for a child, the world does not continue to be exhilaratingly fresh. A pattern of living is soon imposed upon him: and, even the child, great as his zest may be, eventually comes to feel this as monotonous. Along with the desire for fresh experience (the obverse of the medal) is the desire to escape from the tedium of the over-familiar. This is doubtless a simplified account of what actually happens in the mental development of the child. I am not putting it forward as a theory about child psychology. I merely wish to disentangle two familiar and universal states of mind, which do manifest themselves fairly early, and which I believe to be important in the development of humour.

For each of these desires is gratified by a particular type of rather elementary humour. On the one hand we have the exploring of new avenues, the opening up of fresh possibilities. Making faces and playing with words are both examples of this. To make a face is to explore the possibilities of an odd and somewhat limited medium. Other bodily contortions may be indulged in for the same reason. The child's desire to find out all that can be done with his own body is of course often an intent and serious purpose, as when he is learning to walk. Even here the freshness of the experience may exhilarate him to the point of laughter. But, as has been so often noted, a serious purpose usually drives out laughter. It is when he is 'playing' —i.e., trying new experiments just to see where they will lead him—that he will laugh most.

It is the same with words. A child will try seriously enough to master language, to put words together into sentences. But he will also play with words, distort them, mispronounce them, try out new combinations. He may turn a word upside down, like 'dillydaffy'. He will be delighted at the varied possibilities of the same vocable, as in jingles like 'a noisy noise annoys an oyster'. From this he will go to elementary puns. It is not always easy to tell when a child is serious in his word-play. Kimmins quotes a three-year old who, told that he was going to Jersey, asked: 'Do the people wear jerseys there?' He made much the same comment on Kew Gardens: 'Do they grow cucumbers there?' Both these may well have been serious enquiries: but there is no doubt that they could also (probably at a later age) be conscious attempts at humour. Compare the popular riddle about Mississippi borrowing Missouri's New Jersey, etc. Exploring the possibilities of words develops side by side with the attempt to master them, and is no doubt a necessary part of the process.

But in all this we can also detect the other element: the desire to escape from monotony. Making a face is both a bodily exercise and a means of varying a too familiar sight. Much the same is true of distorting or mispronouncing words. It is almost impossible to keep the two wholly separate. Parents sometimes induce children to eat their porridge by encouraging them to make a game out of it. The milk becomes a sea surrounding an island of porridge: the child watches with interest the new shapes that form as he demolishes the island spoonful by spoonful, and the white seas pour in upon it. Here we see both processes at work: the delight in a new game, and the transformation of an old material.

Much childish make-believe is of the same type. The child who indulged in etymological speculations about Jersey is also recorded as taking part in the following dialogue:—

> 'Won't you give me a kiss?'
> 'I haven't the new ones in yet.'
> 'Haven't you any left over from last night?'
> 'Only one or two and they are rather dirty and have
>   holes in them.'

Here we have a quite conscious and playful attempt to carry over into one sphere what is appropriate to another. The child knows quite well that kisses are not merchandise: but it amuses him to see how far he can apply to them the expressions he has overheard in the draper's shop. Here he is playing with ideas rather than words: but once again he is both exploring new possibilities and varying the familiar domestic ritual of kissing

mother. But there is also a third element here: and one that
grows naturally and spontaneously from the other two. This is
the linking of disparates: the importing into one sphere, of ideas
which belong in another. This too, as we have seen, has an
important part to play in humour. And here again it is not
always easy to tell when this linking is conscious make-believe
and when it is serious speculation. If you treat a toadstool as
a fairy's dinner-plate, or rain as angel's tears, you may be a
primitive animist groping towards an explanation of the universe, or you may be A. A. Milne being whimsical. A child can
fill either role, or both. The point of departure occurs when the
two ideas are *felt* as disparates. In exploring new possibilities
it is natural enough to apply to one sphere what has been found
in another. A very young child may suppose, naturally
enough, that animals talk. But after he has learnt that they do
not, he may still find it fun to suppose that they could. He is
still 'exploring an avenue', still investigating possibilities, but
playfully: and a powerful incentive is the desire to escape from
the familiar facts which he knows too well. We can see all
this clearly enough in the fairy tale.

It may be objected that we have now got right away from
humour. But we are still dealing only with the foundations,
with proto-humour. And at least it can be said that this kind
of make-believe, if not exactly funny, is usually considered
'quaint' or 'whimsical'. It belongs, in fact, on the fringes of
humour.

Quaintness or whimsy passes over into humour proper when
our attention is focused on the difference between the two
spheres which are linked. The art of the fairy tale is to create
an atmosphere in which it seems natural for dogs to talk, or
beanstalks to reach to Heaven. The art of humour is to obtrude
these disparities suddenly, unexpectedly, so that the contrast is
evident. This is why shock and surprise have been stressed so
much in all theories of humour.

We can explain a good deal of humour without going any
further than this. The linking of disparates, with due attention
to the element of contrast, is in itself a good formula for humour.
One application of it is seen in a recent comedy *Arsenic and
Old Lace*. This turns on the notion that a couple of old maids,
conventionally sweet, kindly and innocent, should also be homicidal maniacs. The notion must be made plausible: an atmos-

phere must be built up in which the audience believes in this odd conjunction, at least superficially. But the plausibility must not go too far: the audience must not believe too deeply, or we would have a pathological study and not a comedy. Given the necessary minimum of credibility, the emphasis is all on the contrast. Notice that we have present here all three of our elements: the exploring of new possibilities, the breaking away from the familiar stereotype of the maiden aunt, the abrupt collision of two utterly different concepts.

As further examples of the inappropriate, consider these three jokes, taken practically at random from the same number of the *New Yorker* (4 May 1944).

(a) A lascivious Peter Arno business man is pursuing a luscious Peter Arno typist round a desk in his office. Wastepaper basket and stool have been overturned: obviously she has been keeping him at bay with the desk between them, for some time. He is saying heatedly: 'Young woman, do you know my time is worth thirty dollars a minute?'

(b) A beaming wife is watching an obviously reluctant husband shovel the snow away from the front door. Gazing round at the snow-clad scene, she says brightly: 'Like fairyland, isn't it, dear?'

(c) Two clergymen are talking. The caption reads: 'Tell me frankly, Doctor, do you find that your prayers bring home the bacon?'

It is possible to find other elements in each of these: sexual references, the misfortunes of others, the unmasking of pretences. But apart altogether from these, each joke turns on an inappropriate sentiment: one which, while relevant to some features of the situation, is very far from fitting the situation as a whole.

But in order to see how varied are the applications of this formula, we must realise how much of our thinking really is controlled by stereotypes and conventions. The maiden aunt is one such stereotype. Popular fiction presents us with many others: the ruthless capitalist, the comic curate, the absent-minded professor, and so on. Consciously or unconsciously, our judgments of real people tend to be influenced by these lay figures. The newspapers find it easier to evoke these ready-made figures in our minds than to describe real people. When Lord Nuffield visited New Zealand, the newspapers published descriptions of him which were really mere evocations of the Napoleon of commerce of the popular success story. One report, praising his boundless energy, said that he seldom slept more than three or four hours a night. This drew forth an immediate denial from Lord Nuffield, who protested indignantly that he was 'completely normal', and needed as much sleep as anybody else. But it is seldom that millionaires, generals, politicians, film stars or royal personages bother to destroy the images which are created in their names.

Where the stereotype is less flattering, of course, the victim often has no opportunity of protesting. Richard Wright's novel *Native Son* is a careful study of the mind of a negro murderer. When he appears in court the newspapers feature the story: they all describe him as 'brutal', 'sub-human', 'degenerate', with physical appearance to match: hulking body, narrow forehead, thick, powerful, foreshortened arms, and so forth. The reader, who knows something of the true inwardness of the story, realizes how inadequate these descriptions really are.

Some of this distortion can be explained as what is now commonly called propaganda, i.e. lying. But this is too simple an explanation. Generally it merely means that the reporter follows the path of least resistance. It is easy to conjure up a stereotype, difficult to describe reality. More simply still, it is quicker to write in hack phrases. And hack phrases exist because conventional stereotypes exist.

Moreover, we all tend to see what we look for. There are a whole series of popular magazines which claim that the stories they contain have all really happened. Perhaps they have. Nevertheless they are, in a sense, more untrue than good fiction ever is. The facts may be there, but the interpretation is always in terms of popular mythology. The characters are represented as conventional stereotypes: they feel the crude, unsubtle emotions of popular melodrama. The stories may be told in good faith: but it takes some subtlety and insight to know what is really going on in life, even to oneself. By forgetting some facts and highlighting others, all of us tend to impose on life the concepts we have gained from films, books and current mythology.

It is not merely characters which are stereotyped in this way. We all of us have our notions of the 'correct' behaviour in a given situation: some of it, of course has been carefully instilled by parents and teachers. It applies not merely to outward behaviour, but also to our feelings. It is 'right' to be grateful here, humble there, uplifted in this situation, sorrowful in that. Nobody would ever fall in love, it has been said, if he hadn't read about it. This does not mean of course that he would not have sexual desire: it does mean that his emotional attitude to his desire and to the object of his desire would be quite different.

Hack phrases crystallize these conventional attitudes: often enough they are mere symbols which serve to evoke them. And hack phrases have always been a happy hunting ground for humour. By altering them slightly it is possible to jolt the reader right out. of the conventional response: to introduce a discordant element which destroys the whole attitude. 'The youth of to-day', says Oscar Wilde, 'are quite monstrous. They have absolutely no respect for dyed hair.' Here we have a familiar sentiment, suggesting a familiar train of ideas: the proper subordination of youth to age, the respect due to wisdom and experience, and so forth; and, by the alteration of a single word, a totally different train of thought is evoked. The result is a collision, very unsettling to the man of fixed ideas.

In rather a different way, P. G. Wodehouse gains most of his effects by the deft manipulation of hack phrases. I think this explains why Wodehouse keeps his appeal, in spite of stereotyped characters, and mechanically contrived plots. His charm is in his style. And his style consists almost entirely in chivvying clichés.

A very simple example is seen in this sentence: 'He may not have been actually disgruntled, but he was certainly far from gruntled.' This is an adult example of the process we have called exploring possibilities. It does not go beyond this first stage of humour.

But Wodehouse's favourite trick is to mix the cliché with the most irreverent slang. This entirely destroys the atmosphere of lush sentiment or false heroics which the cliché trails along with it.

If part of Wodehouse's purpose is to debunk the hack phrase, it is a very small and incidental part, and one which hardly enters the consciousness of most of his readers. It is enough for them that this odd mixture of styles is somehow funny.

For us it illustrates the general point that humour depends on a fixed background of conventional beliefs, attitudes, behaviour. Humour upsets the pattern by abruptly introducing something inappropriate.

But it must not be wholly inappropriate. There must be some

hidden propriety as well. This may go no further than mere plausibility, as in *Arsenic and Old Lace*. There is no suggestion here that sweet old maids are really homicidal maniacs at bottom: the author is merely exploring, 'for fun', the unexpected possibilities, the odd contrasts, that might arise if they were. But often enough the humorist may be drawing attention to the inadequacy of the popular picture: to those aspects of reality which have been suppressed in order to paint it. We have already seen that Bernard Shaw is an exponent of this type of humour. He sees the whole romantic view of life in all its manifestations as grossly unreal; and he is continually exposing it by dragging to light those inconvenient facts which just do not fit in.

The high heroic attitude to life usually depends on the suppression of inconvenient details. The king, in the *New Yorker* drawing, stands at the balcony in full ceremonial robes, taking the salute as the troops march past. It is a solemn, impressive moment. The king is observed to say something in low tones to a member of his suite. Some comment on the fine bearing of the men, perhaps? Some historic aphorism on the glory of the empire? Actually he is saying: 'All I have on underneath this is my underwear.' Shaw's type of humour insists on dragging to light the underwear beneath the robes of state. It exists; it is there, it is part of the picture: but it disrupts the pattern, because it destroys the pose.

There is another route through which criticism, or satire, may creep into humour. We have said that humour focuses attention on contrast. But when our emotional attitude to two things is in marked contrast, it is usually because we find one 'great', or 'beautiful', or 'sacred' — of high value — and the other 'low', or 'common' or 'vulgar' — of low value. Hence we have Bain defining humour as 'degradation', and Spencer defining it as 'descending incongruity'. But while humour generally links the high and the low, it need not always do so. Consider Sully's example of a girl climbing a mountain in high-heeled shoes. You may regard mountaineering as a healthy ennobling sport, and fashionable shoes as frivolous, unhealthy, and probably immoral. Or you may regard high-heeled shoes as elegant and womanly, and mountain boots as clumsy, boorish and unsexing. But most people would be content to say that the boots look clumsy and ugly in a ball-room, and the shoes tawdry and insufficient on a mountain-side. The point is not that one is intrinsically degraded and the other ennobling, but that each has its appropriate sphere.

It is true, however, that there is nothing wildly funny about this conjunction. And this is precisely because our emotions are not deeply involved. Where they are, it is usually because our system of values has been outraged. Something low in the scale has been found to be inseparably linked with something high. Often enough this does imply a degradation.

But it is not always the higher of the pair that is degraded. Consider the story of the American business man who offered the Pope a million dollars if he would substitute the phrase 'Shell Oil' for 'Amen' in all Catholic services. Here we have the linking of two spheres which are poles apart in the current system of values. But, if anyone is criticized in the story, it is the business man who is unable to see the difference between his sordid sphere of activity and the rarefied atmosphere in which the church operates.

On the other hand, H. G. Wells, in *The Sleeper Awakes,* tells of churches with placards outside: 'Souls Saved in Sixty Seconds. Special Lunch-Hour Service for Business Men.' Here, of course, it is the church which is degrading itself.

There are, then, two types of satire. In both, something is represented as clashing with a particular system of values. But this may mean, either that the system of values exposes the inadequacy of the discordant element, or that the system itself is exposed. The business man does not realize the difference between his outlook and the Church's: so much the worse for him. But Wells, by contriving exactly the same collision of values, suggests that there really is no difference; that the church is a business too. Of course, we may say that here the church has departed from true religion; from the system of values it exists to uphold. Something of that sort is always implied, even when the values themselves are attacked: there must always be an appeal to a 'higher' code.

It is quite common criticism of *Punch* that it laughs at the foreigner who shoots a fox, but that it does not laugh at the greater absurdity of the hunting tradition itself. This brings out very clearly the difference between the two types of satire. It also explains why humour may be either conservative or radical in its effects.

We have said that relief from monotony is always one element in humour. With the second, or radical type, this takes
the more definite form of relief from restraint, or inhibition.
Any code of values may be felt as irksome. This applies
especially, of course, to moral codes: but it may be true even, for
instance, of aesthetic ones. Free verse and modernistic art rouse
quite as much enthusiasm and exhilaration in their own sphere
as the revolt of a Samuel Butler or a Bernard Shaw in theirs.
I am not suggesting, of course, that any revolt against any
system of values is in itself funny. It can be used as a vehicle
for humour in the way we have already discussed. The point
is that any attack on established values will exhilarate those
who find the values oppressive. And when the attack is made
by means of satire, this exhilaration will fuse with and heighten
the specifically humorous emotion. That is why it is often difficult to disentangle the satire from the humour.

Take a sustained satire like *Jonathan Wild*. Here the actions
of a highwayman are described in mock admiration, in the language usually bestowed on generals or statesmen. The humour
consists in the linking of disparates: in the skill with which the
phrases associated with a conventionally honourable sphere are
made to fit a totally dishonourable one. Over and above this
is the inescapable conclusion that the two spheres are not
really different after all. This heightens our enjoyment: but
it would be possible to use much the same device for different
ends; and it would still be funny, though perhaps not so funny.

> Many a stately home he's entered,
> But, with unobtrusive tact,
> He has ne'er, in paying visits,
> Called attention to the fact.

F. ANSTEY

Here again larceny is described in innocent, if not positively
laudable terms: but the effect is quite different. There is no
attack on any system of values.

How does this differ from Eastman's view, that point is something extraneous added to humour: a concession to adult lack
of playfulness? There is an important difference. On our
theory the satire rises naturally and inevitably from the
humour. Humour is inappropriateness (though not all inappropriateness is humour): but one particular kind of inappropriate-

ness will inevitably raise doubt about a code of values. The humour and the satire can be distinguished in theory, for the purpose of analysis; they cannot be distinguished in practice. And it by no means follows that pointless humour is the best and 'purest'.

Relief from restraint is most apparent in sexual jokes, because here the restraint is recognized as onerous even by those who approve of it. Moreover, the code forbids, not only the act itself, but any mention of it. Almost any sexual reference, then, is in itself a release from restraint. The typical smutty joke consists in twisting an innocent remark so as to convey a sexual reference. Since there is always, in conventional thought, a wide gulf fixed between the sexual and the non-sexual, this in itself is a linking of disparates. But the joke is better if it is not merely the innocent (i.e., non-sexual) remark that is twisted, but the positively pious (i.e., anti-sexual). That is why clergy-men frequently figure in smutty stories.

Here, then, we may have relief from restraint without an actual attack on the code itself. But often enough, of course, the code is attacked. Since the attitude demanded by the code is highly artificial, this is a tempting field for the device of obtruding the inconvenient facts which convention disregards. There is, however, a wide difference between the humour of smoking-room stories, which are enjoyed often enough by staunch upholders of conventional morality, and satire which implies the inadequacy of those conventions. The admirers of each type often regard the other as immoral.

But relief from restraint is by no means confined to sex. As Freud saw, inhibitions just as strong may surround a natural propensity to malice. Any frankly spiteful or catty remark may be greeted with the same sort of half-shamed laughter as a reference to sex. It is felt as inappropriate, because it does conflict with propriety. But the laughter will be louder if it is directed against a parent, a brother or sister, a husband or wife, or some other person whom, it is felt, we 'should' love or respect. Any such remark may cause laughter, just as any unveiled mention of sex may cause laughter. But it will not be felt as witty so long as it remains a simple insult. The typical malicious joke is an apparently innocent remark which con-tains a secret barb: or, better still, an insult masquerading as a compliment. Sheridan's *School for Scandal* provides a host of examples. The mere spectacle of a group of backbiting gossips is funny, simply in itself; but the loudest laughter is reserved for Mrs. Candour, whose pretended defence of the victims always turns out to be the sharpest thrust.

Freud was wrong in supposing that sex and malice are the only inhibitions released in humour. Any frank revelation of natural emotion may be funny, if it conflicts with the accepted code.

> I'm tired of Love: I'm still more tired of Rhyme
> But Money gives me pleasure all the time.
>
> H. BELLOC

There is no particular reason why that couplet should be funny except that it is felt to be an ignoble, an unfitting sentiment. Frank admission of cowardice, as Eastman points out, is another case in point.

But, here again, the admission of ignoble sentiments is funniest when it is somehow extracted from a profession of more than usual virtue. The hypocrite has always been a comic figure. And this is not necessarily due to the bolstering of our own self-esteem. The unmasking of any pretence, even an innocent one, is likely to be funny. This is probably the real reason why the audience laughs at any contretemps on the stage. The real situation has suddenly emerged from beneath the elaborate pretence. If the demands of morality and convention do not furnish enough poses to be punctured, the comic writer provides artificial situations in which the characters must maintain a pretence. The man who dresses as a woman, or vice versa, the servant who masquerades as his master, and the like, constitute the commonest of comic devices. The situation calls for one type of behaviour, the man's real character for another: this is the formula for humour.

But the formula can be applied without the need of such artificial situations. For any man's progress through life is likely to be a series of poses. The most honest among us cannot hope to avoid them. André Maurois tells us that this universal human trait is one of the greatest problems of the biographer:—

But further, even if we confine our attention to those periods for which we have a diary, how are we to be sure that the diary exactly represented the mind of the man who wrote it? Cer-

tain diaries are written with an eye to posterity; the author
adopts a definite attitude in his writing, and complacently anticipates the effect which his attitude will produce upon the
reader. Even when the diary is honestly not intended to be
read, the writer is very often posing to himself. He has visual-
ised a certain attitude, he finds it pleasing, and he experiences
an aesthetic pleasure in exaggerating it. Every memorialist is
an author, whether he wishes it or not; the ego which he has
established on his writing-paper becomes a separate entity; he
contemplates it at a distance, sometimes with horror, sometimes
with admiration, but in both cases with an aesthetic detachment which gives many diaries a high literary value, but at the
same time completely destroys their value as psychological
documents . . . I should say much the same about correspondence and about conversations reported by witnesses . . . They
are almost always contradictory; all men and women present
very different appearances of themselves to other people. The
Shelley who writes to Godwin is a different creature from the
Shelley who writes to Miss Hitchener or to Hogg. The Byron
who writes to Lady Melbourne is a cynic; the Byron who talks
with Lady Blessington is almost a sentimentalist.

It has been said that in any dialogue there are six participants: there is A as he appears to himself, A as he appears to
B, and A as he really is; and there are the corresponding B's.
This is a much richer situation than any artificial stage mix-up.
There is room here for any amount of misunderstanding, for
the wildest crossing of purposes. And always there is the
shattering of stereotypes, the puncturing of poses, conscious or
unconscious, which comes with the intrusion of inconvenient
facts.

What we have called the god's-eye view consists in seeing
these discrepancies between the real man, the real facts in the
situation, and the men and the facts as they appear to themselves and each other. But this, it may be objected, is also
the material of tragedy. The difference is that in tragedy we
see from the point of view of the characters: see *from* it, where
in comedy we only see it. In tragedy, that is to say, we share
the aims and feelings of the characters: their emotions seem
to us real and important. When they are frustrated by the
harsh, unaccommodating facts, we share with them their despair and disillusion. In comedy we understand and probably
sympathize with the characters: but we never fully identify

ourselves with them, because we are always conscious of a gulf
between their view of life and the facts. This is, I think, the
truth in Bergson's view that the comic character never quite
adapts himself to the infinite flux of reality.

Let us now summarize our conclusions so far.

(a) Humour, we said, consists in its initial stage in *exploring
fresh possibilities*.

Examples: Whately explores the data about Napoleon with
the object of showing that he is a myth. The fun lies in seeing
how far this odd premise can be made to fit the facts. This is
a sophisticated, complex example with an added element of
satire. But the same process can be seen in any pun, even a
very weak one. When a child says: 'I want a muslin dress'
and her brother replies: 'Yes, you do want muzzlin'', he is not
merely trying to be rude. He is also exploring the possibilities
of words, of twisting their obvious meaning into another, more
exciting one. However wearisome it may be in adults, this
sort of word-play is a sign of mental alertness in a child.

(b) Inseparable from this is the desire for *relief from monotony*.

Examples: The twisting of hack phrases, where the familiarity
of the expression adds to the pleasure of exploring new possibilities. Nonsense in all its forms is the most obvious example.

(c) Both (a) and (b) nearly always involve the *linking of
disparates*. The fresh application of a familiar word or phrase
also means that two remote spheres of thought can be connected.

Examples: Children's riddles show this in its simplest form.
'Why is my pig called Maud? Because she *will* come into the
garden.'

At a more adult level, we have George Price's drawing of the
insect exterminator explaining the mysteries of his craft to the
housewife who has called him in: 'Their first reaction is one of
fright and hysteria. Then a strange apathy seems to seize
them and they lose all will to live.'

(d) But this simple device can have disruptive effects on
our whole complex of thoughts and feelings. We all of us prac-

tice a mental compartmentalism: we sort out the facts of our environment into different mental compartments, and decide that a particular attitude or emotion is appropriate to each. The linking of disparates may mean the shattering of this orderly system. We then have *attitude-mixing* or *universe-changing*.

Examples: The drawing just described is a mild example. The disparates linked here are the trade of the bug-exterminator and the attitude of the psychologist. The point is that one *could* be applied, logically enough, to the other. What stands in the way is not so much the facts of the situation as the views we hold about the insect-exterminator's place in society and the cockroach's place in the universe. But this is a mild example, because our emotions are not deeply involved.

The mental partitions are broken down much more violently in a work like *Jonathan Wild*, where the language commonly used of generals and statesmen is shown to apply equally to highwaymen and pickpockets. Parody and the mock-heroic apply the same device to literature.

(e) *Satire*. The linking of disparates has led us to satire, because part of our enjoyment is the criticism which is nearly always implicit in the comparison. But this criticism may be of two kinds:—

(i) *Conservative satire*. Here two disparates are shown to be linked in some unsuspected way: but the linking only brings out the utter disparity between the two in all other respects. This confirms the rightness of the code of values which insists that the two should be kept in different mental compartments. This explains why humour often preserves social institutions against change.

Examples: A simple example is the traveller's tale of the black king who proudly receives European visitors in morning-coat, top-hat, and bare feet. Here the linking of the two civilizations serves to emphasise the real discrepancy between them.

All humour which depends on foreign or lower-class accents, on the inadequacy of the new-rich when attempting to conform to unaccustomed social conventions, or on the vice which is laughed at and not with, is of this type.

(ii) *Radical satire*. But, as we have seen, attitude-mixing often casts doubts upon the validity of the compartmentalism upon which it depends.

Examples: 'African women wear rings in their noses: European women in their ears.' This can be regarded as a companion-piece to the first example above. It also links two civilizations, but its moral is that the two are really alike, after all.

Consider, too, the story of the small boy left in the play-room of a department store while his parents shopped. When they were ready to go, he refused to get off the rocking-horse on which he was mounted. It was time for the store to close, but he still would not leave. His parents, the floor-walkers, the managing director, cajoled and bribed him, but in vain. Finally a young man in the crowd said to the child's father: 'May I try? I have made a special study of child psychology.' 'Please do,' said the father. Whereupon the young man stepped forward and whispered in the child's ear. The boy immediately slid off the horse and said, quite quietly: 'Take me home, please, Daddy.' Afterwards the young man was asked if he would mind revealing the magic formula. 'Not at all,' he said. 'I just said: "Get off that horse, you little ——— or I'll knock your block off!"'

The disparates here are the concept of 'child psychology' as a magic, painless method of controlling children, and the old, unscientific methods of discipline. But, as the effect of linking them is to break down the special aura surrounding child psychology, this is radical satire in our sense, even though the moral is in the normal sense, positively reactionary.

'Radical' and 'conservative' here, of course, have nothing to do with any particular political doctrine. Satire is radical if its effect is to break down a particular code or 'norm'; conservative if its effect is to reinforce it.

(f) Since radical satire is aimed at the current code of values which produces compartmentalism, it gives us the added pleasure of *release from restraint*. And in much humour this becomes the chief element. It naturally takes different forms according to the particular restraint thrown off. The chief of these are:—

(i) *Sexual jokes*. Almost any mention of sex is forbidden by current convention. Hence the linking of the 'innocent' and the sexual is a particular kind of linking of disparates which has for us a special emotional significance.

Example: A young business man is interviewing a prospective typist. 'Your credentials are quite satisfactory,' he says. 'In fact, I'm afraid you may be too highly qualified for a small office like mine. What salary would you expect?'

'Three pounds a week.'

'Oh, that's all right. I'll pay you three pounds a week with pleasure.'

'Oh—er—with pleasure, five pounds a week.'

This is the common device of twisting a familiar phrase so as to obtain an unsuspected meaning. It only differs from other examples of the kind in that sex is, for our society, a subject apart. There is no very direct attack on the code of values here, except the implication that the correct and innocent relation between typist and employer may become an illicit and guilty one. Some such innuendo is behind most smutty jokes.

Compare this, however, with Bernard Shaw's play, *Overruled*, in which the humour turns on a contrast between natural human behaviour and the conduct demanded by convention. This is a direct attack on the code, and a different type of attitude-mixing.

(ii) *Malicious jokes.* In the same way, there is a special pleasure in the twisting of meaning so as to reveal a hidden insult. Rudeness is, like lust, a human propensity which we must curb in the interests of an ordered society.

Example: The playwright in Sheridan's *Critic* says bitterly of a colleague: 'The fellow is an arrant plagiarist. He has stolen the best things from my tragedy and put them in his comedy.'

Here an apparent attack on another conceals a much more damning attack on oneself. The peculiar appeal of this lies in a well-understood fact in the human situation: that we are all constantly engaged in keeping our ends up, magnifying our virtues, concealing our defects. Giving oneself away is therefore a special type of inappropriate behaviour affording the onlookers special pleasure, in which repressed malice certainly plays a part. More obvious examples are the insults masquerading as compliments, which have already been referred to.

(iii) *Any other irksome pretences.* There are other improper and therefore inappropriate emotions besides lust and malice.

'Lord' George Sanger, after describing how he made money out of a particularly brazen hoax, which in our more squeamish time would probably land him in prison on a charge of false pretences, makes this comment: 'There have been times when I have been sad about the deception I practised in connection with these wolves, but a liver pill has invariably restored my equanimity.'

This sort of brazenness is funny.

Other examples are Belloc's couplet, already quoted, and these lines from Gilbert:

> Now I adore that girl with passion tender,
> And could not yield her with a ready will,
>> Or her allot,
>> If I did not
> Adore myself with passion tenderer still!

(g) *Unmasking.* But here again, humour can be conservative or radical in its implications. The contrast between conventional and 'natural' behaviour may be turned to the disadvantage, not of convention, but of the man who is unable to live up to it.

The self-revealed coward may, by his frankness, make us realize that none of us is really as indifferent to danger as convention demands. But if he reveals his cowardice inadvertently, we will laugh at him and not with him. In either case we are laughing at the inappropriateness of the behaviour: at the contrast between what actually happens and what is supposed to happen.

(h) This simple unmasking passes over into the *god's-eye view* of life. The more subtle comedy of character, we decided, depends on the discrepancies between the real facts of the human situation and the innumerable poses in which we all indulge. And not poses merely: there is the whole interplay between human beings driven by different emotions, different aims, different temperaments.

Laughter occurs when two attitudes come into sudden conflict. Normally the two attitudes are our own. We have, as it were, one attitude reserved for objects of class A, and another reserved for class B. Humour involves demonstrating that A and B are really the same class.

The god's-eye view shows us these attitudes at work in other men. We saw that the comic character is often a man with a fixed idea, an animated mannerism. But it would be more accurate to call him an animated attitude. Don Quixote is simply the romantic attitude to life incarnate. Sancho Panza epitomizes the opposite, prosaic attitude to life. Their contrasting reactions to the same situation objectify, as it were, the conflict of attitudes. Precisely the same conflict, between the heroic and the prosaic attitudes, forms the theme of Shaw's *Arms and the Man*. Indeed, most of Shaw's plays depend on this opposition, in one form or other.

The best comic characters are not, of course, mere incarnations of a single attitude. The god's-eye view sees each of us as a bundle of more or less conflicting attitudes; and every bundle, in its turn, comes into conflict more or less with every other bundle. The result is a rich complex of misunderstandings and cross-purposes. This is, in essence, the human comedy.

We can only appreciate the comedy if, on the one hand, we share all the attitudes involved, so that we can fully grasp the contradictions and inconsistencies that ensue; and if, on the other hand, we do not identify ourselves too completely with any single attitude or bundle of attitudes. This explains why humour strikes some people as detached, remote, cruel; and others as infinitely warm, human, sympathetic. We must be detached from the human scene, so that we can see the complex tangle of crossing paths spread out below us, as on a map. But we can never see just how the paths come to cross unless we have a vivid understanding of human values and human emotions.

(i) *Small misfortunes.* How far does this theory cover all the facts of humour? There is one obvious and glaring omission. How are we to account for small misfortunes? We have allowed a place for malice, but does this really enable us to smuggle in all the facts on which the derision theories place so much emphasis? And can we explain the custard-pie film, or why we laugh when someone hits his thumb with a hammer?

I do not know that we can. It is tempting to try; and it is of course possible to make out a fairly good case. We can say, for example, that we have here once again the contrast between man as he imagines himself, the lord of creation, the heir of the ages, only a little lower than the angels, and the hairless ape, who cannot even manage his own limbs, his own tools, without disaster. We could reinforce this argument by pointing out that it is not so much the simple fall, as the fall which follows pride, that makes us laugh. Or else it is the misfortune which comes upon us because of our very efforts to avert it.

There is something in these contentions: but I cannot feel that they are quite conclusive. Ours is, of course, an incongruity theory, and we have found that incongruity theories cannot explain this type of humour quite as convincingly as the derision theories. But I am prepared to regard this charge as not proven. It is after all reasonable enough to say that all small misfortunes are examples of inappropriate behaviour: inappropriate either in the casting off of conventional restraints, as in the custard-pie orgies of Laurel and Hardy, or in the failure to keep up our façade of dignity and efficiency.

With this possible exception, we have I think been able to find a place for most of the varieties of humour uncovered in our survey. We have done this, of course, largely because our theory is a synthesis of a number of existing theories. It is essentially not very different from Schopenhauer's. His rather forbidding logical formula does describe what we have called the linking of disparates. But Schopenhauer's formula needs a good deal of enlarging and explaining, which we have tried to give it. In the process, we have taken in a good deal from Kline, Freud, Bergson, Menon. That is, I think, all to the good. Obviously it is not possible to dismiss all previous theories of humour as simply wrong-headed. We have found much truth in all of them: the difficulty is that they all conflict. What is needed is obviously a synthesis. The foregoing theory is an attempt to supply one.

It may be objected that the authors of these theories are often talking about different things, and that what is needed is not synthesis, but analysis. But then we would still have to say that each of them expresses part of what we mean by humour, but that none of them expresses the whole of what we mean. Whether we call our final account a synthesis or a full analysis does not seem to matter much.

It will not do to say that the contending theories each give a different definition of humour, and that each may be adequate for its own purpose. It is real, not nominal definition with which we are concerned. No definition can afford to ignore the facts about humour—the situations in which men do laugh. If we rule out some of these as 'not really funny', we should at least be able to explain them as mistaken judgments, or something similar.

When we say that what is funny is inappropriate, we are not making a resolution; we are not saying that henceforth we will laugh only at inappropriateness, and dismiss any other alleged joke as not really funny. We are saying that any situation that is normally called funny is also felt to contain an element of inappropriateness. Of course that does not mean that 'funny' *means* 'inappropriate'. We can ask: 'Is the inappropriate funny?' and this is not the same as asking: 'Is the inappropriate inappropriate?' There is a sense in which 'funny' is indefinable. It is a name we give to situations which arouse in us a particular emotion. If we assert that those situations also strike us as containing a special kind of inappropriateness, and that if they did not we would not call them funny, we are making an empirical observation.

Of course we could not in any case simply define 'funny' as 'inappropriate', because all inappropriate things are not funny.

We may, for instance, describe some of them as 'shamefully' or 'distressingly' inappropriate. Only the *laughably* inappropriate, it may be said, is funny. But this still allows us to say that the laughable is a species of the inappropriate. If we go on to ask the differentia, it resides, I suggest, in this, that there is an element of appropriateness in the inappropriate, when it is funny. It is not merely a question of something intruding where it does not belong, but of something which plainly does belong, but is not allowed for by our pre-existing attitude. The result is what Eastman calls 'the collapse of a pattern', or what Kant calls 'frustrated expectation'. The pre-existing attitude is shattered, at least momentarily. It is when it is not shattered, when it still asserts itself, that we feel shame or distress.

In what sense can such an account of humour be called a synthesis of existing theories? Only in the sense that it describes more adequately the facts which they attempt to describe. It is true, for instance, that we find small misfortunes funny. If our theory is sound, this is because it is in the nature of small misfortunes to have the special kind of inappropriateness we have described. It is not clear that this is the case; and that is the weakness of the theory. But the point at issue is one of fact, though of facts about our own feelings and perceptions when we laugh. It is not merely a matter of possible definitions.

The obvious danger is that the synthesis may be far more apparent than real: that by the ambiguous use of the word 'inappropriate' we may have set down two or three different theories side by side. I hope this has been avoided; but it would still be too much to hope that all the difficulties have been overcome, or that the last word on humour has been said.

There are still many questions to be answered. If humour is the inappropriate, why should it cause the peculiar physical manifestations which we call laughter? Why should the same manifestations be called forth by tickling, by laughing-gas, and by nervousness?

Any complete theory of laughter should answer these questions. I do not know the answers. But I believe that this survey of humour has at least uncovered some important facts which must be taken into account in finding them.

BIBLIOGRAPHY

BAIN, Alexander—*The Emotions and the Will.* 3rd ed. London, Longmans, Green, 1888.

BAIN, Alexander—*English Composition and Rhetoric.* 4th ed. London, Longmans, Green, 1908, pp. 74-80.

BAIN, Alexander—*The Senses and the Intellect.* 3rd ed. London, Longmans, Green, 1868.

BERGSON, Henri—*Laughter.* Tr. by Cloudesley Brereton and F. Rothwell. London, Macmillan, 1911.

EASTMAN, Max—*Enjoyment of Laughter.* London, Hamish Hamilton, 1937.

FEIBLEMAN, James—*In Praise of Comedy.* New York, Macmillan Co., 1939.

FREUD, Sigmund—*Wit and its Relation to the Unconscious.* Tr. A. A. Brill. London, Kegan Paul, 1916.

GREGORY, J. C.—*The Nature of Laughter.* London, Kegan Paul, 1924.

GREIG, J. Y. T.—*Psychology of Laughter and Comedy.* London, Allen & Unwin, 1923.

HOBBES, Thomas—*Leviathan.* 1651. In *English Works of Thomas Hobbes,* ed. Molesworth vol. 3. London, Bohn, 1839.

HOBBES, Thomas—*Tripos;* in three discourses: 1. Human nature; 2. The elements of law. 3rd ed. 1684. In *English Works of Thomas Hobbes,* ed. Molesworth vol. 4. London, Bohn, 1840.

KANT, Immanuel—*Kant's Critique of Aesthetic Judgment,* tr. J. C. Meredith. Oxford, Clarendon Press, 1911, pp. 196-203.

KIMMINS, C. W.—*The Springs of Laughter.* London, Methuen, 1928.

KLINE, L. W.—The Psychology of Humor. In *American Journal of Psychology,* vol. 18, pp. 421-441 (1907).

LEACOCK, Stephen—*Humour and Humanity.* London, Thornton Butterworth, 1937 (Home University Library).

LEACOCK, Stephen—*Humour: its Theory and Technique.* London, John Lane, 1935.

LILLY, W. S.—*The Theory of the Ludicrous;* a lecture delivered to the Royal Institution, March 13, 1896. *In Fortnightly Review,* vol. 59 (N.S.), pp. 724-737 (1896).

LUDOVICI, A. M.—*The Secret of Laughter.* London, Constable, 1932.

NOTE: This bibliography is not intended to be exhaustive. or even to include all the books referred to in the preparation of this book. It merely gives the main works of those writers whose theories of humour are discussed in detail.

258   BIBLIOGRAPHY

McDougall, William—*Introduction to Social Psychology*. 25th
  ed. London, Methuen, 1943, pp. 387-397.
McDougall, William—*The Theory of Laughter*. In Nature,
  vol. 67, pp. 318-319 (1903).
McDougall, William—*Outline of Psychology*. 5th ed. London,
  Methuen, 1931, pp. 165-170.
McDougall, William—A New Theory of Laughter. In *Psyche*
  vol. 2 (N.S.), 1922.
Menon, V. K. Krishna—*A Theory of Laughter*. London, Allen
  & Unwin, 1931.
Orwell, George—The Art of Donald McGill. In *Horizon*, vol. 4,
  pp. 153-163 (1941). *Also in* Orwell, George—*Critical Essays*.
  London, Secker and Warburg, 1946.
Schopenhauer, Arthur—*The World as Will and Idea*. Tr. by
  R. B. Haldane and J. Kemp. 2nd ed. London, Kegan Paul,
  1891.
Spencer, Herbert—Physiology of Laughter. In *Macmillan's
  Magazine*, March, 1860; *Also in* Spencer, H. *Essays Scientific,
  Political, Speculative*. London, C. A. Watts.
Sully, James—*Essay on Laughter*. London, Longmans, Green,
  1903.

REFERENCES

The following are works, other than those listed in the bibliography, from which direct quotations have been made. It has not been thought necessary to give detailed page references, or to distract the reader's attention with footnotes. Anyone wishing to follow up a quotation should be able to do so from this list. Care has been taken to indicate the author of each quotation in the text itself.

ANSTEY, F., *pseud. Mr. Punch's Young Reciter.* 1883. Revised ed., *The Young Reciter and Model Music-hall.* London, Methuen, 1931.

BELLOC, Hilaire. *The Higher Criticism.* In *This and That and The Other.* London, Methuen, 1925.

BELLOC, Hilaire. *Sonnets and Verses.* 2nd ed. London, Duckworth, 1938.

BULLETT, Gerald. *The Bubble.* London, Dent, 1934.

CALVERLEY, C. S. *Verses and Translations.* 1862. In *Complete Works.* London, Bell, 1905.

CARROLL, Lewis, *pseud. Through the Looking-glass.* 1872. Many editions.

CHESTERTON, G. K. *The Defendant.* 3rd ed. London, Dent, 1907.

CHESTERTON, G. K. *Tremendous Trifles.* London, Methuen, 1909.

FORSTER, E. M. *Aspects of the Novel.* London, Edward Arnold, 1927.

GILBERT, W. S. *The Mikado.* In *Savoy Operas.* London, Macmillan, 1926.

GRAHAM, Harry. *Ruthless Rhymes for Heartless Homes.* London, Edward Arnold, 1899.

LEACOCK, Stephen. *Model Memoirs.* London, John Lane, 1939.

LYND, Robert. Eggs. In *The Pleasures of Ignorance.* 2nd ed. London, Methuen, 1930.

MAUROIS, André. *Aspects of Biography.* Cambridge University Press, 1929.

SANGER, George. *Seventy Years a Showman.* London, Dent, 1938.

SHAW, George Bernard. *Plays Pleasant and Unpleasant.* London, Constable, 1928.

SHAW, George Bernard. Getting Married. In *The Doctor's Dilemma* (etc.) London, Constable, 1911.

SITWELL, Edith. *Selected Poems.* London, Duckworth, 1936.

WELLS, H. G. A Vision of Judgment. In *The Time Machine and Other Stories.* London, Heinemann, 1895.

INDEX